DOOR COUNTY OUTDOORS

DOOR COUNTY OUTDOORS

*A Guide to the Best Hiking, Biking, Paddling,
Beaches, and Natural Places*

Magill Weber

THE UNIVERSITY OF WISCONSIN PRESS

The University of Wisconsin Press
1930 Monroe Street, 3rd Floor
Madison, Wisconsin 53711-2059
uwpress.wisc.edu

3 Henrietta Street
London WC2E 8LU, England
eurospanbookstore.com

Printed in the United States of America

Library of Congress Cataloging-in-Publication Data
Weber, Magill.
Door County outdoors: a guide to the best hiking, biking, paddling, beaches, and
natural places / Magill Weber.
p.   cm.
Includes bibliographical references and index.
ISBN 978-0-299-28554-8 (pbk.: alk. paper) — ISBN 978-0-299-28553-1 (e-book)
1. Recreation areas—Wisconsin—Door County. 2. Door County (Wis.)—
Description and travel. I. Title.
GV54.W62D66   2011
796.509775´63—dc22
2011016373

CONTENTS

Beaches and Overlooks

Lighthouses

Bike Routes

Paddling Routes

Chapter 3. Baileys Harbor Area

Major Points of Interest

Beaches and Overlooks

Bike Routes

Paddling Routes

Chapter 6. Egg Harbor Area

Major Points of Interest

Beaches and Overlooks

Bike Routes

Paddling Routes

Major Points of Interest

Beaches and Overlooks

Lighthouses

Bike Routes

Paddling Routes

Major Points of Interest

Beaches and Overlooks

Lighthouse

Bike Routes

Paddling Routes

Bike Routes

Paddling Route

MAPS AND ICONS

MAPS

Each of the maps in this book includes symbols for the attractions found on that map. The following symbols appear:

2   major point of interest

Ⓨ   beach and/or overlook

Ⓟ   parking lot

------   hiking trail

▄▄▄   paddling route (P + number)

▬▬   bike route (B + number)

▐   lighthouse (L + number)

●   town center

ICONS

Each entry is marked with one or more icons to give users easy information about the amenities found at the site. The following icons appear:

     beach

     biking

     camping

hiking

 lighthouse

 Native American cultural site

 overlook

 paddling

 picnic area

 restrooms

 walking

 wildflowers

wildlife

ACKNOWLEDGMENTS

Thanks to Garrett for everything. I love you, but especially for being supportive of this endeavor. My gratitude especially goes out to Mom and Joe—their passion for Door County is infectious. Thank you for visiting every site, hiking every trail, driving every set of directions, and marketing the book, long before it was published. Without your hard work, this would never have happened. Thanks to Dad, the old block to my chip, for making me think about writing a book in the first place. And to the whole family, near and far, the Kaprelians, the Webers, the Nichols, the Hansons, the Kalinoskis, the Derderians, the McKnights, and the Mrazeks, for making this book possible in one way or another. I miss you all every day.

Thanks to Lauren Russell, who joined many of the first hikes included in this book, back in the summer of 2005, Jepson guide in hand. Lauren can be credited with making me look at plants occasionally, instead of only birds. Claudia Kalinoski, Charma McKnight, Carol and Norm Seegar, and especially Rita Stahl were excellent hiking companions throughout the fact-checking process. Laurel Hauser provided invaluable feedback on early drafts. I am indebted to my dear friend Kara Peters, for her wise counsel and hand-holding in the early stages of writing. Her considerable talents with the written word were instrumental in turning an idea into an actual book. Thanks to Phillip Billings, who provided a much appreciated photo donation.

Thanks also to all the great people at the University of Wisconsin Press, especially acquisitions editor Raphael Kadushin, Carla Marolt, and

Anna Wehrwein, along with the anonymous reviewers who graciously provided comments to improve the quality of the manuscript. Sheila McMahon and Diana Cook did an outstanding job editing, including the unenviable task of reviewing 167 sets of maps and directions. I am more than slightly in awe of their attention to detail and diligence throughout the process.

And thanks especially to Bob and Lois, incomparable Door County neighbors, who are gone but will not soon be forgotten.

DOOR COUNTY OUTDOORS

Introduction

For generations, visitors have flocked to Door County to get away from it all. Beckoned by family reunions, fish boils, Fourth of July fireworks, and sunset boat rides, they crave the beauty and simplicity of an era that seems to have disappeared elsewhere. While lives change, kids grow up, and the real world seems increasingly unpredictable, somehow Door County manages to remain comfortingly the same.

Much of what has remained constant is Door County's accessibility to the natural world: the pockets of unspoiled nature that someone had the foresight to preserve, that somehow managed to flourish, wedged between the vacation homes, and the secret spots that seem wild, but are just a short walk down the path. With quiet country roads, lush forests, and 250 miles of Lake Michigan shoreline, it's no wonder this place attracts more than two million visitors each year. Door County is Door County because of the special places you just can't find anywhere else.

This book is about those special places. It will help you discover the kind of off-the-beaten-track hikes, views, and paddles that the locals know about. Popular destinations are here too, but the focus is on options away from the crowds that pack the state parks on summer weekends. This book will also acquaint you with the plants and animals you'll encounter along the way. Chapters are organized by regions and towns, so you can select the closest routes for walking, biking, hiking, or paddling, whether you're on the north side of Washington Island or the southeastern beaches of Whitefish Dunes.

THE LAY OF THE LAND

Most of Door County sits on the Door Peninsula, which is about 60 miles long and 18 miles wide at the widest point and surrounded by Lake Michigan on three sides. (The arm of Lake Michigan on the western side of the peninsula is called Green Bay, and this book uses the terms "Green Bay side" and "Lake Michigan side" to refer to the western and eastern sides of the peninsula.) The one-third of the peninsula that is south of the Bayview Bridge in downtown Sturgeon Bay is known as Southern Door. Approaching Southern Door from the south, you'll notice the patchwork of small family farms, oak woodlands, and gently rolling hills. In the southwest part of the county, around the town of Brussels, are many family dairy farms and the largest Belgian community in the United States. Moving east, past the towns of Union, Gardner, Namur, Maplewood, and Forestville, you'll find more family farms growing hay, cherries, apples, corn, and other crops. Sturgeon Bay, on both sides of the bridge, is the only real city on the peninsula, with about ten thousand year-round residents. North of the bridge and inland, around the towns of Carlsville, Sevastopol, and Jacksonport, family farms with cherry and apple orchards, hay, wheat, corn, and other crops dominate the landscape.

As you head north, on the Lake Michigan side of the peninsula—known as "the quiet side"—you'll find coastal forests, small inland lakes, and lots of vacation homes, particularly around the town of Baileys Harbor. One of the oldest settlements on the peninsula, Baileys Harbor maintains its fishing heritage and small town feel to this day. Across the peninsula on the Green Bay side are the bustling summer hamlets of Egg Harbor, Fish Creek, Ephraim, Sister Bay, and Ellison Bay. The north end of the peninsula boasts some remnants of Door County's fishing heritage, with a few working harbors around Rowleys Bay, Gills Rock, and Northport, interspersed with lush forests and more vacation communities.

Door County also includes a chain of large islands known as Grand Traverse Islands. The largest is Washington, a 25-square-mile island about 6 miles off the end of the peninsula, with a small community originally settled by Scandinavian farmers and fishermen. Door County's other islands include Detroit and Chambers, both mostly privately owned, with a few summer residences; Rock Island, a state park just off Washington

Island; and a number of tiny, unsettled islands, which are mostly designated as bird sanctuaries.

From Southern Door to Washington Island, Door County is filled with colorful place names, from the quaint Hedgehog Bay to the tongue-twisting Sevastopol. Some are the legacy of northeastern Wisconsin's original inhabitants, the Potawatomi Indians. The French fur trappers and priests who stopped along the shores of Lake Michigan in the late 1600s also left their mark. The name "Door County" comes from these French explorers, who used the term *Porte des Morts* (Death's Door) to describe the passage between what is now Northport and Washington Island. Still other names came from the host of European settlers, mostly Scandinavian, who came to fish, farm, and harvest the natural resources of Door County in the early 1800s.

GUIDELINES AND ADVISORIES

Whether you're walking the sandy beaches at Newport State Park, inhaling the scent of spruce trees on a Door County Land Trust trail, climbing the steps at Eagle Bluff Lighthouse, or watching bald eagles hunting for fish, Door County is the perfect place to feel like an adventurer.

But even the boldest adventurers need to know where they're going and how to get there. This section provides some recommendations for planning a safe and enjoyable trip in the wilds of Door County.

Levels of Difficulty

Most, if not all, of the hiking trails, and many of the biking and paddling routes included in this book, are completely doable for anyone who can climb a flight of stairs. In short, there are no mountains in Door County! Each entry is rated as easy, moderate, or difficult, and even the harder ones are difficult relative to Door County, not to Mount Everest. Start out with the easy routes and go from there.

Public Access or Private Property?

When venturing off the beaten track, it's important to keep in mind where you're permitted to be. Less than 10 percent of Door County is open to the public. While many locals are relaxed about access, particularly during the off-season, many homeowners, farmers, and business owners are rightfully quite intolerant of trespassers. This book aims to be as specific as possible in providing directions to trails, but in many areas, it's just plain hard to tell if you're on private land. When in doubt, ask permission, and if permission is denied, respect the landowner's right to his or her private property.

Lakes and navigable waterways are held in the public trust. In other words, they belong to everyone to boat, fish, hunt, swim, and enjoy. As a general rule, along Lake Michigan and Green Bay, the public has a right to access and walk along the beaches via public roads, public boat ramps, and public beach access points. From those public access points, you may then walk along the beaches on all lands below the high water mark. You may not use private access roads, stairways, or backyards of private property, or cut through private property to get from a public road to the beach. On streams and rivers, the public is permitted to wade or launch boats at public road crossings or rights-of-way. On inland lakes, including Kangaroo, Clark, and Europe, property owners hold the rights to their shoreline, and the public may not enter. You can access these lakes only via public boat ramps and beach areas, and you must remain in your boat or swimming. For more information on the Wisconsin Public Trust Doctrine, and how it applies to recreational users, see the Wisconsin Department of Natural Resources website at http://dnr.wi.gov.

Paddling

Whether you're a novice or an experienced paddler, Door County offers some of the top kayaking opportunities on the Great Lakes. This book provides access points and routes for some of the most popular and scenic paddles. It is strongly recommended, however, that advanced paddlers seek out detailed nautical charts for offshore excursions and that beginners and intermediate paddlers take advantage of guided trips with one of the many excellent outfitters around the county.

The generally calm and protected waters of inland lakes like Kangaroo, Clark, and Europe are great for beginning canoeing and kayaking. Riebolt's Creek, Richter Bayou on Washington Island, and the Mink River Estuary are also relatively protected for canoeing and kayaking and offer exceptional wildlife viewing opportunities, though they are far more challenging than inland lake paddling. On the Green Bay side of the peninsula, experienced kayakers may want to take a day trip out to one or more of the offshore islands, including the Strawberry Island group, Snake Island and Sand Bay Point, the Sister Islands, Hat Island, or Horseshoe Island. Experts will find plenty to do on the Lake Michigan side of the peninsula, where the sea caves at Cave Point County Park or the journey across Porte des Morts to Washington Island can prove challenging.

This book provides information on access points, but those venturing offshore should consult detailed maps, bring appropriate gear and provisions, and take normal safety precautions. The areas along the coast—especially south of Baileys Harbor, around Jacksonport, off Cave Point County Park, as well as the Porte des Morts crossing—can be particularly treacherous at any time of the year. Unless you are an expert, go with a local outfitter in those areas. It goes without saying that paddling, especially on the open waters of Lake Michigan, is inherently dangerous. Sit-atop kayaks and canoes are not well suited to Lake Michigan, and anyone venturing offshore in them should use extreme caution. Enclosed sea kayaks with spray skirts are the appropriate choice in almost all circumstances on Lake Michigan.

Paddlers of all abilities should take safety precautions, including wearing a Coast Guard–approved, appropriately sized, personal flotation device at all times, as well as bringing food, water, bilge pumps, paddle floats, maps, and a cell phone in a waterproof case. Rain gear and wet or dry suits are recommended, particularly for trips on Lake Michigan, no matter the season. Hypothermia can be a major concern even in the warmest part of summer, so do not underestimate the importance of warm protective gear. Lake Michigan and Green Bay paddlers should be familiar with self-rescue techniques. Use common sense. Paddle with others, keep a close eye on the weather forecast, and always tell someone onshore where you're going and when you'll be back. Paddlers have drowned and succumbed to hypothermia in Door County waters in recent years, and it's never a good idea to overestimate your ability level or underestimate the weather, wind, current, or waves.

Biking

The biking routes in this guide are geared toward families with children and recreational "weekend warriors." Routes that are rated easy and moderate are appropriate for newer bikers, while routes rated difficult are geared toward those with some experience and comfort with longer distances and hills. However, as equipment has improved and road biking has gained popularity, more and more cyclists are comfortable riding 50 to 100 miles in a single outing. If you consider yourself in that category and are interested in racking up higher mileage, you will find challenge in stringing together several of the rides into a longer and more strenuous trip. Serious cyclists may also want to consider joining up with one of the groups that ride out of Sturgeon Bay and Fish Creek, or participate in the Door County Century or Ride for the Ridges cycling events, held during the summer and fall months. Check with the local bike shops for more details.

By state law, bicycles are considered vehicles and bikers are expected to follow all rules of the road, just as if they were driving. Follow appropriate traffic patterns, stop at stop signs, and use hand signals when turning. Keep in mind that in many parts of Door County the roads are narrow and have blind curves. Cars are prone to speeding on most of the peninsula's roads, so no matter where you are, bike defensively. Use extreme caution when biking along or crossing Highways 42 and 57. Above all, use common sense. Wear a helmet and reflective gear, ride single file, and give cars enough room to pass you. Bike rentals and maps are available in many of Door County's sports and bike stores, as well as at many of the resorts.

Hiking and Walking

For many people, the term "hiking" conjures up images of steep mountains and lots of technical equipment. Hiking may seem completely impossible for those of us who haven't been putting in long hours at the gym or are carrying AARP cards in our wallets. Relax—all we're talking about is walking in the woods. Hikes rated as "easy" are suitable for anyone who can walk up a flight of stairs. The few "moderate" and "difficult" hikes included are slightly longer and more strenuous, but are still not going to require the endurance of an Olympic athlete to complete them. Most of the "moderate" and "difficult" hikes were rated so because of their location near the Niagara Escarpment. These trails—particularly those around bluffs and cliffs—can be steeper and rocky.

Keep in mind that Door County is not a wilderness. Hikers are seldom more than a few miles from a road; there is good cellular coverage throughout the region; and trails are generally short and well marked. But don't be lulled into a false sense of security. Take adequate precautions when venturing out. This means preparing for weather, carrying enough water, and telling someone where you're going. A first aid kit, snacks, and a cell phone are always a good idea.

Hunting

Hunting has long been a part of Wisconsin's outdoor heritage. The fall and winter deer, turkey, and waterfowl seasons attract hunters from all over Wisconsin and neighboring states. Many of the sites included in this book are open to hunting. The Door County Land Trust, for example, allows some types of hunting on many of its preserves with proper permission. Many of the Wisconsin Department of Natural Resources (WDNR) sites are also managed for or open to hunting in season. In addition, some landowners invite hunters onto their property to hunt, particularly during the deer season.

Annually, there are about four weeks of gun season and several months of bow season for white-tailed deer in Door County. These seasons generally begin as early as mid-September and run through January. Waterfowl, Ruffed Grouse, and Canada Goose seasons vary from year to year, but are typically also in the fall and early winter. Anyone planning to spend time outdoors in Door County in the fall and winter should check the WDNR's website and become familiar with hunting season schedules. During hunting season, avoid areas with thick vegetation, wear blaze orange, make noise, and be especially cautious in areas open to hunting.

Insects

Wisconsin's Northwoods has a well-deserved reputation for mosquitoes. Door County is not nearly as bad as some other parts of the state, thanks to breezes off Lake Michigan and Green Bay, but mosquitoes still can be thick at times. Door County also has large numbers of biting deerflies, ticks, and other pests during the warmer months. Lyme disease is present in Wisconsin, as is West Nile virus and other insect-borne diseases.

Hikers in wooded or grassy areas should avoid wearing shorts and take such general precautions as tucking pants into socks, spraying with strong insect repellent containing DEET, wearing long sleeves, and doing regular tick checks after hiking. During the summer deerfly season, many local stores sell sticky patches that you can affix to your hat. These make hiking tolerable when large biting flies are out.

Animals

Door County is home to a wide variety of animals. Some species, including rodents, bats, and western fox snakes, are likely to find their way into human dwellings. Other animals, notably white-tailed deer, are present in such large numbers that it is almost impossible to spend time in the county without encountering them. Drive slowly at dusk to avoid collisions. Give wild animals the wide berth they deserve, and enjoy them from a distance. While generally rare, rabies is known to occur in Wisconsin in bats, raccoons, foxes, and skunks. Be cautious of any animal that approaches you, acts sick, or staggers, particularly if it is out during broad daylight. Report any sick animals to local public health officials and the WDNR.

Invasive Species

Dozens of nonnative invasive plants have been introduced across Wisconsin. The most common ones in Door County include phragmites, dame's rocket, forget-me-not, yellow rocket, garlic mustard, purple loosestrife, and common and glossy buckthorn. Invasives can wreak havoc with local ecosystems, where they outcompete native plants.

Hikers, bikers, campers, and boaters should be aware that Wisconsin law prohibits the transport of any invasive plants and animals. Take time to brush off boots and clothes before and after hiking to avoid spreading seeds, hose bikes down after rides, and make an effort to shake out tents and other camping equipment between uses. Boaters should be aware that Wisconsin law requires them to wash and drain their boats at the beginning and end of each trip, to avoid spreading invasive plants and animals from lake to lake.

If you're spending a lot of time outdoors in Door County you may want to consider helping to remove invasive species, by participating in regular volunteer events, including those hosted by The Ridges Sanctuary or the Door County Invasive Species Team. More information on how to identify and prevent the spread of invasive species can be found at the invasives section of the Wisconsin Department of Natural Resources website (http://dnr.wi.gov/invasives).

Maps

The maps in this book will help you find and enjoy some of Door County's premier natural attractions. They are not comprehensive, however. Always consult the maps and trailhead signs at parks and trails. Free road maps are available from the Wisconsin Department of Transportation and from local visitors' bureaus. Online map databases also have excellent coverage of Door County. Additionally, boaters venturing offshore will want to order copies of the National Oceanic and Atmospheric Administration (NOAA) nautical charts covering Door County.

Weather

Weather can change rapidly, and Door County is prone to unpredictable summer lightning storms, high winds, spring and fall blizzards, and the occasional tornado. Dressing in layers is the key no matter the season. Keep an eye on the forecast, and if you get caught out in bad weather, take appropriate cover.

DOOR COUNTY'S NATURAL FEATURES

The great writer and environmentalist Rachel Carson wrote, "Those who dwell, as scientists or laymen, among the beauties and mysteries of the earth are never alone or weary of life." People come to Door County to experience the rejuvenating camaraderie of nature, but it doesn't have to remain a mystery. Whether you're a botanist or a casual hiker who simply likes to smell the flowers, a basic knowledge of the area's geology, plants, animals, and birds can greatly enhance your appreciation of Door County's considerable natural beauty. The following sections will help to acquaint you with Door County's topography, wildlife, and changing seasons. Perhaps this knowledge will deepen your respect for the earth's rich natural cycles and complex interrelationships and underscore the importance of treading lightly.

In the interest of preserving Door County's scenic beauty, there has been significant effort in the last few decades to preserve some of the most ecologically sensitive, historic, and quintessentially "Door County-esque" places. Organizations like the Door County Maritime Museum, Door County Historical Society, Door County Land Trust, The Ridges Sanctuary, and The Nature Conservancy are working to protect many of these unique areas and have opened many of them to the public. State, county, and local governments, including the Wisconsin Department of Natural Resources, the Door County Parks System, and towns and villages, also have a large number of parks that are open to the public, many of which are free of charge.

Please do your best to protect sensitive plants and animals and their habitats. When you consider that about two million people visit Door County annually, even the smallest impact by each person can have a major aggregate effect on the region's rare plants and animals. We encourage you to support the organizations that make these places possible, and respect the places you visit so that they may be kept open for others to enjoy.

The Niagara Escarpment

One of Door County's most prominent features is the geologic ridge known as the Niagara Escarpment. The islands are outcroppings of the Niagara Escarpment—literally, places where the earth was pushed up and out of the bottom of Lake Michigan about four hundred million years ago. The distinctive tall bluffs and rocky outcrops are most noticeable on the Green Bay side of the peninsula and along the Lake Michigan shoreline. The 650-mile-long ridge, which got its name from its prominence around Niagara Falls, runs from east to west, beginning in upstate New York near Buffalo, continuing along Lake Ontario and Lake Erie across southern Ontario, through Lake Huron and Georgian Bay, across the northern portion of Lake Michigan, and then underground through southern Wisconsin to northern Illinois.

The Niagara Escarpment was formed by the weathering of lower layers of rocks, exposing the upper layers of dolomite limestone. Areas of the Niagara Escarpment cracked and eroded during the Pleistocene epoch, when the last of the major Great Lakes glaciations covered the region in a massive ice sheet. When you are hiking along or standing on top of the escarpment you will notice crumbly cliff faces. The tall bluffs and rocky outcrops associated with the Niagara Escarpment provide critical habitat for a variety of plants and animals and give Door County its distinctive views and promontories. Many of these areas have been protected as parks and land trust holdings.

The geology of the Niagara Escarpment has heavily influenced Door County's forests. For example, in most parts of the world, white cedar forests are found only in wet places. In Door County, however, you'll find white cedars growing even on the rockiest outcrops of the escarpment. The reason for this is the unique soil chemistry of the area. The Niagara Escarpment creates a highly fractured, alkaline soil. White cedar forests grow well in alkaline conditions and can tap into moisture stored in small fissures in the rocks. In other areas, cracks in the bluffs and outcrops of the escarpment create small seeps, or areas where water drips out of the rock. Areas around these seeps are home to specific types of plants and animals. These distinctive ecological communities are discussed in more detail below.

Ecological Communities

"Ecological communities" or "natural communities," as scientists call them, describe a group of species—trees, flowers, plants, animals, birds, insects—that live in the same place and interact with one another. Over the years, Wisconsin's leading ecologists have come up with some general names that describe certain collections of plants and animals. This book uses these names to characterize the plants and animals living in a particular area. Keep in mind that no two sites are exactly the same, and the ecological community is just a general guide to what kinds of plants and animals you might find in it. The following sections describe the community types most frequently encountered in Door County.

Northern Wet-Mesic Forest

The northern wet-mesic forest is one of the most widespread communities in Door County. Examples of northern wet-mesic forest can be found at Rock Island State Park, North Bay, Newport State Park, Mud Lake State Natural Area, Toft Point State Natural Area, and Peninsula

State Park. This community is also common in Door County's populated areas.

White cedar dominates; other trees include balsam fir, black ash, white
spruce, tamarack, paper birch, and black spruce. It may also have sedge
meadows dominated by soft-leaf sedge and three-sided sedge in wetter
areas, as well as plants like blunt-leaved orchid and heart-leaved tway-
blade. Also look for plants growing on the forest floor, or understory,
including Canada mayflower, wild sarsaparilla, wood fern, and yellow
trout lily. Common animal and bird species include red squirrel, spotted
salamander, blue-spotted salamander, Ruffed Grouse, Red-breasted Nuthatch, porcupine, American mink, and white-tailed deer.

NORTHERN MESIC FOREST

The northern mesic forest community is widespread in Door County.
Examples can be found at Newport State Park, Europe Bay Woods
State Natural Area, Whitefish Dunes State Park, Cave Point County Park,
Toft Point State Natural Area, Rock Island State Park, and Peninsula
State Park. It is common on private residential lands around Door
County's towns.

Dominant trees are sugar maple, hemlock, and often beech, particularly near Lake Michigan, along with basswood, black maple, red maple,
mountain maple, yellow birch, paper birch, white ash, red oak, and white
pine. Some parts of the peninsula, particularly those without large white-
tailed deer populations, still have intact layers of forest floor plants,
including Canada yew and Canada mayflower, but for the most part deer
grazing has eliminated them. Wildlife of northern mesic forests includes
wood frog, meadow vole, raccoon, red fox, Wild Turkey, gray squirrel,
snowshoe hare, American Redstart, Red-eyed Vireo, Great Crested Flycatcher, and American Robin.

NORTHERN DRY-MESIC FOREST

The northern dry-mesic forest community is dominated by white pine,
red pine, red maple, and red oak. Trees like bigtooth aspen and trembling
aspen also appear in some areas. It is associated with sandy soils, which
are found in many parts of northern Wisconsin but less so in Door
County. Pine plantations, particularly in Southern Door, represent this

community. Examples can also be found at Potawatomi State Park, Newport State Park, Gardner Swamp State Wildlife Area, Chambers Island, the southern portions of Washington Island (particularly around Detroit Harbor), Plum Island, and Rock Island State Park.

Understory may include wild sarsaparilla and Canada mayflower. Wildlife found in northern dry-mesic forests includes Wild Turkey, Hermit Thrush, Eastern Bluebird, Brown-headed Cowbird, gray squirrel, and porcupine.

BOREAL FOREST

Boreal forests are typically found across Canada, northern New England, and the very northern parts of Minnesota, Michigan, and Wisconsin. In Door County, the cooling influence of Lake Michigan creates localized climate conditions, or microclimates, that allow these northern forests to thrive. Cool microclimates support some of the southernmost examples of boreal forest communities, particularly along the nearshore coastline between Baileys Harbor and Newport State Park, at North Bay, Moonlight Bay Bedrock Beach State Natural Area, Jackson Harbor Ridges State Natural Area, Baileys Harbor Boreal Forest and Wetlands State Natural Area, Cana Island, Toft Point State Natural Area, and The Ridges Sanctuary. In addition to cool temperatures, this area has the thin soils over dolomite bedrock necessary to support a healthy boreal forest.

Dominant trees are white spruce and balsam fir, along with white cedar and white pine. Other tree species, including balsam poplar, quaking aspen, and white birch, may be present in small areas. This community generally lacks brushy understory, mostly due to poor soil and lack of light filtering down to the forest floor, but mosses and lichens may be present. Boreal forest animals and birds include porcupine, Olive-sided Flycatcher, Northern Waterthrush, red squirrel, Winter Wren, black bear, Ovenbird, White-throated Sparrow, and snowshoe hare.

NORTHERN HARDWOOD SWAMP

The northern hardwood swamp community is characterized by forested wetlands dominated by trees, including black ash, red maple, yellow birch, and green ash, often in association with balsam fir conifer swamp

and occasionally alder species. Examples can be found at Franke Park,
Ephraim Wetlands Preserve, Lautenbach Woods Preserve, Moonlight
Bay Bedrock Beach State Natural Area, Mud Lake State Natural Area,
Bayshore Blufflands Preserve, Gardner Swamp State Wildlife Area, on
private land along the Door–Kewanee County border, and in pockets
around Sturgeon Bay. Northern hardwood forests occur in Door County
only in fragmented, or isolated, stands, particularly in the southern part
of the county.

This community typically has marsh understory, including *Carex*
sedges and a variety of native ferns. Weeds like invasive garlic mustard
can be problematic in many spots. Animals found in this community
include Wood Duck, raccoon, white-tailed deer, spotted salamander,
Red-eyed Vireo, and Gray Catbird.

Boreal Rich Fen

Boreal rich fens are generally treeless and distinguished by wet moss
peatlands. These mosses, including such species as campylium, drepan-
ocladus, scorpidium, or sphagnum, form a thick, solid floating mat of
vegetation over an underlying calcareous (calcium-based) bedrock and
till (a loose glacial gravel and sand). Door County has some of Wisconsin's finest examples of boreal rich fen communities, namely, at The
Ridges Sanctuary; the headwaters of Piel Creek, which feeds Kangaroo
Lake; Big and Little Marsh and Coffey Swamp on Washington Island; and
Mud Lake State Natural Area.

Plants typical of this community in Door County include wooly sedge,
coast sedge, rush aster, twig-rush, beaked bladderwort, Hudson Bay cot-
ton grass, bog birch, sage willow, speckled alder, round-leaved sundew,
pitcher plant, livid sedge, showy ladyslipper, leafy white orchid, tufted
club-rush, and long-spurred violet. Typical animals include white-tailed
deer, deer mouse, Great Blue Heron, and numerous species of dragonflies, including Hine's emerald.

Shore Fen

As the name suggests, shore fen communities are found near the Great
Lakes coastline, typically near creeks and rivers. They are characterized by large, floating mats of sedges. Like boreal rich fens, shore fens

are thick, and you can walk on top of them. Shore fen plants include wooly sedge, twig-rush, sweet gale, and buckbean. Look for birds such as Red-winged Blackbird, Blue-winged Teal, Common Goldeneye, and Common Yellowthroat, and a variety of dragonflies, including Hine's emerald. White Cliff Fen, Little Lake, and Kellner Fen are all excellent examples of shore fen communities in Door County.

EMERGENT AND SUBMERGENT MARSH

Emergent marshes are typified by shallow, standing water with lots of cattail and bulrush species. They often contain invasive plants like giant reed (phragmites). Submergent marshes include areas with deeper water that have vegetation growing on the surface, generally including pond-weed and duckweed. Emergent and submergent marshes can be found at Detroit Harbor, Clark Lake, Kangaroo Lake, Europe Lake, Mud Lake, North Bay, and the Mink River Estuary.

Animals and birds found in Door County's marshes include muskrat, Great Blue Heron, Canada Goose, Red-winged Blackbird, Common Yellowthroat, beaver, painted turtle, and Sandhill Crane.

GREAT LAKES ALKALINE ROCKSHORE

This community's wave-eroded dolomite bedrock cliffs and flat rock ledges, known as pavements, have been pounded down to a smooth surface over thousands of years by Lake Michigan's crashing waves. Great Lakes alkaline rockshores are associated with the Niagara Escarpment and are found primarily on the eastern side of the Door Peninsula, for example, at Moonlight Bay, Toft Point, and Baileys Harbor.

These rugged shoreline areas are generally treeless with low shrubs along the lakeshore. They are often adjacent to mature white cedar, white pine, or white spruce. Typical plants include ninebark, shrubby cinquefoil, gentian species, Indian paintbrush, and low calamint. Birds of the Great Lakes alkaline rockshore include Ring-billed Gull, Common Goldeneye, and Common Merganser.

GREAT LAKES BEACH AND DUNE

Door County has a number of sandy beaches, particularly along the eastern side of the peninsula. Dune communities are present in some of these areas, most notably at Whitefish Dunes State Park and the nearby Glidden Drive beaches (White Pine, Goldenrod, Hemlock, Deer Path, and Evergreen), which represent some of the best examples of this community in Wisconsin; others in Door County are at Jackson Harbor Ridges State Natural Area, Sturgeon Bay Ship Canal Nature Preserve, Newport State Park, and North Bay. These expanses are covered by low plants like beach grass, seaside spurge and American sea rocket, as well as rare species such as dune goldenrod, sand-binding marram grass, and dune thistle. Along the shore, look for Killdeer, Song Sparrow, and Bank Swallow.

Examples of forested dunes can be found in such areas as Meridian County Park, Lyle-Harter-Matter Sanctuary (adjacent to Meridian), and around Europe Bay Woods State Natural Area.

Northern Sedge Meadow

Northern sedge meadows are open, treeless wetlands dominated by sedges and grasses. In Door County they can be found at Meridian County Park, around Kangaroo Lake, Toft Point, North Bay, parts of Mink River Estuary, and Moonlight Bay. They can include tussock sedge and Canada bluejoint grass, hairy sedge and Northwest Territory sedge, or wooly sedge and coast sedge. Wildlife includes beaver, muskrat, Common Yellowthroat, meadow vole, painted turtle, and Sandhill Crane.

Great Lakes Ridge and Swale

This unique community is characterized by a set of sandy ridges alternating with swales, or low wet areas, running parallel to Lake Michigan. The north-south oriented ridges, including those near the Sturgeon Bay Ship Canal and at Jackson Harbor Ridges State Natural Area, were formed as glaciers receded, and the earth gradually rebounded to form new beaches and later ridges. The east-west oriented ridges, including those at The Ridges Sanctuary, were formed by the wind and wave action of Lake Michigan. The ridges and swales tend to be open with low vegetation, though some ridges are forested. At certain locations, including The Ridges Sanctuary, the inland ridges support a boreal forest of white spruce, black spruce, and white pine. The swales are wet and often marshy, and are typically fed by springs or streams. Swales may support emergent or submergent marsh vegetation, northern sedge meadows, or, farther inland, shrubby alder thickets.

These swale areas can also be good for rare plants like showy ladyslipper, yellow ladyslipper, and dwarf lake iris. Wildlife includes Common Goldeneye, *Dorcas* copper butterfly, northern ring-necked snake, Blackthroated Green Warbler, eastern cottontail, snowshoe hare, red bat, and Hine's emerald dragonfly.

Other excellent examples of this community are found at Toft Point State Natural Area and at Cave Point County Park, as well as private lands along the Shivering Sands State Natural Area.

Clay Seepage Bluff

Clay seepage bluffs are small communities, generally a few dozen feet wide or on a single rocky bluff slope. They occur along Lake Michigan shorelines and inland lakes near Lake Michigan. In Door County, examples can be found at Meridian County Park, along Kangaroo Lake, and at Bayshore Blufflands Preserve.

Clay seepage bluffs are characterized by forested dolomite outcrops of the Niagara Escarpment, typically with underground springs that create damp conditions. In Door County these areas are often dominated by white cedar, white birch, white pine, or small alder trees. Due to the wet seeps and springs, this community often has a well-developed understory of Canada goldenrod, buffaloberry, and pearly everlasting.

Moist Cliff

The moist cliff community is found in a few areas along the northernmost part of the Door Peninsula along Green Bay, typically in northern wet-mesic forests along the Niagara Escarpment. These areas are characterized by dolomite rock cliff faces with seeps, or underground springs that drip out of cracks in the rocks of bluff faces. Look for this community along rock faces at Potawatomi State Park, Bayshore Blufflands Preserve, Washington Island, Plum Island, and Rock Island State Park. Moist cliff communities provide appropriate conditions for mosses, fragile ferns, and wood ferns. Common animals and birds are typical of those found in northern wet-mesic forests: red squirrel, White-breasted Nuthatch, and Black-capped Chickadee.

THE DOOR COUNTY OUTDOOR YEAR

No matter the month, you can find a quiet place in Door County to experience the magic of nature. Certainly the summer is the most popular time to visit Door County. The woods, meadows, and marshes are alive with breeding songbirds and dragonflies, and the warm days beckon visitors to the beaches and lakefronts. You may have to look a bit harder, but if you seek summer solitude you will find it at many of the places in this book.

As the locals know, the off-season, particularly the late spring and early fall, has pleasant weather and far fewer crowds. In the spring the trees awaken, and each day brings new arrivals of the season—wood frogs croak, Red-winged Blackbirds display their plumage in the marshes, and the ice slowly melts off the lakes. In the fall, flocks of Sandhill Cranes stalk the farm fields and marshes, autumn leaves crunch underfoot, migrating Canada Geese honk overhead, and small mammals bustle about, stocking up for a long winter. Winter has its own appeal, especially if you're enjoying its stark beauty by cross-country ski or snowshoe. You may catch a glimpse of a white snowshoe hare, hear the scolding call of a Black-capped Chickadee from the top of a snowy spruce tree, watch rafts of Common Goldeneye diving for mollusks just offshore, or listen to the chitter of a red squirrel stirring from its nest on a sunny day.

A month-by-month guide to what you can expect to see, hear, and experience in Door County's natural world follows.

January and February

Typically cold and snowy, with significant ice packs on inland lakes and below-zero temperatures, sunny January and February days are ideal for exploring Door County's parks and back roads by cross-country ski or snowshoe. Look for tracks of small rodents, ermine, gray fox, red fox, fisher, cottontail rabbit, and raccoon. Large rafts of ducks, including Long-tailed Duck, Common Merganser, Redhead, Greater Scaup, Bufflehead, Common Goldeneye, and an occasional scoter flock may be present off Cave Point County Park, the ferry docks, and Washington Island. Look for Bohemian Waxwings in flocks of cedar waxwings, and Pine Grosbeaks, particularly around ornamental plants in Sturgeon Bay and other urban areas. Watch for Snowy Owls on the beaches and breakwaters. At feeders, winter finches, including Evening Grosbeaks, Common and

Hoary Redpolls, and Pine Siskins, may be present in significant numbers. White-winged Crossbills may also appear in conifer forests and edges. On warm days, red squirrels and chipmunks may be active, particularly around backyard feeders.

March

Early March brings the arrival of the first spring birds. The *kon-kaa-ree* of Red-winged Blackbirds is a welcome sound early in the month, with flocks of American Robins and Sandhill Cranes following shortly thereafter. As waterways start to thaw, wood frogs and Killdeer arrive. By late March, the ice on Green Bay loosens its winter grip, though temperatures remain cool, and migrant waterfowl float in large rafts in bays and off promontories. Look for large flocks of Common Goldeneye and Red-breasted Mergansers off Peninsula State Park, Newport State Park, and Whitefish Dunes State Park. Toward the end of the month, American Woodcocks *peent* and sky-dance in woodland clearings, and silver maple and skunk cabbage begin to flower.

April

By early April, Ruffed Grouse drum from downed logs and stumps, northern spring peepers call from thawed pond edges and wetlands, and flocks of Tundra Swans turn up in the bays north of Baileys Harbor where the ice has melted. As the ice leaves smaller wetlands, look for salamanders migrating across roads and trails after rain showers to reach these ponds. Woodchucks and eastern chipmunks begin to emerge, and caterpillars explore the resurgent vegetation. Leopard frogs call, and Song Sparrows, Eastern Meadowlarks, Tree Swallows, and Eastern Phoebe return. By mid-April, as flying insects become more numerous, the first bats of the season begin winging across the evening sky. The first warbler of spring, the Yellow-rumped Warbler, stops over in Door County on its way to northern breeding grounds. Noisy Canada Geese return and congregate in bays, lakeshores, and golf courses in nesting pairs. As April comes to a close, ice disappears from the lakes, rivers, and wetlands. A multitude of plants poke through the ground, garter snakes slither in the grass, migrant songbirds begin to arrive, and mourning cloak and Milbert's tortoiseshell butterflies flutter through the spring air.

May

Around the first week in May, painted turtles emerge from hibernation, and red maple and paper birch begin flowering with fuzzy catkins. Returning Winter Wrens sing from dense forests, and green frogs croak from wetlands. The second and third weeks in May are noteworthy not only for the budding vegetation, but for the numbers of migrant wood warblers buzzing from every tree, in search of caterpillars. On a good mid-May day, a walk in the woods might yield up to twenty-five or more warbler species, all in brilliant breeding plumage. By mid- to late May, you can spot monarch and tiger swallowtail butterflies and hear American toads. Great white trillium flowers and jack-in-the-pulpit abound in the woodlands and along the roads, and cherry orchards and Indian paintbrush bloom. Toward the end of the month, most waterways are free of ice, and mosquitoes start buzzing in decent numbers. Fruit trees flower, and many mammals and birds begin breeding.

June

The beginning of June is still cool in Door County, but wood lilies, yellow ladyslipper orchid, and pink ladyslipper orchid are in flower, drawing orchid enthusiasts and photographers to roadsides across the county. A walk in the woods will be accompanied by the sounds of male warblers defending their breeding territories. Baltimore Orioles build pendulous nests from overhanging branches; Rose-breasted Grosbeaks sing and chip in the forests; Indigo Buntings twitter from their perches, and Great Crested Flycatchers rattle from the treetops. The first white-tailed deer fawns are born around midmonth, and a lush carpet of ferns begins to blanket the forest floor. Pitcher plants abound in wet forests. Mushroom hunters also begin to find their quarry in a variety of species. By mid-June, the first of the rare Hine's emerald dragonflies emerge from their underground burrows around Kangaroo Lake, The Ridges Sanctuary, and other breeding areas. By the end of the month, lightning bugs and June bugs are common nighttime sights. Yarrow, milkweed, chicory, dogwood, and showy ladyslipper are flowering. The marshes are alive with nesting snapping and painted turtles, Common Yellowthroats, and Song Sparrows, while pitcher plants flower and bulrushes and cattails grow tall.

July

Early July brings an influx of summer visitors to Door County, and the woods and fields abound with blooming wildflowers and meadow plants like orange jewelweed, Canada thistle, wild parsnip, stinging nettle, Queen Anne's lace, and black-eyed Susan. Purple loosestrife, an invasive species, blooms from ditches, roadsides, and wetlands, while butterflies descend on the meadows to feast on them. By mid-July dragonflies flit through wetlands: Hine's, brush-tipped, and Williamson's emerald, and wandering glider skimmer and twelve-spotted skimmer. The songbirds are quieter as they focus energy on feeding their young. Gulls and terns soar over beaches and cliff overlooks, where they forage for fish to bring back to chicks at the offshore colonies. Deerfly numbers increase in locations like Mud Lake State Natural Area, Whitefish Dunes State Park, and Newport State Park. Grassland birds have fledged and parent birds are busy teaching their young how to fend for themselves. In the interior of the peninsula, the orchards are full of fruit, and farmers begin harvesting. Thunderstorms rumble across the peninsula many afternoons and evenings, and temperatures are on the rise, particularly inland and on the Green Bay side.

August

By August, the summer season is in full swing, and with temperatures rising, visitors begin to flock to Lake Michigan and Green Bay beaches. Meadow plants like black raspberry, Canada thistle, common and Canada ragweed, and zigzag and giant goldenrod flower in fields, drawing butterflies in to forage. The wetlands continue to buzz with dragonflies: brush-tipped emerald, Canada darner, chalk-fronted corporals, four-spotted skimmers, Hine's emerald, and Williamson's emerald. Tadpoles emerge as full-grown wood frogs, and small families of ducks and geese with rapidly growing offspring frequent lakes and wetlands. Turkey hens are in the woodlands with troops of growing young birds, called polts. Gulls and terns soar over beaches and cliff overlooks. August temperatures are variable. In some years days are in the eighties and nineties; in other years days are in the sixties and nights in the forties. Afternoon and evening thunderstorms are common.

September

September mornings are crisp, a harbinger of cold weather. Goldenrod and ragweed continue to bloom; big bluestem and fringed gentian begin to flower. Dragonflies, like the white-faced meadowhawk skimmer, flit about meadows and wetlands. Flocking blackbirds begin to appear, particularly around agricultural areas during harvesting. Colonial nesting birds such as Great Blue Heron, Double-crested Cormorant, and several species of swallow begin to depart nesting grounds, gathering in flocks along shorelines. Staghorn sumac changes colors, and dogwoods bear fruit. Canada Geese and Sandhill Cranes head south. By mid- to late September, deciduous forests across Door County begin to turn orange, gold, and red, and highbush cranberries are in full fruit. By month's end, Blue Jays are more noticeable in large, noisy migrant flocks, and other boreal forest breeding birds, like White-throated Sparrow and Yellow-rumped Warbler, are beginning to migrate in considerable numbers.

October

Door County's fall colors are at their peak around mid-October, depending on precipitation and temperature. The first snow and hard freeze of the season usually occur in early October, though exact dates vary. All but the last of the neotropical migrants and summer crowds have gone south, leaving Door County's human winter population to breathe a collective sigh of relief from the hectic pace of the tourist season. Turtles and frogs tuck into the mud for winter hibernation as the temperatures start to dip, and Canada Geese, Ruddy Ducks, Blue-winged Teal, and Tundra Swans move through en route to warmer climes. Tamarack is in full yellow color toward the middle of the month. Migrant birds like White-crowned and Fox Sparrow descend on the peninsula by mid-month, while flocks of winter residents like Dark-eyed Junco and American Tree Sparrow begin to appear toward the end of the month.

November

By early November, sugar maples, beech, shagbark hickory, and a few species of oak still have color, though other species have long since dropped their leaves. Painted turtles and mourning cloak butterflies take their last opportunities to bask in the sun on warm days. Intermediate wood fern may still remain green, peeking out from the early snowfalls. Chipmunks have begun to hibernate, gray squirrels finish their nests and stash nuts for winter, and other small mammals and rodents disappear to warmer nooks. The first large flocks of the wintering waterfowl begin to appear around the peninsula and Washington Island, with scoters, Common Merganser, Redhead, Long-tailed Duck and Bufflehead rafting offshore. Other winter birds, including Pine Siskins and American Tree Sparrows, appear in larger flocks at feeders alongside resident species.

Late November and December

Late November and December herald another influx of winter visitors, drawn to Door County for cross-country skiing, hunting, and snowmobiling. The weather can be variable. In some years, winter begins in earnest. Trees are bare, and many shallow ponds, wetlands and bays are frozen. In other years, sunny, warmer days persist as autumn takes longer to draw to a close. As winter progresses, larger bodies of water begin to freeze. Watch for the northern lights on cloudless nights. Snowy Owls may appear along the lakeshores, particularly on dunes and breakwaters and along frozen fields. Snowshoe hare and ermine have turned white for the year. Watch for Common Ravens flocking on deer carcasses and for the return of wintering Rough-legged Hawks and Northern Shrikes patrolling open agricultural areas. At feeders, look for the first of the winter finches to appear, including Evening Grosbeaks, Common and Hoary Redpolls, and Pine Siskins.

1

Washington Island

Washington Island, the largest of the Grand Traverse Islands, was settled in the mid-1800s by Scandinavian farmers, loggers, and fishermen. About 650 hardly souls, many of Icelandic descent, call Washington Island home today. Washington Island is accessible by private boat or by ferry from the Door Peninsula. The Island Clipper from Gills Rock to Washington Island is a passenger-only ferry, and is ideal for cyclists because you can take your bike on the ferry for no additional charge (http://www.islandclipper.com, (920) 854-2972). The Washington Island Ferry Line from Northport is the car ferry, and also allows walk-on passengers and cyclists (http://www.wisferry.com, (800) 223-2094). Both ferry services drop passengers off on the island within a few hundred feet of one another at the main public docks along Detroit Harbor, in the town of Washington, the only "urban" part of the island. The rest of the island consists mostly of farms, interspersed with homes, shops, churches, a few restaurants, motels, museums, boatyards, and a nine-hole golf course. While a few tourist attractions have sprung up in recent years, the island is still a quiet place, well suited for family biking trips along back roads, and trips to the beach on warm summer days.

MAJOR POINTS OF INTEREST

1. Rock Island State Park

≋ 🛆 🏃 ⌂ 🎿 🗒 🚻

Rock Island, part of the Wisconsin State Park System, offers camping, swimming, hiking, and kayaking from May to October. It is located just northeast of Washington Island and is reached by the passenger-only ferry from Jackson Harbor on Washington Island. (Note that cars and bikes are not allowed on Rock Island.) The ferry has many daily sailings during the summer season, so you can visit Rock Island as a day trip or as an overnight camping trip (reserve well in advance). It can be busy on summer weekends; visit midweek or during the off-season if you want to feel as if you're on your own private island.

In the fall and winter, Rock Island is a popular destination for deer hunting and winter recreation. It is accessible by private boat or by snow-mobile when Jackson Harbor freezes solid.

The island, less than 1,000 acres, was originally settled in the early 1900s by the Thordarson family. In the mid-1960s, the family sold the island to the State of Wisconsin. Today, the entire island is a state park. It has no hotel facilities, no cars, no roads, and no houses. Visitors will find a traditional Icelandic-style boathouse built by the Thordarson family, a seasonal campground with a summer naturalist, a water tower, historic Pottawatomie Lighthouse and museum, and the remains of a few historic buildings. You can buy souvenirs at the small park store, but not much

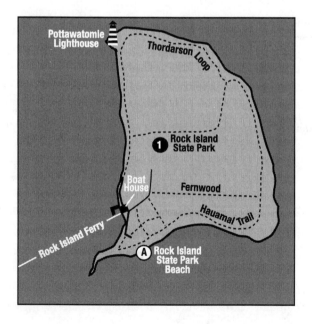

more. There is a source for drinking water, but for extended stays, plan to bring all of your food and supplies from the mainland.

The island has more than 10 miles of loop trails, 5,000 feet of sandy beaches, and a campground with 40 sites. More than half of the island is designated as a State Natural Area, for its majestic groves of spruce, maple, cedar, and beech along rocky outcrops in its interior. Wet places along these rocky outcrops, known to ecologists as moist cliff communities, are fed by underground springs, or seeps. These rare communities are home to a host of fern species and large-flowered trillium. The plants on outcrops and along the forest floor provide habitat for northern ring-necked snake and ground-nesting birds, such as Ovenbird and Mourning Warbler.

The campground, beach, and boathouse area boasts a large Cliff Swallow colony, and Caspian Terns and gulls drift past the docks in summer. A summer walk around the island will reveal breeding birds, like Northern Parula, Black-throated Green Warbler, Canada Warbler, Blackburnian Warbler, and American Redstart. In the fall, Rock Island can be an exceptional place to watch fall songbird and raptor migrations.

Trails

The Thordarson Loop Trail (6.5 miles) traverses the perimeter of the island, passing the Pottawatomie Lighthouse, built in 1836 and one of the oldest on the Great Lakes. The trail from the boathouse to the lighthouse (about 2.5 miles round-trip), which includes part of the Thordarson Loop Trail, is the most popular hike on the island. The Fernwood Trail (1.5 miles) and the Hauamal Trail (1.5 miles) run across the middle and southern third of the island, respectively, and both link up with the Thordarson Loop Trail. Generally flat, the trails are easy to moderate hiking. Shorter loop hiking and nature trails are located in the southwestern portion of the island around the camping areas. No bicycles or motorized vehicles are allowed on the trails. Check at the park visitor center for more detailed trail information.

Contact Information and Directions

Wisconsin Department of Natural Resources, Rock Island State Park, 1924 Indian Point Road, Washington Island, WI 54246-9728, (920) 847-2235, http://dnr.wi.gov/org/land/parks/specific/rockisland/. Friends of Rock

Island: http://uniontel.net/~cmarlspc/. Ferry to Rock Island: (920) 535-0122. From the main ferry docks at Detroit Harbor on Washington Island, head north on Lobdell Point Road/County W for 1.7 miles to Main Road/County W. Turn left and head north on Main Road/County W 2.6 miles to Jackson Harbor Road/County W. Turn right and head east on Jackson Harbor Road/County W for 3.7 miles to Indian Point Road. Follow Indian Point Road to the ferry landing at Jackson Harbor. Park in the lot, and take the passenger ferry to Rock Island. Rock Island is also accessible by private boat. Campsites must be reserved through the Wisconsin State Park System. Fee for ferry. Fee area.

2. Domer-Neff Nature Preserve and Bird Sanctuary

The 0.5-mile birding trail in this preserve is maintained in the summer months by the Door County Land Trust (DCLT) for birding and nature viewing. Mowed through fields, it provides good opportunities to see

grassland birds, including Field Sparrow, Clay-colored Sparrow, and Eastern Meadowlark. The trail is also an easy walk for those who have difficulty walking long distances or are walking with small children.

CONTACT INFORMATION AND DIRECTIONS

Door County Land Trust, P.O. Box 65, Sturgeon Bay, WI 54235, (920) 746-1359, http://www.doorcountylandtrust.org/. From the ferry docks at Detroit Harbor head north on Lobdell Point Road/County W for 1.7 miles to Main Road/County W. Turn left onto Main Road/County W and proceed 1.3 miles to Town Line Road. Turn right on Town Line Road and proceed about 0.3 mile to the yellow Door County Land Trust signage. The birding trail is next to Stavkirke, a Norwegian stave church, and across the road from Trinity Lutheran Church. Parking is available at both churches, space permitting. Access the trail at the DCLT signage on Town Line Road or from the Stavkirke prayer path marked Birding Path. No fee.

3. Jackson Harbor Ridges State Natural Area and Carlin's Point

Jackson Harbor Ridges State Natural Area includes a town park, owned and operated by the Town of Washington, and the small peninsula area locally known as Carlin's Point. The park is located in the sleepy harbor settlement of Jackson Harbor on the far northeast side of Washington Island. The park and beach are great for swimming and picnicking, as well as for launching canoes and kayaks for day trips around Carlin's Point, Rock Island, or Hog Island. In addition to a nine-acre sandy swimming beach, there are two short trails, which connect with one another.

This area was named after the series of twelve low wooded ridges and swales found in the region. These forested ridges and wetland swales, like others in Door County, were formed by glaciations and historic water level changes in Lake Michigan. The wooded area along Jackson Harbor is predominantly boreal forest, with dense spruce trees, as well as some cedar-dominated northern wet-mesic forest and maple-dominated northern mesic forest. Along Lake Michigan, you will find large dunes and sandy beaches. The upper dunes areas are home to several endangered

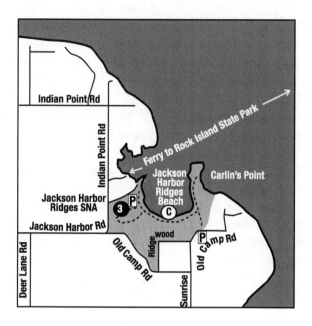

and threatened plants, including dune goldenrod and dune thistle. Jackson Harbor also contains a rare interdunal wetland, that is, damp areas between the dunes that contain a number of plants atypical of Door County, including such rare species as bladderwort, Baltic rush, twigrush, bird's-eye primrose, low calamint, and slender bog arrow-grass. In the summer look for the flashy blue dwarf lake iris in the wooded areas and nesting conifer-specialist warblers, such as Blackburnian, Canada, and Yellow-rumped. During spring migration, scan the sand spit along the harbor for migrant shorebirds.

TRAILS

Jackson Harbor Ridges has nature trails, along the shore and out to Carlin's Point, that are well maintained and less than a mile long. The main Jackson Harbor Ridges Trail meanders along the harbor for about 0.5 mile and provides lake views and views of Hog Island, part of the Green Bay National Wildlife Refuge. From the 0.3-mile Carlin's Point Trail you can see the boathouse on Rock Island. Trails are limited to nonmotorized access. Trailheads and detailed trail maps can be found on kiosks near the Jackson Harbor Ridges beach.

CONTACT INFORMATION AND DIRECTIONS

Town of Washington, Town Offices, 910 Main Rd., P.O. Box 220, Washington Island, WI 54246, (920) 847-2522, http://www.washingtonisland-wi .gov. Visitors can pick up the trails by parking at either the Jackson Harbor Maritime Museum or the Carlin's Point access. To reach the Maritime Museum from the ferry landing, take Lobdell Point Road/County W north for 1.7 miles, then turn left and go north on Main Road/County W for 2.6 miles to Jackson Harbor Road/County W. Turn right and go east for 3.7 miles to the intersection of Old Camp Road. As the road turns to the left and becomes Indian Point Road, bear right on the continuation of Jackson Harbor Road as it continues toward the water. Park at the Maritime Museum lot, just past the Jackson Harbor Inn. To reach the Carlin's Point access, take Old Camp Road from the intersection of Jackson Harbor Road, follow the turn to the left and then right (don't get on Sunrise). Watch for a Carlin's Point sign on the left side of the road. Park off the shoulder of the road. The access trail is 0.1 mile to the point where it meets the Jackson Harbor Ridges Trail. Turn right to hike to the end of Carlin's Point (0.3 mile). No fee.

4. Little Lake State Natural Area

Little Lake, a shallow 24-acre lake, was a bay of Lake Michigan thousands of years ago. The bay was cut off from Lake Michigan as silt, sediment, and cobble rock were gradually deposited at its mouth. This area is an important Native American cultural site, and many cultural artifacts collected from this site are on display at Washington Island's acclaimed Jacobsen Museum. The Door County Land Trust (DCLT) owns most of the shoreline on the northern two-thirds of the lake, which is home to pockets of deciduous northern wet-mesic forest, within a large northern sedge meadow wetlands and fen area. In the summer look for nesting Black-throated Blue Warbler, Red-shouldered Hawk, breeding blue-spotted salamander, little brown bat, and northern leopard frog. In the

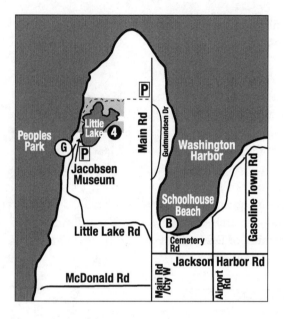

shallows along the lakeshore, watch Great Blue Herons hunting for frogs and fish. Given its unique geography, during spring and fall migration this spot along the edge of Washington Island can be an excellent place to look for migrant songbirds that "fall out" after flying over Lake Michigan and stop on the first available land.

TRAILS AND ACCESS

This site offers a moderate day hike that can also be done in combination with Paddling Route P2. A round-trip hike of about 2.4 miles includes 0.8 mile of trails on the preserve, and 0.4 mile on an access easement road. Note that the trail can be rocky in spots. From Main Road, follow the access easement road west for about 0.4 mile to the beginning of the preserve, and then continue another 0.8 mile on the trail to the trail's end at the shore of Little Lake. Retrace your steps to return.

CONTACT INFORMATION AND DIRECTIONS

Door County Land Trust, P.O. Box 65, Sturgeon Bay, WI 54235, (920) 746-1359, http://www.doorcountylandtrust.org/. From the ferry landing, head north on Lobdell Point Road/County W for 1.7 miles to Main Road/County W. Turn left on Main Road/County W and head east for 3.9 miles to 2288 Main Road, just past the intersection with Gudmundsen Drive. Park off the shoulder and look for a DCLT trail sign on the west side of the road to access the trail. No fee.

5. Detroit Harbor State Natural Area

Detroit Harbor State Natural Area includes large parcels of land on Washington Island and Detroit Island that have been collectively designated a State Natural Area. The Washington Island section is spread across a number of DCLT holdings to the north and west of the ferry dock, along Detroit Harbor. These land holdings include the Detroit Harbor Nature Preserve on Lobdell Point Road and the Richter Community Forest Preserve on Green Bay Road.

The Detroit Harbor Nature Preserve has about 0.5 mile of hiking trails, along an old logging road, maintained by DCLT volunteers in the summer

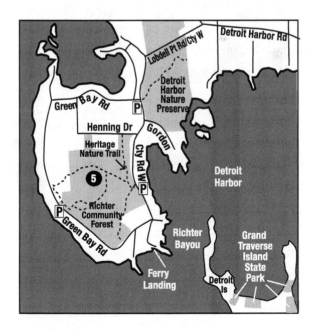

months. Trails may be muddy during the spring, and appropriate footwear is recommended. The site is noteworthy for its stands of ancient
hemlock and yellow birch, and abundance of understory plants including
rare native ferns, Canada yew, and wild sarsaparilla. Listen for American
Redstart, Indigo Bunting, and Black-capped Chickadee. Leashed dogs are
permitted. Bikes, horses and motorized vehicles are prohibited. Hunting
is authorized in some areas subject to DCLT guidelines and permission.

The Richter Community Forest Preserve contains large stands of old
cedar trees in a northern wet-mesic forest, along with sections of northern mesic forest, which provides nesting habitat for Winter Wren, Cedar
Waxwing, and American Redstart. Pockets of northern dry-mesic forest,
particularly along the lake, are primarily red pine and white pine, which
provide habitat for hoary bat and ermine. In late spring and early summer, you can find several species of rare orchids, including pink and
yellow ladyslipper. The highlight of the Richter tract is several scenic
trails maintained by DCLT volunteers, which link up with the 1.0-mile
Heritage Nature Trail. The latter is dedicated to early civic leaders and
their families, is managed by the Town of Washington, and provides a
natural history and historical introduction to Washington Island. These
trails are an easy walk for all ages.

Contact Information and Directions

Door County Land Trust, P.O. Box 65, Sturgeon Bay, WI 54235, (920)
746-1359, http://www.doorcountylandtrust.org/. Town of Washington,
Town Offices, 910 Main Rd., P.O. Box 220, Washington Island, WI 54246,
(920) 847-2522, http://www.washingtonisland-wi.gov. There are two trail-
heads for the Richter Community Forest tract: the DCLT trailhead on
Lobdell Point Road and the Heritage Nature Trail trailhead on Green Bay
Road. To reach the DCLT trailhead, from the ferry landing take Lobdell
Point Road/County W north 0.1 mile to Green Bay Road. Turn left on
Green Bay Road and proceed 0.7 mile to a yellow DCLT sign across from
301 Green Bay Road. Park alongside Green Bay Road, and look for the
trail sign on the east side of Green Bay Road. To reach the Heritage
Nature Trail trailhead, from the ferry landing take Lobdell Point Road/
County W north for 0.3 mile, where you will see trail signs. The trail ends
on Henning Road. You can access the trail from either end. No fee.

6. Mountain Park Lookout Tower

Mountain Park Lookout Tower, located near the highest point on Washington Island in an area known as Little Mountain, should be a stop on any Washington Island itinerary. The tower has 184 steps and two main viewing platforms—one at the top and a lower one—and several benches where you can rest and appreciate the views. From the top you can see all of Washington Island; many of the Grand Traverse Islands, including Rock Island; St. Martin Island, Michigan; and, on clear days, the Escanaba area of the Upper Peninsula of Michigan. The lookout tower is also a great place to watch for migrant songbirds during spring and fall migrations. This park has parking and picnic tables but no trails.

CONTACT INFORMATION AND DIRECTIONS

Washington Island Town Office, 910 Main Rd., P.O. Box 220, Washington Island, WI 54246, (920) 847-2522, http://www.washingtonisland-wi.gov. From the ferry landing, go north on Lobdell Point Road/County W for

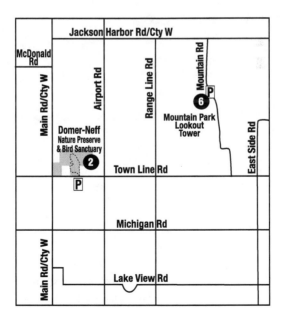

1.7 miles to Main Road/County W. Turn right and head east on Main Road/County W for 2.6 miles to Jackson Harbor Road/County W. Turn right on Jackson Harbor Road/County W and go east for 1.5 miles to Mountain Road/County W. Take a right on Mountain Road/County W and go south for 0.5 mile to the park entrance. No fee.

BEACHES AND OVERLOOKS

A. Rock Island State Park Beach

The sandy beach at Rock Island State Park can be accessed via the Rock Island Ferry from Memorial Day through early fall. The site has restrooms, changing shelters, boating opportunities, and a historic boathouse.

CONTACT INFORMATION

Wisconsin Department of Natural Resources, Rock Island State Park, 1924 Indian Point Rd., Washington Island, WI 54246-9728, (920) 847-2235,

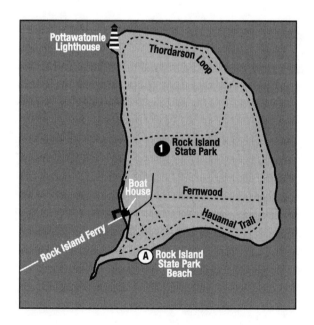

http://dnr.wi.gov/org/land/parks/specific/rockisland/. Rock Island Ferry: (920) 847-3322 or (920) 535-0122. Fee area.

B. Schoolhouse Beach

This scenic limestone cobble beach is located in a protected shallow cove. The cobbles are smooth, fist-sized rocks that have been worn down by the waves of Lake Michigan over time. The beach has a swimming area, diving raft, restrooms, and a picnic area with grills. This is one of the few cobble beaches in Door County. Removing cobbles is prohibited.

CONTACT INFORMATION AND DIRECTIONS

Washington Island Town Office, 910 Main Rd., P.O. Box 220, Washington Island, WI 54246, (920) 847-2522, http://www.washingtonisland-wi.gov/. From the ferry landing, proceed north on Lobdell Point Road/County W for 1.7 miles to Main Road/County W. Turn left on Main Road/County W and go north for 2.6 miles to Jackson Harbor Road/County W. Turn

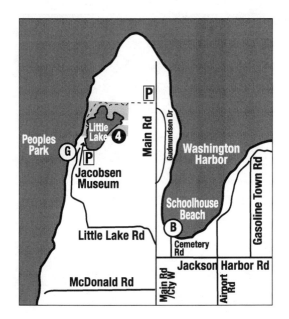

right on Jackson Harbor Road and go east 0.2 mile to Cemetery Road. Take a left on Cemetery Road, which leads to the beach entrance. No fee.

C. Jackson Harbor Ridges Beach

Jackson Harbor Ridges Beach is a protected harbor beach with warm water. Canoes and kayaks can be launched from the swimming beach for a trip over to Rock Island or around Carlin's Point. This area has parking at the Maritime Museum and restrooms.

CONTACT INFORMATION AND DIRECTIONS

Washington Island Town Office, 910 Main Rd., P.O. Box 220, Washington Island, WI 54246, (920) 847-2522, http://www.washingtonisland-wi.gov/. From the ferry landing, go north on Lobdell Point Road/County W for 1.7 miles to Main Road/County W. Turn left and follow Main Road/County W for 2.6 miles to Jackson Harbor Road/County W. Turn right and go east on Jackson Harbor Road for 3.7 miles to the intersection with

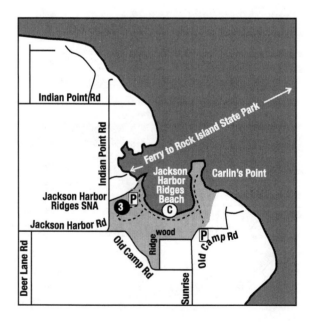

Old Camp Road. As the road turns to the left and becomes Indian Point Road, bear right to continue on Jackson Harbor Road. Park at the Maritime Museum, just past the Jackson Harbor Inn. No fee.

D. Percy Johnson County Park Beach

Percy Johnson County Park has a shallow, sandy beach with rock ledges and a rocky bottom. It has a picnic area with grills and restrooms. Experienced paddlers can launch canoes or kayaks for a trip around Hog Island or over to Rock Island.

CONTACT INFORMATION AND DIRECTIONS

Door County Parks System, 3528 Park Dr., Sturgeon Bay, WI 54235, (920) 746-9959, http://map.co.door.wi.us/parks/. From the ferry landing, head north on Lobdell Point Road/County W for 1.7 miles to Main Road/County W. Turn left on Main Road/County W and proceed 0.4 mile to Lake View Road. Turn right at Lake View Road and go east for 3.1 miles,

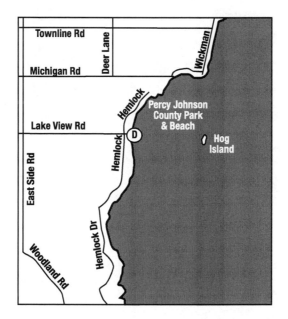

until the road ends at a parking area overlooking Hog Island, at 601 Lake View Road. No fee.

E. Gislason Beach

Wide and sandy Gislason Beach is located in Red Barn Park, which has a playground, picnic area with grills, restrooms, volleyball courts, trails, and a summer theater. When lake levels are low, the beach is generally unsuitable for swimming but the area is often good for seeing wading birds, ducks, and marsh birds.

CONTACT INFORMATION AND DIRECTIONS

Washington Island Town Office, 910 Main Rd., P.O. Box 220, Washington Island, WI 54246, (920) 847-2522, http://www.washingtonisland-wi.gov/. From the ferry landing, take Lobdell Point Road/County W east around Detroit Harbor for 2.9 miles (the road will become Detroit Harbor Road) to Range Line Road. Turn right and follow Range Line Road south for

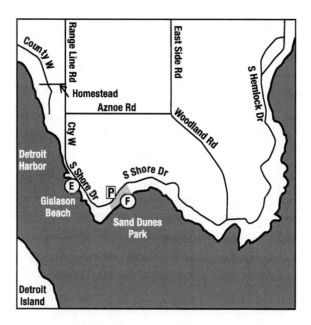

0.7 mile (the road will become South Shore Drive) until you reach the beach. The beach is located next to the Shipyard Marina. No fee.

F. Sand Dunes Park and Beach

In recent years, as lake levels have dropped, Sand Dunes Beach has filled in with marsh vegetation. When lake levels are low, the beach is generally unsuitable for swimming, but the area is often good for seeing wading birds, ducks, and marsh birds. Recent efforts have been made to improve this beach. The park has restrooms, and the beach can be accessed by walking over a sandy trail.

CONTACT INFORMATION AND DIRECTIONS

Washington Island Town Office, 910 Main Rd., P.O. Box 220, Washington Island, WI 54246, (920) 847-2522, http://www.washingtonisland-wi.gov/. From the ferry landing, head east on Lobdell Point Road/County W for 2.9 miles around Detroit Harbor (the road will become Detroit Harbor Road) to Range Line Road. Turn right and proceed south on Range Line Road for 1.4 miles (the road will become South Shore Drive) past the Shipyard Marina. The park is located at 1291 South Shore Drive. No fee.

G. Peoples Park

This wooded bluff overlook is a popular spot for photographing sunsets over Green Bay.

CONTACT INFORMATION AND DIRECTIONS

Washington Island Town Office, 910 Main Rd., P.O. Box 220, Washington Island, WI 54246, (920) 847-2522, http://www.washingtonisland-wi.gov/. From the ferry landing, head north on Lobdell Point Road/County W for 1.7 miles to Main Road/County W. Turn left and follow Main Road/County W for 2.7 miles to Little Lake Road. Turn left at Little Lake Road and proceed 1.4 miles to the parking area for the beach, near the Jacobsen Museum. No fee.

LIGHTHOUSE

L1. Pottawatomie Lighthouse

Pottawatomie Lighthouse, also sometimes shown as "Potawatomi Lighthouse," is located on Rock Island. First established in 1836, this lighthouse is one of the oldest on the Great Lakes. The current, inactive lighthouse was built in 1858, and an active automated navigation tower was built nearby in 1989. A group known as Friends of Rock Island has put in a significant volunteer restoration effort. Volunteer docents from the group live at the lighthouse during the summer tourist season, run a small museum and visitor center, and provide free daily lighthouse tours during the summer months. From the ferry landing you can walk to the lighthouse (approximately 2.2 miles round-trip). The state park and the lighthouse grounds are open year round, but ferry service is seasonal, from early summer through early fall.

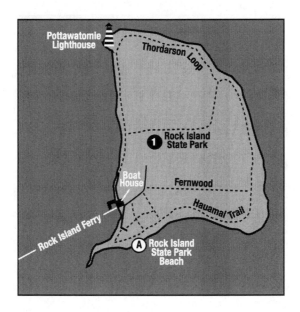

CONTACT INFORMATION

Wisconsin Department of Natural Resources, Rock Island State Park, 1924 Indian Point Rd., Washington Island, WI 54246-9728, (920) 847-2235, http://dnr.wi.gov/org/land/parks/specific/rockisland/. Friends of Rock Island: http://uniontel.net/~cmarlspc/. Rock Island Ferry: (920) 535-0122. Fee area.

BIKE ROUTES

B1. Detroit Harbor to Sand Dunes Park
(8.6 miles total—easy)

This easy bike route is mostly flat and is suitable for beginners of all ages. It starts at the ferry landing at Detroit Harbor, goes past the Detroit Harbor State Natural Area and the urban part of the Town of Washington, and then continues on around Detroit Harbor. The woodlands of the Detroit Harbor State Natural Area provide glimpses of Lake Michigan, the marshes of Richter Bayou, and Detroit Island offshore.

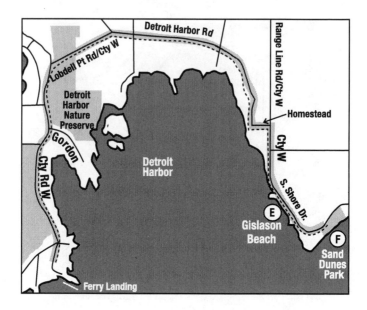

ROUTE

From the ferry landing, head east on Lobdell Point Road/County W for 2.9 miles around Detroit Harbor (the road will become Detroit Harbor Road) to Range Line Road. Turn right and proceed south on Range Line Road 1.4 miles (the road will become South Shore Drive) past the Shipyard Marina. Sand Dunes Park will be on your right at 1291 South Shore Drive. Retrace your route to return.

CONTACT INFORMATION

Washington Island Town Office, 910 Main Rd., P.O. Box 220, Washington Island, WI 54246, (920) 847-2522, http://www.washingtonisland-wi.gov/. No fee.

B2. Detroit Harbor to Schoolhouse Beach Park

(8.6 miles total—easy)

This route begins at the ferry landing in Detroit Harbor and heads north through Washington Island's main commercial center, past homes,

Little Lake Rd

Jackson
Harbor Rd/ Cty W

McDonald Rd

Main Rd/Cty W

Airport Rd

Town Line Rd

2

Michigan Rd

Main Rd/Cty W

Lake View

Lobdell Pt Rd/Cty W

Detroit Harbor

Ferry Landing

businesses, the golf course, the airport, and farm fields, before ending at Schoolhouse Beach Park. The route is mostly flat and suitable for cyclists of all ages and abilities.

ROUTE

From the ferry landing, proceed north on Lobdell Point Road/County W 1.7 miles to Main Road/County W. Turn left on Main Road/County W and go north for 2.6 miles to Jackson Harbor Road/County W. Turn right and go east 0.2 mile to Cemetery Road. You can take a left on Cemetery Road, which leads to the beach entrance, or retrace your route back to the ferry landing. Schoolhouse Park has restrooms.

CONTACT INFORMATION

Washington Island Town Office, 910 Main Rd., P.O. Box 220, Washington Island, WI 54246, (920) 847-2522, http://www.washingtonisland-wi.gov/. No fee.

B3. Detroit Harbor to Jackson Harbor to Mountain Park Lookout Tower

(17.8 miles total—moderate)

This route makes a nice day trip, whether done in its entirety or in shorter stretches, providing cyclists with a full Washington Island experience. The route begins at the ferry landing in Detroit Harbor and heads north along Washington Island's main drag, past homes, businesses, the golf course, the airport, and farm fields, before reaching Schoolhouse Beach Park. It then heads east on Jackson Harbor Road, past a mix of agricultural areas and cedar forests, to the ridges, swales, and dunes of Jackson Harbor Ridges. The route then retraces Jackson Harbor Road and heads south, climbing the hill near Mountain Park Lookout Tower. This middle stretch is challenging and best suited to experienced cyclists. The route then comes down the middle of the island, in the heart of the farming region, on Town Line and Range Line Roads; cuts over on Detroit Harbor Road, providing glimpses of Lake Michigan; and runs past the

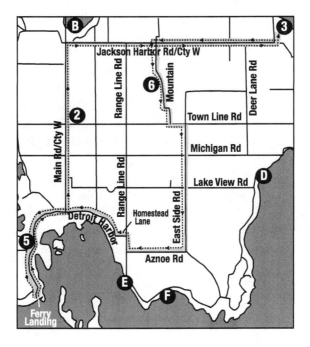

mixed cedar and deciduous forests of Detroit Harbor State Natural Area, before returning to the ferry area.

ROUTE

From the ferry landing at Detroit Harbor, head north on Lobdell Point Road/County W for 1.7 miles to Main Road/County W. Turn left and go north on Main Road/County W for 2.6 miles to Jackson Harbor Road/County W. Take a right on Jackson Harbor Road/County W and follow this road 0.2 mile to Cemetery Road, the entrance road to Schoolhouse Beach Park. You can take a detour into the park, or continue on Jackson Harbor Road/County W for 3.5 miles to Jackson Harbor Dunes Park. Retrace your route back down Jackson Harbor Road/County W for 2.2 miles to Mountain Road and turn left. You will reach Mountain Park Lookout Tower in about 0.5 mile. Proceed past the tower, about 1.0 mile, until Mountain Road ends at Town Line Road. Turn left on Town Line Rd. and continue for about 0.3 mile to East Side Road. Turn right onto East Side Road and follow it for about 2.0 miles to Aznoe Road. Turn right onto Aznoe Road and proceed for about 1.0 mile to Range Line Road. Turn right on Range Line Road and proceed 0.3 mile to Homestead Lane. Turn left onto Homestead Lane and proceed for about 0.2 mile to Detroit Harbor Road. Turn right onto Detroit Harbor Road and follow it along the shores of Detroit Harbor for about 1.0 mile to Main Road/County W. Cross Main Road/County W and continue about 0.1 mile to a split. Bear left at the split onto Lobdell Point Road and proceed for about 2.7 miles to the ferry dock. Jackson Harbor Ridges and Schoolhouse Beach have restrooms.

CONTACT INFORMATION

Washington Island Town Office, 910 Main Rd., P.O. Box 220, Washington Island, WI 54246, (920) 847-2522, http://www.washingtonisland-wi.gov/. No fee.

PADDLING ROUTES
P1. Rock Island State Park
(2.0–8.0 miles total—difficult)

Only experienced kayakers should undertake this trip out to or around Rock Island. Paddling the area requires either bringing a kayak and gear over from the mainland to Washington Island on the ferry, or departing from the Door Peninsula and crossing Porte des Morts. Paddlers can either launch from Jackson Harbor Ridges Beach or Percy Johnson County Park on Washington Island or take another ferry to Rock Island for an extended trip with a base camp at Rock Island State Park. The crossing from Jackson Harbor to the southeastern tip of Rock Island is about 1.0 mile, and the trip around Rock Island is about 6.0 miles. The 8.0 miles round-trip should be attempted only in good weather. Water can be rough, especially during windy periods or inclement weather. As with other parts of Door County, weather can change rapidly, and the areas around Rock Island should not be attempted during approaching storms or windy weather. The exterior of Rock Island is mostly craggy limestone, and landing opportunities are limited to sites near the state park boathouse and beach areas on the southeast side of the island. Despite the effort to get here, the scenery, bluffs, sunsets, and solitude

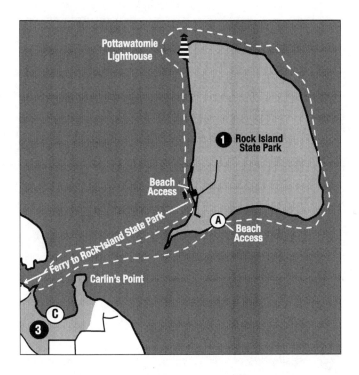

make the trip worthwhile. There is a small seasonal concession at Rock Island State Park, but paddlers must bring all equipment, foul weather gear, warm clothes, water, and food from Washington Island or the mainland Door Peninsula.

ROUTE

From the dock at Jackson Harbor, proceed across to the southeastern tip of Rock Island, about 1.0 mile. While the crossing can sometimes be rough, the boathouse on Rock Island is an easy landmark. You can land either at the dock and boathouse area, or on the sand beaches of the swimming area. From there, you can proceed on an extended trip around Rock Island, about 6.0 miles, although there are few places to land along the perimeter of the island. Keep a close eye out for the ferry and other power boats in the harbor.

Wisconsin Department of Natural Resources, Rock Island State Park, 1924 Indian Point Rd., Washington Island, WI 54246-9728, (920) 847-2235, http://dnr.wi.gov/org/land/parks/specific/rockisland/. Rock Island Ferry: Washington Island Ferry Line, P.O. Box 39, Washington Island, WI 54246, (800) 223-2094 or (920) 847-2546, http://www.wisferry.com/. To reach Jackson Harbor from the ferry landing, head north on Lobdell Point Road/County W for 1.7 miles to Main Road/County W. Take a left on Main Road/County W and go 2.6 miles to Jackson Harbor Road. Turn right and go east on Jackson Harbor Road/County W for 3.7 miles to the intersection of Old Camp Road. As the road turns to the left and becomes Indian Point Road, bear right on the continuation of Jackson Harbor Road. Park at the Maritime Museum lot, just past the Jackson Harbor Inn. Rock Island is a fee area.

P2. Little Lake State Natural Area
(less than 1.0 mile—easy)

Little Lake, a shallow 24-acre lake, was a bay of Lake Michigan thousands of years ago. The bay was cut off from Lake Michigan as silt, sediment, and cobble rock were gradually deposited at its mouth. Today the lake is well suited for easy kayaking or canoeing when lake levels are sufficient. Even in wet years, the lake is rarely more than six feet in the deepest spots, which makes it an excellent place for beginning paddlers to learn the ropes, or for keen wildlife watchers to explore the shorelines by canoe or kayak. During dry times, the lake levels drop, and the area is more of a wetland. The Door County Land Trust (DCLT) owns the land on the north side of the lake, which is home to pockets of deciduous northern wet-mesic forest, within a large northern sedge meadow wetlands and fen area. The State Natural Area designation includes this site and the lake.

You can view the lake and the State Natural Area, and put in canoes or kayaks, from Little Lake Road on the south shore of the lake. This area is also an important Potawatomi Indian archaeological site. Paddling the site requires bringing a kayak or canoe over from the mainland on the ferry.

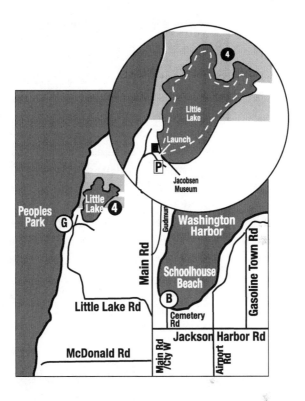

Contact Information and Directions to Launch Site

Door County Land Trust, P.O. Box 65, Sturgeon Bay, WI 54235, (920) 746-1359, http://www.doorcountylandtrust.org/. From the ferry landing, head north on Lobdell Point Road/County W for 1.7 miles to Main Road/ County W. Take a left on Main Road/County W and head north for 2.7 miles to Little Lake Road. Follow Little Lake Road as it jogs west and then north for about 1.4 miles. Limited parking is available at the nearby Jacobsen Museum. Peoples Park along Lake Michigan, operated by the Town of Washington, is nearby and provides some limited parking. No fee.

P3A. Detroit Harbor and Richter Bayou

(2.0 miles round-trip—moderate)

The area between Washington Island and Detroit Island, locally known as Richter Bayou, is part of Detroit Harbor State Natural Area. In recent years, as lake levels have dropped, the marshes and sand bars have become larger, providing close-up opportunities for wildlife viewing while paddling. Along the shore, Richter Bayou's marshes and flats provide habitat for ducks and shorebirds. Also look for Hine's emerald dragonfly, Bald Eagle, American White Pelican, and Osprey, along with gulls and terns. Richter Bayou and Detroit Harbor also provide significant habitat for spawning smallmouth bass. A kayak trip around Detroit Harbor, through the Richter Bayou, and across to Detroit Island (Paddling Route P3B) is appropriate for experienced kayakers only, though most of the route is generally protected from the wind. Paddling the site requires bringing a kayak over from the mainland on the ferry.

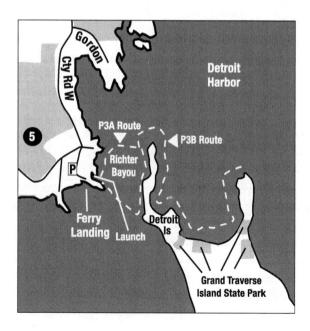

ROUTE

From the docks around the ferry landing, you can paddle directly across to Richter Bayou, just off the main town docks, about 0.5 mile. Keep a close eye out for ferry boats and other power boats on this route, particularly around the docks.

DIRECTIONS TO LAUNCH SITE

The public docks and sand flats around Detroit Harbor provide excellent launching points for a kayak trip through the marshes of the Richter Bayou and over to Detroit Island. Washington Island locals tend to be relaxed about beach access, and you can put in anywhere along the docks and main harbor off Green Bay Road or Lobdell Point Road, but avoid trespassing or parking your vehicle on private property. There is a public boat ramp with a shallow, protected entry point just north of the northernmost ferry dock (the Island Clipper), which is the best place to put your boat in. Generally speaking, you can park in the Welcome Center parking lot right across from the ferry docks, but ask permission if you plan to leave your car there for an extended period. Pay any appropriate launching fees where applicable, and ask permission if in doubt. No fee.

P3B. Detroit Harbor and Grand Traverse Island State Park

(2.5 miles round-trip—moderate)

From Detroit Harbor, experienced kayakers can pair the trip around Detroit Harbor and Richter Bayou (Paddling Route P3A) with a paddle out to Detroit Island. Detroit Island is generally private, with a small summer community loosely organized under the Detroit Island Property Owners Association. The Wisconsin Department of Natural Resources (WDNR) owns several parcels of undeveloped property on the northern end of the island, at Detroit Harbor, which are open to the public, and designated as Grand Traverse Island State Park. This undeveloped property is a state park in name only and lacks the facilities normally found in state parks. At the beaches you can enjoy a picnic lunch and stretch your legs after kayaking over from Washington Island. The WDNR parcels are primarily northern wet-mesic forest community, with large stands of cedar. Along the Lake Michigan shore is an ecological community known as alkaline rockshore, characterized by well-worn rock ledges and some sandy beaches, depending on water levels of Lake Michigan. Grand Traverse Island State Park protects a number of rare plants and animals, including Hine's emerald dragonfly, Crawe sedge, low calamint, and dwarf lake iris. Property owners on the island are generally welcoming, but it is important that visitors stay on WDNR land. Stick to the beaches, to avoid trampling vegetation inland. This area contains many protected rare and endangered plants and animals, and is maintained as a roadless natural area. There are no public facilities or services on Detroit Island.

Route

From Richter Bayou, you can paddle around to the natural harbor at the top of Detroit Island, which forms a small "C"-shaped bay. You can land on the beach areas along the middle of this bay, part of Detroit Harbor. Check the maps to find parcels owned by WDNR, and avoid heading inland. The trip across Detroit Harbor is less than 1.0 mile from Richter Bayou. Keep a close eye out for ferry boats and other power boats on this route, particularly around the docks at Washington Island.

Contact Information and Directions to Launch

Wisconsin Department of Natural Resources, 101 S. Webster St., P.O. Box 7921, Madison, WI 53707, (608) 266-2621, http://www.dnr.wi.gov/. The public docks, boat ramps, and sand flats around Detroit Harbor provide excellent launching points for a kayak or canoe trip through the marshes of Richter Bayou and over to Detroit Island (see Paddling Route P3A for more launching information). Camping is not allowed on Detroit Island. Contact WDNR for more information on access to Grand Traverse Island State Park. Access to WDNR properties is subject to the agency's rules and regulations. No fee.

2

Liberty Grove

Northport, Gills Rock, Ellison Bay, and Sister Bay

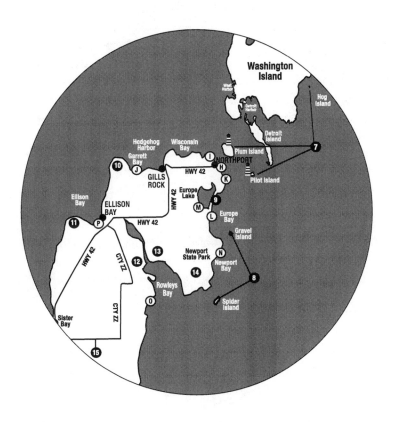

Liberty Grove generally refers to the northern end of the Door Peninsula. It includes the rural, sprawling Town of Liberty Grove, which spans the unincorporated settlements of Ellison Bay, Northport, Rowleys Bay, and Gills Rock, along with the Village of Sister Bay. It is a popular destination for second-home owners and vacationers, but this part of the county is far less developed than areas to the south, consisting primarily of forests and farmland. Inland, you'll find family farms growing wheat, corn, cherries, apples, and pumpkins. The hamlets of Northport and Gills Rock are known for their working harbors, small fleets of fishing boats, and ferries to Washington Island. Ellison Bay is home to the Clearing Folk School and a few shops. Sister Bay is by far the most built up, with many attractions and services. It has a decent-sized grocery store, so if you're planning to do any camping or offshore boating, this is your last real place to stock up.

The Town of Liberty Grove has more than 45 miles of shoreline, hidden beaches, lighthouses, and quiet trails, making it an ideal destination for off-the-beaten-track excursions. Newport State Park draws hikers, campers, and mountain bikers. Offshore, sand and gravel bars and low-lying islands scattered on both the Green Bay and Lake Michigan sides of the peninsula comprise Green Bay and Gravel Island National Wildlife Refuges. Paddling out around these islands is a great day trip for experienced kayakers.

MAJOR POINTS OF INTEREST

7. Green Bay National Wildlife Refuge

The Green Bay National Wildlife Refuge consists of three islands: Pilot, Plum, and Hog. Over a century ago, lighthouses were built on Pilot and Plum Islands, and these became important landmarks for ships navigating the dangerous Porte des Morts straits between Northport and Washington Island. Over time, improvements in navigation and changes in shipping routes made these light stations obsolete. Eventually the buildings fell into disrepair and nature began to take hold. Large colonies of Double-crested Cormorants and nesting gulls took over, and in 2007 the Green Bay National Wildlife Refuge was designated by U.S. Congress, providing protection to the birds. Efforts are underway to preserve the historic lighthouse buildings on the two islands; the U.S. Fish and Wildlife Service, along with a volunteer friends group effort, is planning for a future that includes both protecting wildlife and preserving the buildings.

The 325-acre Plum Island, one of the Grand Traverse Islands, with its historic Coast Guard station and range lights, is located in Death's Door, the narrow and dangerous water passage that connects Green Bay to Lake Michigan. The buildings and 1897 lighthouse are visible from the ferry to Washington Island. While Plum Island has some mature deciduous forests, more and more of the trees are dying back as Double-crested Cormorant populations increase. The island also contains areas of moist cliff, a unique plant community that includes a number of rare ferns and wild sarsaparilla.

Tiny 3.75-acre Pilot Island is located southeast of Detroit Island, also in Death's Door. It is mostly open, with a ground vegetation layer of low red raspberry, Canada yew, and red elder, which provides nesting cover for Black Duck and Canada Geese. Pilot Island has Double-crested Cormorant and Herring Gull nesting colonies, and in some years hosts a

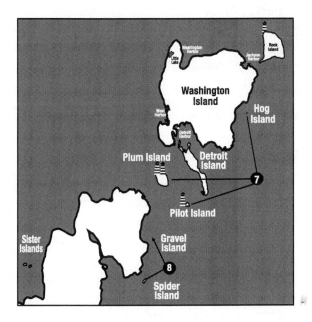

small breeding rookery of Great Blue Herons and Black-crowned Night Herons. From the Washington Island ferry you can see two buildings: the former lighthouse keeper's residence and the Pilot Island Lighthouse, built in 1858. The island was once completely covered with mature forests, but roosting Double-crested Cormorants are gradually killing off the trees.

Even tinier is two-acre Hog Island, located directly east of Percy Johnson Park on Washington Island. It is mostly open with low red raspberry, Canada yew, and red elder shrubs. Federally protected for breeding birds since the early 1900s, it is home to an active herring gull colony.

Trails, Access, and Facilities

Access to these islands is restricted, but you can take private boats or kayaks out around them. Several charter boat captains in the area offer day trips to view the lighthouses, and the Door County Maritime Museum offers tours. The ferries to Washington Island pass close to Plum and Pilot Islands, providing good viewing opportunities. The breeding bird colonies should not be closely approached during waterbird nesting seasons (late spring through August)—the smell of bird guano and the possibility of being covered in it by birds defending their breeding grounds will be enough to deter anyone from setting foot on the islands. That said, it's quite an impressive sight to watch large numbers of birds leaving the colonies in search of fish, as you sit in your boat or watch from the mainland at a safe distance.

Contact Information

Green Bay National Wildlife Refuge is managed by Horicon National Wildlife Refuge, W4279 Headquarters Rd., Mayville, WI 53050, (920) 387-2658, http://www.fws.gov/Refuges/. Friends of Plum and Pilot Islands: http://www.plumandpilot.org/. No fee.

8. Gravel Island National Wildlife Refuge

Gravel Island National Wildlife Refuge consists of two islands: Spider and Gravel. Gravel Island and Hog Island, part of Green Bay National Wildlife

Refuge, together have an additional federal wilderness designation: the Wisconsin Islands Wilderness Area. Spider Island (23 acres) and Gravel Island (4 acres), both located off of Newport State Park, have enjoyed federal protection since the early 1900s. Both are nesting colonies, primarily for Double-crested Cormorants and Herring Gulls, but in some years also for breeding Caspian Terns, Red-breasted Mergansers, and Black-crowned Night Herons. Spider Island was once a maple and beech forest, but over the last few decades, as Double-crested Cormorant colonies expanded, the trees have died back. Today these islands are mostly open sand and gravel with a few areas of scrubby low vegetation and dead trees.

Setting foot on these islands is prohibited, but you can take private boats or kayaks out around them. The breeding bird colonies should not be approached during waterbird nesting seasons (late spring through August), nor would you want to, for the same reasons described above (Green Bay National Wildlife Refuge). Foraging adults are best observed from the water by boat or along the mainland, as they leave the colonies.

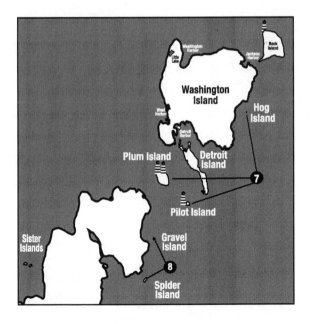

Gravel Island National Wildlife Refuge is managed by Horicon National Wildlife Refuge, W4279 Headquarters Rd., Mayville, WI 53050, (920) 387-2658, http://www.fws.gov/Refuges/. No fee.

9. Europe Bay Woods State Natural Area

Europe Bay Woods State Natural Area sits along a narrow strip of land between Lake Michigan and Europe Lake within Newport State Park. Its 200 acres include quiet Europe Lake shoreline on one side and Lake Michigan beaches on the other. It is accessible from the Newport State Park trail system via the Europe Bay/Hotz Loop Trail.

This area is an exceptional spot for those seeking a quiet walk along a scenic Lake Michigan beach or solitary wildlife watching opportunities. The undeveloped beach has low dunes and large eroded stone ledges when water levels are low. It is fine for swimming, albeit a little chilly even in the late summer! This is one of the quietest sand beaches in all of Door County, perfect for anyone looking to get away from the crowds.

Inland, if you're seeking wildlife viewing opportunities along the hiking trails, take Newport State Park's Europe Bay/Hotz Loop Trail. You'll walk across forested woodlands situated atop ancient ridges and swales, low wooded ridges interspersed with wetlands. Europe Bay Woods contains

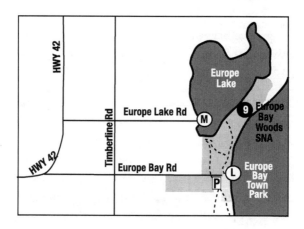

a mix of ecological communities, including spruce-dominated boreal forest, mixed deciduous northern mesic forest, and pine-dominated northern dry-mesic forest. Plants found along the forest floor include dwarf lake iris, beaked hazelnut, wild sarsaparilla, wintergreen, and Canada mayflower. Europe Bay Woods is home to striped skunk, ermine, porcupine, gray fox, red fox, red bat, hoary bat, Black-throated Blue and Cape May Warblers, Ruffed Grouse, snowshoe hare, and Wild Turkey.

TRAILS, ACCESS, AND FACILITIES

The Europe Bay Trail/Hotz Loop provides about 7.0 miles of hiking and biking trails and includes the trails through the State Natural Area portions of Newport State Park. Several primitive camping sites, also part of the state park, are located along the trail system on the northern edge of Europe Bay Woods. While Newport State Park provides picnic areas, restrooms, drinking water, and shelters, Europe Bay Woods State Natural Area has such no facilities. Campsites may be reserved through the Wisconsin State Park System.

CONTACT INFORMATION AND DIRECTIONS

Newport State Park, Wisconsin Department of Natural Resources, 475 County Highway NP, Ellison Bay, WI 54210, (920) 845-2500, http://www .dnr.wi.gov/. From the south (the easiest access point), at the intersection of Highway 42 and Mink River Road in Ellison Bay, head north on Highway 42 for 2.6 miles to Europe Bay Road. Go east on Europe Bay Road for about 2.0 miles. Park at Europe Bay Town Park, a small Liberty Grove park, at the end of Europe Bay Road. You can also access Europe Bay Woods by entering Newport State Park (see directions for Newport State Park) and parking at Lot 3. From Lot 3, pick up the Europe Bay Trail and head north. The Newport State Park visitors' center has trail maps. Fee area.

10. Door Bluff Headlands County Park

Door Bluff Headlands is a 155-acre county park located at the northwestern-most point of the Door Peninsula near Ellison Bay. It is noteworthy for its spectacular limestone bluffs towering over Green Bay, and

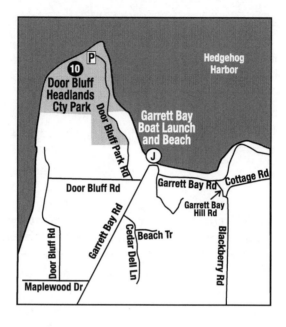

is thought to be the site of conflicts between the Iroquois and Potawatomi tribes. Federally registered Potawatomi pictographs are located in
the general area around this park, visible by boat from Lake Michigan.

It's easy to imagine being one of those early inhabitants as you walk
the dark and damp trails. Enormous old white cedar trees block out the
sunlight even on the hottest summer days, making Door Bluff Headlands
seem particularly remote. The park contains some of the highest eleva-
tions in Door County, and you can glimpse Washington Island and the
Plum Island Range Lights through the massive, ancient forests growing
precariously from the fragile soil atop the bluffs. This park is great for
those in search of adventure. While trails are not marked or maintained
by the county, there is an extensive network of trails on the property, and
intrepid hikers can find several miles of steep, often rocky trails down
to views of the lake. Given the small size of the park, it's difficult to truly
get lost, but remember to be cautious, as there are many dangerous outcrops and slippery slopes without guardrails. In the summer, listen for
Indigo Bunting, Great Crested Flycatcher, Hermit Thrush, Rose-breasted

Grosbeak, and Red-eyed Vireo. Lucky visitors may also spot big brown bats flying at dusk, Virginia opossum, or raccoon. During spring migration, look for migrant songbirds in the trees and along the park roads.

Trails, Access, and Facilities

The park has a seasonal portable toilet, parking along the road, and a network of unofficial hiking trails throughout the property. There are currently no marked trails.

Contact Information and Directions

Door County Parks System, 3528 Park Dr., Sturgeon Bay, WI 54235, (920) 746-9959, http://map.co.door.wi.us/parks/. From the intersection of Highway 42 and Mink River Road in Ellison Bay, go northeast on Highway 42 for 0.1 mile to Garrett Bay Road. Turn slightly left and go north on Garrett Bay Road for 2.2 miles to Door Bluff Road. Turn left at Door Bluff Road and, after about 300 feet, bear right onto Door Bluff Park Road, and go north for 0.3 mile into the park, to 12900 Door Bluff Park Road. No fee.

11. Ellison Bluff County Park

Owned and operated by the Door County Parks System and designated a State Natural Area, this scenic 174-acre park provides excellent views of Green Bay from atop 180-foot dolomite Ellison Bluff. The overlook platform on top of the bluff offers views of Chambers Island, Horseshoe Island, the Strawberry Islands, and, on clear days, the Upper Peninsula of Michigan. These bluffs, part of the Niagara Escarpment, support significant northern wet-mesic and northern mesic communities, including 25 species of snails. The viewing overlook tends to draw crowds, but visitors interested in a bit more can walk the short gravel trails. Along the trails are Canada mayflower, large-flowered trillium, wood betony, bracken fern, and wild sarsaparilla. Listen for birds such as Scarlet Tanager, Rose-breasted Grosbeak, Great Crested Flycatcher, and Winter Wren, and keep an eye out for gray fox, raccoon, northern flying squirrel, and ermine.

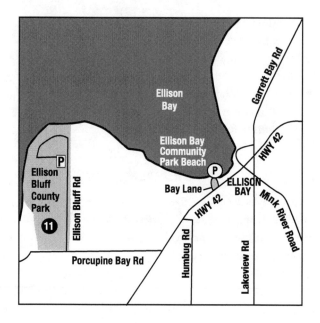

TRAILS, ACCESS, AND FACILITIES

The park has a network of short, easy hiking trails off a central 1.0-mile loop trail. The trails are gravel and well marked. The park has lots of parking, picnic areas, restrooms, and an overlook platform.

CONTACT INFORMATION AND DIRECTIONS

Door County Parks System, 3528 Park Dr., Sturgeon Bay, WI 54235, (920) 746-9959, http://map.co.door.wi.us/parks/. From the intersection of Highway 42 and Mink River Road in Ellison Bay, go south on Highway 42 for about 0.9 mile to Porcupine Bay Road. Go west on Porcupine Bay Road for 0.8 mile to Ellison Bluff Road, then north for about 0.4 mile to the parking lot, at 12050 Ellison Bluff Road. No fee.

12. Mink River Estuary—West Side

Few places on the Door Peninsula have inspired outdoor lovers quite like the Mink River Estuary. The trails are quiet, passing through forests strewn with mossy logs, over gently rolling hills, past hidden wetlands, and finally ending along the banks of the Mink River. You have an excellent chance of seeing wildlife, and it's a great spot to reconnect with the natural world, no matter the season. The Nature Conservancy owns substantial holdings on both the east and west sides of the Mink River down to the river mouth at Rowleys Bay. The west side is a bit less traveled and highly recommended for any Door County hiker.

The spring-fed Mink River, more of a bay of Lake Michigan than a true river, forms a large estuary as it empties into Rowleys Bay. Along the river you'll find a large emergent marsh community, dominated by bulrush, wild rice, and cattail. The estuary is a critical spawning area for some of Lake Michigan's popular sport fish species. Water levels in the Mink River and the estuary's marshes fluctuate, depending on seasons and weather conditions, and are often flooded by seiches—back and forth sloshing waves—from Lake Michigan. Inland and along the Mink River, vegetation is northern sedge meadow community, bordered by willow and alder thickets, which gradually gives way to a northern wet-mesic

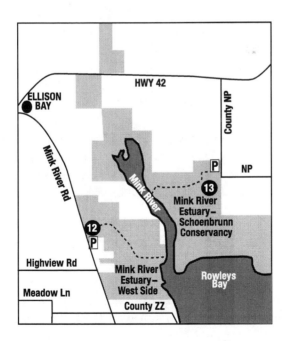

forest. Look for Hine's emerald dragonfly, beaver, muskrat, northern flying squirrel, meadow jumping mouse, northern spring peeper, and an occasional river otter, along with nesting Wood Duck, Blue-winged Teal, Great Blue Heron, Wood Thrush, Tundra Swans, Sandhill Cranes, and migrant waterfowl.

Trails, Access, and Facilities

There are about 5.0 miles of trails on the west side of the river on Nature Conservancy property. The uncrowded, scenic Maple Ridge Trail winds through the property, branching off into several other trails, including the Rowleys Bay, Mink River, and Little Pond Trails. The trails are wide two-track, with the exception of the overgrown, narrow Little Pond Trail.

An easy to moderate walk (about 2.3 miles round-trip), from the parking area to the river, passes through an impressive mix of towering old white cedar forests and mixed deciduous northern mesic communities and ends with spectacular views of the emergent marshes. From the parking on Mink River Road, follow the Maple Ridge Trail to the Mink River Trail to the river. Retrace your steps to return to the parking area. There are no signs at the trailheads but a few throughout the property. The preserve has no facilities. Bikes, dogs, and motorized vehicles are prohibited on these trails.

Contact Information and Directions

The Nature Conservancy, 242 Michigan St., Ste. B103, Sturgeon Bay, WI 54235, (920) 743-8695, http://www.nature.org/. From the intersection of Highway 42 and Mink River Road in Ellison Bay, head south on Mink River Road for about 1.0 mile to a small parking lot for The Nature Conservancy preserve, located across the street between the green address signs for 11713 and 11723 Mink River Road, near the junction with Sylvan Lane. No fee.

13. Mink River Estuary—Schoenbrunn Conservancy and Rowleys Bay

Like the west side of the Mink River Estuary, the east side, also known as the Schoenbrunn Conservancy, is an exceptional spot for a quiet hike,

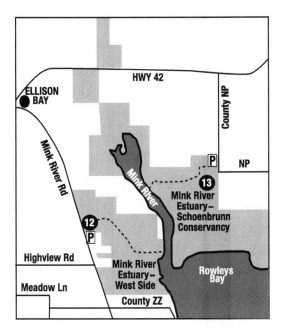

and Rowleys Bay is an ideal launching point for a sublime paddling experience (see Paddling Route P5 for details). The ecological communities and wildlife of the east side are virtually the same as those of the west side.

Trails, Access, and Facilities

There are several miles of easy trails in the Schoenbrunn Conservancy and along Rowleys Bay. You can access these trails from a parking area at the bend of County NP about 1.0 mile south of Highway 42, where County NP makes a 90-degree turn to the east. The main one is the Hemlock Trail (1.75 miles round-trip), which begins at the parking lot and heads directly to the banks of the Mink River. Along the way, you'll pass through towering northern mesic forests, including several stands of large old-growth hemlock trees. The trail ends in an open area along the river and provides excellent views of the marshes. The conservancy has no facilities. Bikes, dogs, and motorized vehicles are prohibited on these trails.

The Nature Conservancy, 242 Michigan St., Ste. B103, Sturgeon Bay, WI 54235, (920) 743-8695, http://www.nature.org/. From the intersection of Highway 42 and Mink River Road in Ellison Bay, go east on Highway 42 for about 2.2 miles to County NP. Turn right and go south on County NP for about 1.0 mile to the parking area at the 90-degree turn of County NP. No fee.

14. Newport State Park

Finding solitude at Door County's state parks, particularly in the busy summer months, can sometimes be a challenge. Newport State Park offers one of the best chances for a more remote nature experience. Even during the high season, its trails and wide, wind-swept Lake Michigan beaches are generally empty. During the middle of the week you'll practically have the place to yourself. Newport provides plenty of opportunities

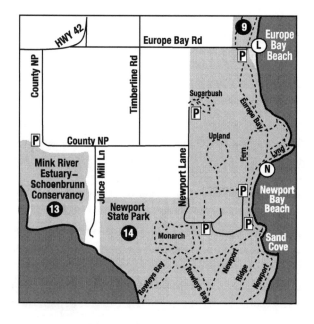

for camping, hiking, mountain biking, and kayaking. It is also one of the coolest places on the peninsula, temperature-wise. This area has extensive northern mesic forest and some pockets of boreal and northern wet-mesic forests. In the forests, watch for porcupine, mink, gray fox, hoary bat, northern flying squirrel, red squirrel, snowshoe hare, White-throated Sparrow, Warbling Vireo, Winter Wren, Red-shouldered Hawk, Cooper's Hawk, Merlin, Magnolia, Ovenbird, Hermit Thrush, American Redstart, and Chestnut-sided, Yellow-rumped, and Black-throated Green Warblers. Canada Warbler is also present in low numbers. Along the lake, look for Common Merganser, Red-breasted Merganser, Wood Duck, and Common Goldeneye. In addition, Cormorant and Ring-billed and Herring Gulls can be observed nesting offshore at Spider and Gravel Islands, and Bald Eagle and Osprey may be observed. In some years, the Ruffed Grouse population is substantial.

TRAILS, ACCESS, AND FACILITIES

The Newport State Park trail system is the most extensive in Door County. It includes one of the most scenic spots in the park, the moderate Europe Bay Trail/Hotz Loop (7.0 miles), which runs through the Europe Bay Woods State Natural Area; the moderate Rowleys Bay Loop (4.0 miles); and the easy Upland Loop (2.0 miles). Especially recommended is the moderate Newport Loop (5.0 miles), which passes through the Newport Conifer-Hardwoods State Natural Area, a northern mesic forest situated atop a long rocky dolomite ledge, complete with boulders and ancient dunes. Some of these trails allow mountain biking; others are limited to hiking. Check with the park visitors' center for specific rules. Lake Michigan swimming beaches are accessible from the trail system. Kayaks can be launched directly from the beach. Newport State Park provides camping, picnic areas, restrooms, drinking water, and shelters. Campsites may be reserved through the Wisconsin State Park System.

CONTACT INFORMATION AND DIRECTIONS

Newport State Park, Wisconsin Department of Natural Resources, 475 County Highway NP, Ellison Bay, WI 54210, (920) 845-2500, http://www.dnr.wi.gov/. From the intersection of Highway 42 and Mink River Road in Ellison Bay, go east on Highway 42 for about 2.1 miles to County

NP. Go south and follow County NP for 1.0 mile to the 90-degree turn in road. Turn right and go 0.5 mile to the park entrance. Fee area.

15. Harold C. Wilson Three Springs Nature Preserve

This 420-acre parcel, managed by the Door County Land Trust (DCLT), sits within the North Bay wetlands complex and includes the headwaters, or beginning point, for Three Springs Creek, which feeds into North Bay. Harold C. Wilson Three Springs Nature Preserve contains a diversity of habitat types, including northern wet-mesic forest, ephemeral (seasonal) streams, northern sedge meadows, and emergent and submergent marshes. The area harbors a variety of plants and animals, including Bald Eagle, American Bittern, Belted Kingfisher, muskrat, meadow vole, white-tailed deer, rare orchids, Hine's emerald dragonfly, and dwarf lake iris. Three Springs Creek and the adjacent wetlands are also important for Door County fish populations, providing significant habitat for smallmouth bass, brown trout, chinook salmon, yellow perch, and northern

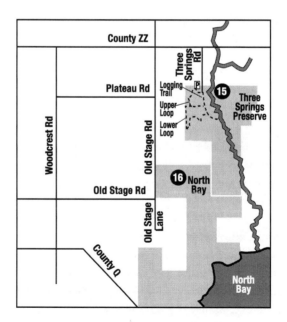

pike. The creek itself feeds into North Bay, a major spawning ground for Lake Michigan whitefish. The meadows and wetlands at Three Springs Preserve are also great for butterflies and dragonflies from May through September.

TRAILS, ACCESS, AND FACILITIES

The property has a newly developed easy 1.8-mile round-trip walking trail and kiosk at the trailhead. The trail winds from the parking area past scenic meadows and historic buildings and ends at a viewing platform overlooking marshes around the springs. Retrace your steps to return to your car. The preserve has no facilities. Hunting is authorized pursuant to DCLT guidelines and permission.

CONTACT INFORMATION AND DIRECTIONS

Door County Land Trust, P.O. Box 65, Sturgeon Bay, WI 54235, (920) 746-1359, http://www.doorcountylandtrust.org/. From the intersection of Highway 42 and County ZZ in Sister Bay, go east on County ZZ/Maple Drive (toward Mill Road) for about 2.0 miles to Three Springs Road. Go south on Three Springs Road, a gravel road with a few houses along it. At the end of Three Springs Road you will see a Door County Land Trust sign and access to the parking area and the trailhead. No fee.

BEACHES AND OVERLOOKS
H. Northport Ferry Terminal (Washington Island Ferry)

The Northport dock and harbor, overlooking the famed Porte des Morts strait at the very end of the Door Peninsula, is usually a stop along the way, borne of necessity while waiting for the ferry to Washington Island, rather than a destination. However, this spot is worth visiting for other reasons. In the winter, the harbor is a good place to look for flocks, known as rafts, of diving ducks, including Long-tail Duck and Red-breasted and Common Merganser, plus the occasional scoter, as well as rare gulls like Thayer's, Lesser Black-backed, or Iceland along the harbor, breakwater, and offshore. During spring migration watch for groups of Broad-winged Hawks and other raptors navigating up the Lake Michigan

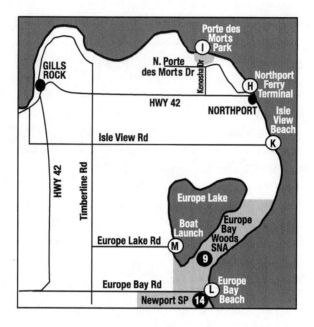

coastline. In the summer, look for Caspian and Common Terns, gulls, and various swallows and Purple Martins cruising the harbor and roosting on the breakwater. The ferry itself can provide good views of offshore species and islands, including the Double-crested Cormorant and gull colonies at Pilot and Plum Islands. For experienced kayakers, this is an excellent launching site for kayaking trips around Plum Island and Pilot Island, or across Porte des Morts to Washington Island.

CONTACT INFORMATION AND DIRECTIONS

Washington Island Ferry Line, P.O. Box 39, Washington Island, WI 54246, (920) 847-2546 or (800) 223-2094, http://www.wisferry.com/. To reach the Northport Ferry Terminal, from the intersection of Highway 42 and Wisconsin Bay Road in Gills Rock, go north on Highway 42 about 1.9 miles until it dead-ends near the end of the peninsula. Follow signs to Washington Island Ferry parking lot. Northport harbor access and observation are from the private parking lots around the ferry dock area. No fee.

I. Porte des Morts Park

Porte des Morts Park, also known as Kenosha Park, can be a good place for observing migrant song birds and raptors, particularly during spring and fall migration. Overlooking Lake Michigan, it is a nice spot for a summer picnic. It has no trails or lake or beach access. The park is minimally developed with seasonal portable toilet and picnic tables. Note that dogs are not allowed in the park.

CONTACT INFORMATION AND DIRECTIONS

Town of Liberty Grove, 11161 Old Stage Rd., Sister Bay, WI 54234, (920) 854-2934, http://libertygrove.org/. From the intersection of Highway 42 and Wisconsin Bay Road in Gills Rock, head north on Highway 42 1.8 miles to Kenosha Drive (which may appear as Park Drive on some maps), just before the ferry lot. Take a left on Kenosha Drive and follow it until it ends at the park. No fee.

J. Garrett Bay Boat Launch and Beach

Garrett Bay Boat Launch and Beach is a 50-foot public access point with limited parking and a concrete boat ramp. This beach is primarily cobble, or smooth rocks, polished by the wave action of Lake Michigan. It is an excellent spot for launching kayaks for excursions past Door Bluff Headlands County Park and the Clearing Folk School. Removing cobbles is prohibited.

CONTACT INFORMATION AND DIRECTIONS

Town of Liberty Grove, 11161 Old Stage Rd., Sister Bay, WI 54234, (920) 854-2934, http://libertygrove.org/. From the intersection of Highway 42 and Mink River Road in Ellison Bay, go northeast on Highway 42 for 0.1 mile to Garrett Bay Road. Turn slightly left on Garrett Bay Road and proceed for about 2.4 miles, almost to the end of Garrett Bay Road, where it makes a sharp turn to the east. The boat launch address is 1310 Garrett

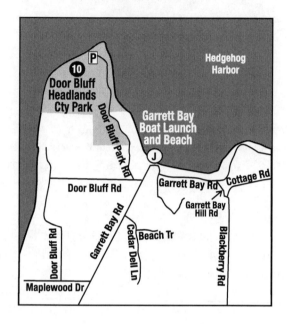

Bay Road. There is parking for a few cars, with additional parking along Garrett Bay Road. No fee, except to launch boats.

K. Isle View Beach

Isle View Beach, adjacent to the Town of Liberty Grove's Hotz Memorial Park, is one of the most scenic in all of Door County, with views of Pilot, Plum, and Detroit Islands. While the park sits above the shoreline, it is possible to climb down the cliffs a few yards to the beach below. The beach is sand and rock, with lots of quagga and zebra mussel shells. It is open to the public below the high water mark, but note that this public stretch of beach is bordered by private homes—avoid trespassing. The park has parking for five or six cars and picnic tables with grills. Note that dogs are not allowed in the park.

CONTACT INFORMATION AND DIRECTIONS

Town of Liberty Grove, 11161 Old Stage Rd., Sister Bay, WI 54234, (920) 854-2934, http://libertygrove.org/. From the intersection of Highway 42

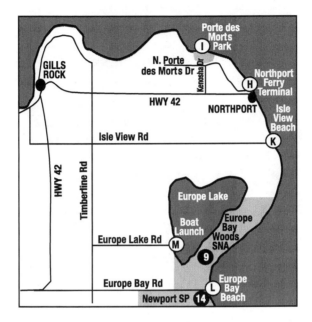

and Mink River Road in Ellison Bay, go north on Highway 42 for 4.2 miles to Isle View Road. Turn right and follow Isle View Road for 2.2 miles until it ends at the parking area at Hotz Park. No Fee.

L. Europe Bay Beach

This wide, scenic, uncrowded, sandy Lake Michigan beach, adjacent to Newport State Park, is a feature of Europe Bay Town Park, which has parking, restrooms, picnic tables, and beach access. Experienced kayakers can use this as a launching point for trips out to Plum Island, Pilot Island, or Detroit Island. Note that dogs are not allowed in the park.

CONTACT INFORMATION AND DIRECTIONS

Town of Liberty Grove, 11161 Old Stage Rd., Sister Bay, WI 54234, (920) 854-2934, http://libertygrove.org/. From the intersection of Highway 42 and Mink River Road in Ellison Bay, go north on Highway 42 for 2.6 miles to Europe Bay Road. Take a slight right and go east on Europe Bay Road

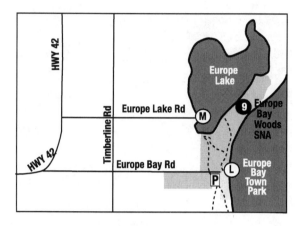

for 1.8 miles, to the end and the entrance to the town park. There is no fee to enter the town park or beach. You can also access the beach by walking up the beach from Newport State Park (a fee area).

M. Europe Lake Boat Launch and Beach

Europe Lake, a quiet inland lake, is bordered by Newport State Park and a number of private residences. This lake is ideal for a relaxing paddle on calm, protected waters, with ample opportunity for wildlife-watching in the marshes. The Town of Liberty Grove maintains a small public boat ramp that provides excellent access for canoeing and kayaking, as well as swimming, although the lake is very rocky and has a limited beach along the shoreline. If you're going to swim, consider wearing water shoes to protect your feet. This site has a parking lot, picnic tables, grills, seasonal portable toilets, a dock, and a boat ramp.

CONTACT INFORMATION AND DIRECTIONS

Town of Liberty Grove, 11161 Old Stage Rd., Sister Bay, WI 54234, (920) 854-2934, http://libertygrove.org/. From the intersection of Highway 42 and Mink River Road in Ellison Bay, go north on Highway 42 for 2.6 miles to Europe Bay Road. Turn right and follow Europe Bay Road east for 0.7 mile to Timberline Road. Turn left and follow Timberline Road for 0.5

mile to Europe Lake Road. Turn right and follow Europe Lake Road for
0.9 mile to the end and the entrance to the parking area. No fee, except
to launch boats.

N. Newport Bay Beaches

The wide, sandy, windswept, Lake Michigan beaches within the boundaries of Newport State Park, including Sand Cove, are collectively referred to as the Newport Bay Beaches. Facilities, including restrooms, are
located within the park. These lovely sand beaches are some of the most
scenic and uncrowded in all of Door County.

CONTACT INFORMATION AND DIRECTIONS

Newport State Park, Wisconsin Department of Natural Resources, 475
County Highway NP, Ellison Bay, WI 54210, (920) 845-2500, http://www
.dnr.wi.gov/. From the intersection of Highway 42 and Mink River Road
in Ellison Bay, go north on Highway 42 for about 2.1 miles to County NP.

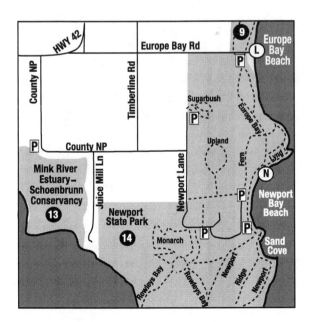

Follow County NP about 3.0 miles into the park. Once inside the park, follow directions to the beach access off Newport Park Road. Fee area.

O. Sand Bay Town Park Beach

Sand Bay Town Park has a very narrow, protected, sandy beach on Rowleys Bay. This Town of Liberty Grove park has a picnic area with grills, restrooms, and a playground. Dogs are prohibited.

CONTACT INFORMATION AND DIRECTIONS

Town of Liberty Grove, 11161 Old Stage Rd., Sister Bay, WI 54234, (920) 854-2934, http://libertygrove.org/. From the intersection of Highway 42 and Mink River Road in Ellison Bay, go southeast on Mink River Road for 3.5 miles until it ends, at Waters End Road. Go east on Waters End Road for 0.4 mile to North Sand Bay Lane. Go north on North Sand Bay Lane for 0.3 mile to the park entrance on your right. No fee.

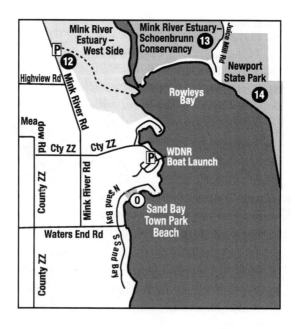

P. Ellison Bay Community Park Beach

Ellison Bay Community Park is on the south end of town, at the bottom of the hill. It has a small sand wading beach, restrooms, picnic areas with grills, a pavilion, a large playground, and tennis courts. The beach is good for launching kayaks for a trip past Ellison Bluff County Park, where you can see some of the tallest bluffs in Door County.

CONTACT INFORMATION AND DIRECTIONS

Town of Liberty Grove, 11161 Old Stage Rd., Sister Bay, WI 54234, (920) 854-2934, http://libertygrove.org/. From the intersection of Highway 42 and Mink River Road in Ellison Bay, go south on Highway 42 for about 0.4 mile to Bay Lane (called Bayview Road on some maps). Turn right on Bay Lane and proceed to the park entrance. No fee.

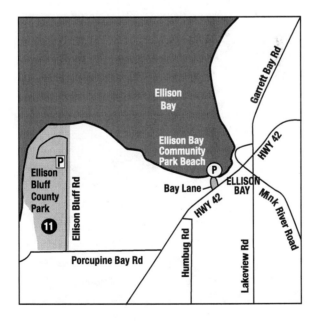

LIGHTHOUSES

L2. Plum Island Range Lights

Plum Island, first established as a light station in 1848, gained its now historic range lights in 1896, when crews began construction on the lights, docks, barn, boathouse, and residential buildings. Now in disrepair, the buildings are the target of preservation efforts by a local group called Friends of Plum and Pilot Islands. The island is now part of the Green Bay National Wildlife Refuge, for breeding birds, and is off-limits to landing by the public. It can be seen from the Washington Island Ferry and the Island Clipper, and boat tours to view the range lights are offered annually through the Door County Maritime Museum. Local festivals and events also offer tours to the islands, particularly during the summer, as do local charter boat captains. Check with the visitors' bureau for more information. Kayaking around Plum Island, launching from Northport, is a great day trip for advanced paddlers (see Paddling Route P4).

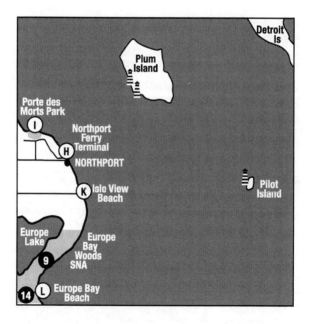

Green Bay National Wildlife Refuge is managed by Horicon National Wildlife Refuge, W4279 Headquarters Rd., Mayville, WI 53050, (920) 387-2658, http://www.fws.gov/Refuges/. Door County Maritime Museum, 120 N. Madison Ave., Sturgeon Bay, WI 54235, (920) 743-5958, http://www.dcmm.org/. Friends of Plum and Pilot Islands, http://www.plum andpilot.org/. No fee.

L3. Pilot Island Lighthouse

Pilot Island was first established as a light station in 1846. Built of Cream City brick in 1846, the lighthouse that stands today and buildings can be seen in the distance from the ferries to Washington Island. Active navigation beacons are now fully automated, and the lighthouse has since fallen into disrepair and the buildings neglected. Restoration efforts are underway by Friends of Plum and Pilot Islands. Like Plum Island, Pilot Island is part of the Green Bay National Wildlife Refuge, for breeding birds, and off-limits to landing by the public. For boat tours and events related to the lighthouse, and for contact information, see Plum Island Range Lights (above). A kayaking trip around Pilot Island, launching from Northport, is a great day trip for advanced paddlers (see Paddling Route P4).

BIKE ROUTES

B4. Ellison Bay to Sand Bay Town Park Beach
(8.5 miles round-trip—easy)

This mostly easy biking route is suitable for beginners of all ages or for a family interested in a beach outing a bit off the beaten track. It travels quiet roads, passes northern wet-mesic forests and a few farm fields, and ends at Lake Michigan.

ROUTE

From the intersection of Highway 42 and Mink River Road in Ellison Bay, go southeast on Mink River Road for 3.5 miles to Waters End Road. Turn

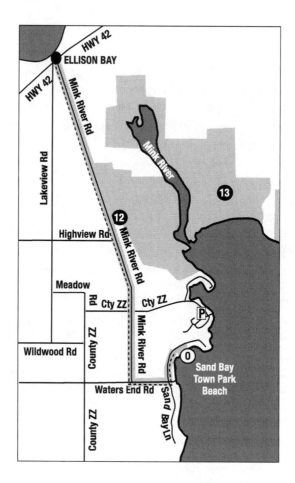

left and follow Waters End Road for 0.4 mile to Sand Bay Lane. (Note that you will see a large dock, as Waters End Road continues a few hundred feet to Lake Michigan.) Turn left and follow Sand Bay Lane about 0.35 mile to the town park entrance. Retrace your steps to return to Ellison Bay. Sand Bay Town Park has restrooms.

CONTACT INFORMATION

Town of Liberty Grove, 11161 Old Stage Rd., Sister Bay, WI 54234, (920) 854-2934, http://libertygrove.org/. No fee.

B5. Ellison Bay to Newport State Park

(13.2 miles round-trip—moderate)

This straightforward biking route is suitable for cyclists of all ages, but is rated moderate for its distance. The route begins in Ellison Bay, enters a patchwork of northern wet-mesic forests and farmland, and ends at the main entrance road to Newport State Park. If you have a mountain or

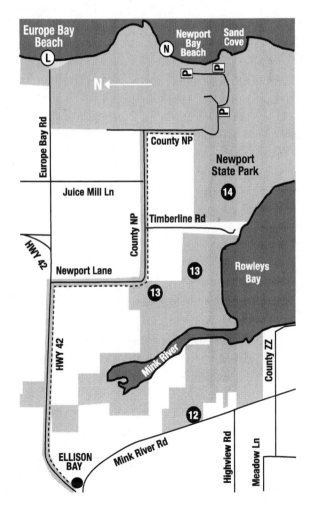

hybrid bike, you can pick up any of Newport State Park's bike trails from this point, or just head along the paved park roads to the beach.

ROUTE

From the intersection of Highway 42 and Mink River Road in Ellison Bay, head north on Highway 42 for 2.2 miles to County NP. Turn right and follow County NP as it heads south and then jogs east and then south again, for about 3.0 miles, to the entrance of Newport State Park. Continue on the main road into the park for about 0.3 mile to hook up with park trails or proceed another 0.9 mile on paved park roads to the beach. Retrace your route to return to Ellison Bay. Newport State Park has restrooms.

CONTACT INFORMATION

Newport State Park, Wisconsin Department of Natural Resources, 475 County Highway NP, Ellison Bay, WI 54210, (920) 845-2500, http://www .dnr.wi.gov/. Newport State Park is a fee area.

B6. Newport State Park Mountain Biking

(12.0 miles round-trip—moderate)

A portion of Newport State Park's trail network is open to mountain biking. The trails run through an extensive northern mesic forest with some pockets of boreal and northern wet-mesic forests. You'll also pass through the Newport conifer hardwoods, a northern mesic forest situated atop a long dolomite ledge, complete with boulders, ancient dunes, and views of Lake Michigan. This trail network is challenging enough to keep experienced mountain or hybrid bikers occupied for a few hours. Those with road bikes should stick to the park's main paved roads.

ROUTE

Once inside Newport State Park, the recommended mountain biking route begins by picking up the Europe Bay Trail at Parking Lot 2, following that trail up to the Hotz Loop, and then retracing the route back to the parking area, a total of about 7.0 miles round-trip. At this point, you

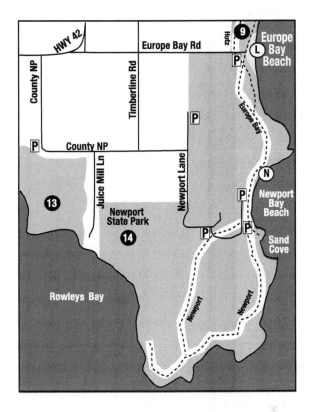

have the option to continue south on the Newport Loop, a 5.0-mile trail that brings you full circle back near Parking Lot 2. Trails open to biking are subject to change. Check with the visitors' center for the most current information on bike trails within Newport State Park. The park has restrooms.

CONTACT INFORMATION

Newport State Park, Wisconsin Department of Natural Resources, 475 County Highway NP, Ellison Bay, WI 54210, (920) 845-2500, http://www .dnr.wi.gov/. Fee area.

88 Liberty Grove

B7. Bluff to Bluff: Gills Rock to Ellison Bluff

(16.8 miles round-trip—difficult)

This difficult cycling route encompasses the hilliest and most challenging terrain in all of Door County. The route, which spans the top of two
of Door County's highest bluffs, is best suited for experienced road
cyclists and is not recommended for beginners or mountain bikers. It
offers spectacular fall colors in most years and impressive views of Lake
Michigan at both Ellison Bluff and Door Bluff Headlands County Parks.
The route begins in Gills Rock, a quiet fishing community, and heads
west along Cottage Road and Garrett Bay Road, two hilly, well-shaded,
summer cottage–lined roads with plenty of hidden driveways and tight
curves, to Door Bluff Headlands County Park. Cyclists can pause for
views of Lake Michigan and Washington Island, or continue south down
wooded, hilly Garrett Bay Road to downtown Ellison Bay. From Ellison
Bay, the route winds its way to Ellison Bluff County Park, another scenic
overlook point, before returning to Gills Rock. Cyclists may find enough

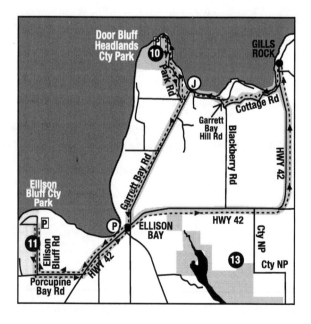

challenge in climbing only one bluff and cut the route in half as an option. Ellison Bluff County Park has year-round restrooms; Door Bluff has seasonal portable toilets.

ROUTE

From downtown Gills Rock at the intersection of Highway 42 and Cottage Road, head west on Cottage Road and proceed up and down the steep curves of Cottage Road for 1.1 miles. Take your second right onto Garrett Bay Hill Road. Follow the steep Garrett Bay Hill Road for 0.2 mile to Garrett Bay Road. Take a left on Garrett Bay Road and cruise down it for 0.7 mile. Take your second right on Door Bluff Road and another right almost immediately onto Door Bluff Park Road. Follow the scenic, shaded entrance road into Door Bluff Headlands County Park, and then back out, 2.2 miles round-trip. Turn left out of the park and proceed 0.1 mile on Door Bluff Road to Garrett Bay Road. Take a right on Garrett Bay Road and cruise up and down the rolling hills for 2.1 miles into downtown Ellison Bay, where Garrett Bay Road ends at Highway 42. Go south on Highway 42 for 1.1 miles to Porcupine Bay Road. Take a right and follow Porcupine Bay Road for 0.8 mile to Ellison Bluff Road. Take a right and follow Ellison Bluff Road north until it ends at the park, 1.1 miles. Return on Ellison Bluff Road, retracing your route to Porcupine Bay Road. Take a left on Porcupine Bay Road and follow it for 0.8 mile back to Highway 42. Take a left on Highway 42, and return to downtown Gills Rock, about 5.5 miles.

CONTACT INFORMATION

Door County Parks System, 3528 Park Dr., Sturgeon Bay, WI 54235, (920) 746-9959, http://map.co.door.wi.us/parks/. No fee.

PADDLING ROUTES

P4. Plum Island and Pilot Island
(3.0–5.75 miles round-trip—difficult)

A trip from Northport out around 325-acre Plum Island or 3.75-acre Pilot Island is suited for very experienced kayakers only. The waters of

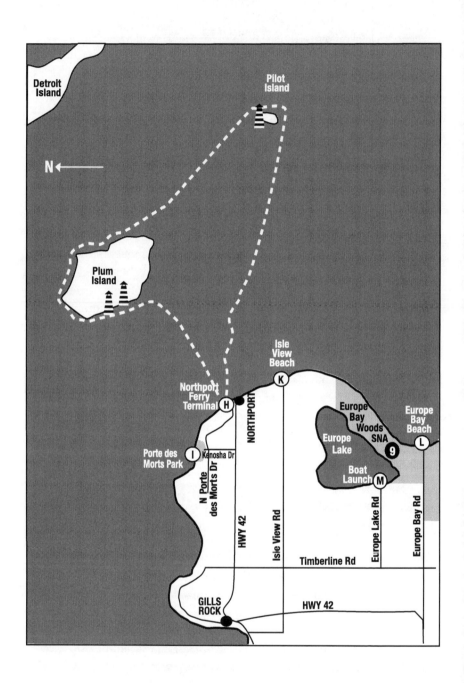

Porte des Morts have claimed the lives of many and can be treacherous even under the best of weather conditions. Do not attempt the trip unless you are extremely experienced and have taken adequate safety precautions, and take along appropriate foul weather gear, warm clothes, water, and food. Pay special attention to the ferries that run close to this route. From Northport the distance to Plum Island is about 1.5 miles and to Pilot Island about 2.5 miles. The two islands can be combined into a longer trip; they are about 1.75 miles apart. Landing on either of these islands is prohibited—both are part of Green Bay National Wildlife Refuge—but a trip around the islands during the summer months will provide great looks at nesting bird colonies. At all times of the year, paddlers will enjoy seeing the historic lighthouses and crumbling buildings. There are also several shipwrecks just off Pilot Island, in depths of 15 to 40 feet, including the schooners *Forest, J. E. Gilmore,* and *A. P. Nicholas,* which make the area popular among divers. Launch from the beach near the ferry terminal. Parking and restrooms are available there.

ROUTE

From Northport, head northeast across Death's Door to Plum Island. You should be able to make out the Plum Island Range Lights for orientation as you get closer to the island. The crossing is about 1.5 miles and, depending on wind direction, can be very strenuous. As you approach Plum Island, begin heading northwest, keeping the island on your right-hand side. As you round Plum Island, you can either head back to Northport or continue on to Pilot Island to the southeast. Keep a close watch for ferries and other boat traffic, particularly around Northport, on this heavily traveled route.

CONTACT INFORMATION AND DIRECTIONS TO LAUNCH SITE

Washington Island Ferry Line, P.O. Box 39, Washington Island, WI 54246, (920) 847-2546 or (800) 223-2094, http://www.wisferry.com/. Green Bay National Wildlife Refuge is managed by Horicon National Wildlife Refuge, W4279 Headquarters Rd., Mayville, WI 53050, (920) 387-2658, http://www.fws.gov/Refuges/. To reach the Northport Ferry Terminal, take Highway 42 north until it dead-ends near the end of the peninsula. Follow signs to Washington Island Ferry parking lot. No fee.

P5. Mink River Estuary

(4.5–6.0 miles round-trip—moderate)

Kayaking the Mink River Estuary offers some of the premier wildlife viewing in the Upper Midwest. This trip is suitable for intermediate and experienced kayakers and canoers and should be at the top of the list for a Door County paddling itinerary. Several local kayak outfitters offer day

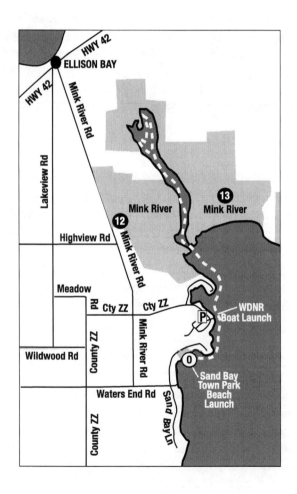

trips to this area. Located east of Ellison Bay, the spring-fed Mink River forms a large estuary as it empties into Rowleys Bay on Lake Michigan. Paddling the area's extensive bulrush, wild rice, and cattail marshes may give you up-close views of Bald Eagle, Black Tern, Common Goldeneye, beaver, Sandhill Crane, and Hine's emerald dragonfly. The estuary is also a critical spawning area for some of Lake Michigan's popular sport fishing species.

Water levels in the Mink River and the estuary's marshes fluctuate, depending on seasons and weather conditions. The river is often flooded by seiches—sloshing waves—from Lake Michigan, but when water levels are low, some portaging may be required. Paddling conditions from morning to afternoon can also fluctuate, so before venturing out to the Mink, check the weather. On most days, the estuary is calm, well protected, and suitable for intermediate kayakers and for canoeing. When there is a strong south wind, however, only experienced paddlers should attempt the trip, as it involves strenuous paddling to exit the estuary and return to either of the launching sites.

ROUTE

From either launching site, Sand Bay Town Park Beach or the Rowleys Bay Resort (located on private land and formerly called Wagon Trail; some land and docking facilities were recently acquired by the Wisconsin Department of Natural Resources [WDNR] and will be available for public access for a small fee), head north along the shoreline and up the mouth of the estuary through the marshes. From Sand Bay Town Park, launch at the sandy beach and head northeast toward the point just northeast of the park, about 0.1 mile (look for the large breakwater dock). Follow the shoreline north around the point and continue up the shoreline about 0.3 mile. You'll see the marina for Rowleys Bay Resort and Crescent Bay on your left. (If you're starting from the Rowleys Bay dock, pick up the directions here.) Unless you feel like extending your route by following the shoreline into tiny Crescent Bay, continue toward the tip of the crescent—the point of land due north—for about 0.2 mile. As you round the tip of the crescent, you will see the entrance to the Mink River just up the shoreline, 0.4 mile on your left. Depending on water levels, you can generally paddle up the Mink River about 1.5 miles more. Retrace your route to return to your launch site, keeping close to the shoreline as you head south.

CONTACT INFORMATION AND DIRECTIONS TO LAUNCH SITE

Town of Liberty Grove, 11161 Old Stage Rd., Sister Bay, WI 54234, (920) 854-2934, http://libertygrove.org/. Wisconsin Department of Natural Resources, 101 South Webster Street, Madison, WI 53707, (608) 266-2621, http://www.dnr.wi.gov. No fee to launch at Sand Bay Town Park; small fee to launch at the Rowleys Bay Resort dock. To reach Sand Bay Town Park Beach from the intersection of Highway 42 and Mink River Road in Ellison Bay, go southeast on Mink River Road for 3.4 miles until it ends at Waters End Road. Turn left and follow Waters End Road for 0.4 mile to North Sand Bay Lane. Turn left and proceed north for 0.3 mile into the park, on your right. To reach the Rowleys Bay Resort dock from the intersection of Highway 42 and Mink River Road in Ellison Bay, head south on Mink River Road for 2.6 miles to County ZZ. Turn left and proceed 100 feet to the entrance. Restrooms are available at both Sand Bay Town Park and the Rowleys Bay Resort.

P6. Door Bluff Headlands

(6 miles round-trip from Garrett Bay to Ellison Bay—moderate)

This popular kayaking route is suitable for intermediate and experienced kayakers, particularly during the summer months. Conditions can be very rough during windy weather, so, to avoid being tossed into the rocky bluffs, watch the weather reports and wind conditions. Generally speaking, however, Hedgehog Harbor and Garrett Bay are protected from the wind. This route passes by an 1880s shipwreck, has great views of the bluffs and Washington Island, and even goes past some ancient Potawatomi Indian pictographs.

On summer weekends, you will have plenty of company—the area off Door Bluff Headlands County Park is one of the best salmon fishing spots in Door County. Watch out for powerboats, which may be traveling fast in these areas.

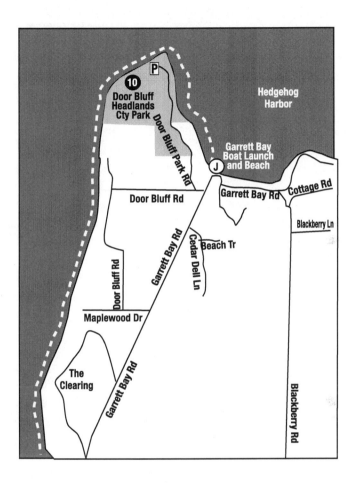

ROUTE

Launch from the Garrett Bay Boat Launch site, a 50-foot public access point with limited parking, a rocky cobble beach, and a concrete boat ramp. Head northwest up the coast. About 250 feet from the boat launch you will pass over an old shipwreck, *Fleetwing*, which is sitting at depths of 5 to 25 feet on the bottom of Hedgehog Harbor. Part of the schooner's skeleton is visible as you pass over it. Continue north along the coast for about 1.0 mile to the towering limestone bluffs of Door Bluff Headlands County Park. You'll enjoy views of the bluffs in the county park for about 0.6 mile as you round the bend to the south. Keep an eye out for Indian pictographs on the cliffs near the park. As you pass around the park peninsula, you can continue heading south along the shoreline about 2.6 miles, past the Clearing Folk School, to Ellison Bay. Retrace your route to return to the launching site.

CONTACT INFORMATION AND DIRECTIONS TO LAUNCH SITE

Town of Liberty Grove, 11161 Old Stage Rd., Sister Bay, WI 54234, (920) 854-2934, http://libertygrove.org/. From the intersection of Highway 42 and Mink River Road in Ellison Bay, go north on Highway 42 for 0.1 mile to Garrett Bay Road. Turn slightly left on Garrett Bay Road and proceed about 2.4 miles. The beach is near the end of Garrett Bay Road, where it makes an almost 90-degree turn to the east. The boat launch is at 1310 Garrett Bay Road. The launch has no facilities. No fee.

P7. Europe Lake

(2.1 miles around the lake—easy)

Europe Lake is a perfect spot for beginners to learn kayaking or canoeing and makes a great family paddling trip. Swimmers can also enjoy a dip on hot days. The shallow, sandy, 273-acre lake warms up quickly in the spring, making it an ideal spot for a late spring or summer trip. Europe Lake is generally protected, but beginners will want to keep an eye on wind conditions. The lake is bordered by Newport State Park to the east, and there are some scattered summer cottages along the north and west shores, but you will generally have the place to yourself. You can launch from the Europe Lake Boat Launch at the end of Europe Lake Road and spend a few hours paddling along the shoreline. There is also a small wetlands at the north end of the lake, where wildlife watching can be excellent. Look for families of Common Goldeneye, Common Merganser, Canada Geese, and painted turtle along the shore. The boat launch has a parking lot, picnic tables, grills, seasonal portable toilets, and a dock.

CONTACT INFORMATION AND DIRECTIONS TO LAUNCH

Town of Liberty Grove, 11161 Old Stage Rd., Sister Bay, WI 54234, (920) 854-2934, http://libertygrove.org/. To reach the boat launch from the intersection of Highway 42 and Mink River Road in Ellison Bay, take Highway 42 north for 2.6 miles to Europe Bay Road. Turn right and follow Europe Bay Road east 0.7 mile to Timberline Road. Go north on Timberline Road for 0.5 mile to Europe Lake Road. Turn right and follow Europe Lake Road 0.9 mile to the end and the entrance to the parking area. Small fee to launch boats.

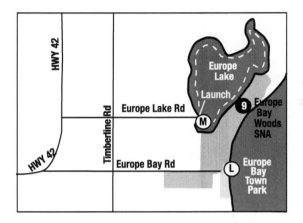

3

Baileys Harbor Area

With easy access to outstanding natural areas like the Ridges Sanctuary and Toft Point, Baileys Harbor makes a great home base for a multitude of Door County hiking, boating, and beach excursions, as well as for diving and exploring lighthouses and shipwrecks.

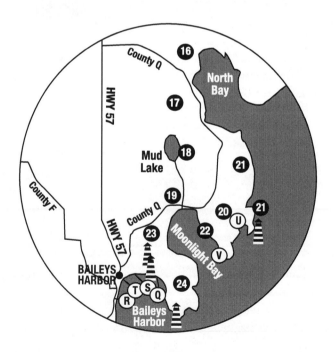

Historically, Baileys Harbor played a key role in Great Lakes shipping. Both the town and the harbor were named for ship captain Justice Bailey, who first took refuge in the protected harbor during a large storm in 1848, while hauling loads of timber and stone between Milwaukee and Detroit. Captain Bailey recognized the timber and quarrying potential of the region, and soon his employer sent crews to settle the area, cutting down the forests, quarrying the limestone, and convincing the federal government to construct the first lighthouse. In the years that followed initial settlement, Scandinavian, German, Polish, and British settlers moved into the area, establishing mercantile shipping businesses, sawmills, lime kilns, commercial fisheries, and family farms, including the cherry orchards that are still common in the area today.

More than a century and a half later, the region's rich maritime history is still evident. The Old Baileys Harbor Lighthouse is still standing, many shipwrecks litter the bottom of the harbor, and Hickey Brothers Fisheries, with family fishing roots dating back more than a century in Door County, is still in existence. Though most of the forests around Baileys Harbor were logged during those early days, today much of that forest has regenerated, and the area probably looks much as it did when Captain Bailey first saw it. Today's visitors can enjoy the scenic beauty of towering northern wet-mesic and boreal forests, historic lighthouses, expansive beaches, and rocky shores of Lake Michigan, which draw hikers, bikers, boaters, and natural history enthusiasts of all ages.

MAJOR POINTS OF INTEREST
16. North Bay

Those seeking a remote spot to ponder the wonders of nature and enjoy spectacular views of Lake Michigan should look no further than North Bay. The Nature Conservancy and state and private landowners have worked hard over the last few decades to protect this area for its incredible ecological diversity and the plants and animals that live here. Today, more than 4,700 acres, including 8,500 feet of Lake Michigan frontage, have been preserved.

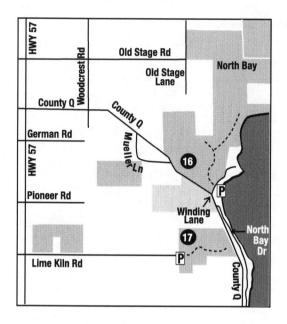

North Bay has a nice moderate hiking trail, perfect for a half-day excursion. After a mile of hiking through lush, damp northern wet mesic and boreal forests, you will come to a large northern sedge meadow complex fringed with tamarack trees, dwarf lake iris, and a variety of other rare plants, as well as expansive views of North Bay. Depending on the season, you can walk into the meadow toward the shoreline. While the first mile of trails is routine, with dark cedar forests and slippery trails, the views at the trail's end are quite memorable. North Bay features a large number of ecological communities: ephemeral, or seasonal, wetlands and streams, shore fens, northern sedge meadows, Great Lakes beach and dune, Great Lakes ridge and swale, emergent and submergent marshes, northern wet-mesic forest, and boreal forest. Along Lake Michigan, shallow North Bay is gradually filling in with marsh vegetation, making it one of the major spawning grounds for Lake Michigan's whitefish populations. Look for a variety of rare orchids, dwarf lake iris, muskrat, northern spring peeper, eastern American toad, painted turtle, snapping turtle, northern leopard frog, Bald Eagle, Sandhill Crane, Great Egret, Common Goldeneye, and Hine's emerald dragonfly.

Trails, Access, and Facilities

From the parking area, the moderate 2.5-mile round-trip trail meanders through a white cedar swamp for about 1.0 mile before reaching a fork. If you head left, the trail will end at an adjoining private property in about 0.25 mile (not recommended). If you head right, as is recommended, the trail will go another 0.25 mile to a large sedge meadow along Lake Michigan. Retrace your steps to return to the parking area. The trail may be wet and has uneven sections and small wooden bridges, which may be slippery, so appropriate footwear is recommended. There are no facilities at North Bay. Bikes, dogs, and motorized vehicles are prohibited on these trails.

Contact Information and Directions

The Nature Conservancy, 242 Michigan St., Ste. B103, Sturgeon Bay, WI 54235, (920) 743-8695, http://www.nature.org/. From the intersection of Highway 57 and County F in Baileys Harbor, head north on Highway 57 for 6.5 miles to the north end of County Q. Turn right on Q and proceed for 2.5 miles to Winding Lane. Turn left on Winding Lane and proceed 0.25 mile to a Nature Conservancy sign and gate on the west side of the road across from the green sign for 9804 Winding Lane. Park off to the side of Winding Lane and pick up the trailhead at the gate. No fee.

17. Mud Lake State Natural Area—Upland Section

The upland section of the 1,200-acre Mud Lake State Natural Area is just inland from North Bay and is operated by the Wisconsin Department of Natural Resources (WDNR). This section does not have access to or views of Mud Lake, but it can still provide good wildlife viewing opportunities, as in other parts of the State Natural Area. A 0.5-mile-long easy hiking path from the end of Lime Kiln Road provides access to the meadows and wetlands, through old fields, northern wet-mesic forest with pockets of northern hardwood, and boreal forest, as well as wetlands areas. Listen for breeding Winter Wren, White-throated Sparrow, Alder Flycatcher, and Olive-sided Flycatcher. Breeding warblers include Magnolia, Canada, Golden-winged, Chestnut-sided, Yellow-rumped, and Black-throated Green, along with Ovenbird, Common Yellowthroat, Northern Waterthrush, and American Redstart. Mammals found here include ermine, hoary bat, northern flying squirrel, white-tailed deer, meadow vole, and mink.

Trails, Access, and Facilities

From the end of Lime Kiln Road, the trailhead is located at the parking area near the WDNR sign. From the end of the parking area, the trail goes about 1.0 mile round-trip (requiring retracing of your steps to return to your vehicle). It provides access to the meadows, but no lake views. This site has no facilities. Insect repellant is a must here during the warmer months, as mosquitoes and deerflies can be fierce at times. This site is popular for fall deer and turkey hunting.

Contact Information and Directions

Wisconsin Department of Natural Resources, 101 S. Webster St., P.O. Box 7921, Madison, WI 53707, (608) 266-2621, http://www.dnr.wi.gov/. From the intersection of Highway 57 and County F in Baileys Harbor, head north on Highway 57 for 4.9 miles to Lime Kiln Road. Turn right, and follow it for 1.5 miles to the end and a large WDNR sign. No fee.

18. Mud Lake State Natural Area—Wetlands and Lake Section

Located north of Baileys Harbor, the lake section of Mud Lake State Natural Area is a hidden treasure. It's a bit poorly marked and a bit tough to find, but rarely will you encounter another person. This location feels especially remote, even though it is a relatively quick drive from downtown Baileys Harbor. Still, the area feels wild, and one can easily imagine black bear roaming the wet northern sedge meadows. The namesake lake is generally shallow with a muddy bottom, but water levels vary, depending on precipitation and time of year. This is a good area for Sandhill Cranes, Great Egrets, Great Blue Herons, ducks, and geese, particularly in the fall. The lake is surrounded by emergent and submergent marsh vegetation, like bulrush and yellow water lily, and a few standing dead

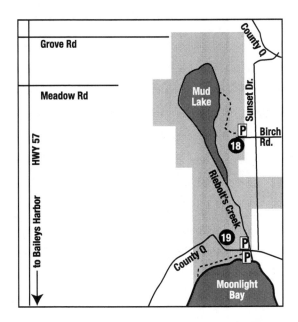

trees. Upland from the lake, northern wet-mesic forest and northern hardwood swamp communities are interspersed with pockets of boreal forest. Look for breeding Northern Waterthrush, White-throated Sparrow, Common Goldeneye, Wood Duck, Alder Flycatcher, and Hine's emerald dragonfly. A trail to the lake travels through old fields and a white cedar forest and ends in a northern sedge meadow at the lake.

TRAILS, ACCESS, AND FACILITIES

A 1.0-mile round-trip trail between two private properties leads to Mud Lake from the end of Birch Road. From the trailhead across from the green address sign at 1836 Birch Road, follow a double-track access road (unsigned) sloping slightly downhill. There are no facilities. This area is popular with hunters in the fall.

CONTACT AND DIRECTIONS

Wisconsin Department of Natural Resources, 101 S. Webster St., P.O. Box 7921, Madison, WI 53707, (608) 266-2621, http://www.dnr.wi.gov/. From the intersection of Highway 57 and County F in Baileys Harbor, head north on Highway 57 for 0.6 mile to County Q. Take a right on County Q and head northeast for 3.0 miles to Sunset Drive. Turn left at Sunset Drive and follow it for 1.2 miles to Birch Road. Turn left and follow Birch Road to the end, about 0.2 mile. The trailhead is across from a green address sign at 1836 Birch Road. No fee.

19. Mud Lake State Natural Area—Riebolt's Creek Section

In this section of the State Natural Area, Riebolt's Creek flows from Mud Lake down to the wetlands of Moonlight Bay at Lake Michigan. Along the creek are extensive areas of red osier dogwoods, willows, and shrubby northern sedge meadow. The area around the mouth of the creek includes extensive wetlands of emergent marsh vegetation, which is home to breeding Common Yellowthroat, Red-winged Blackbird, Song Sparrow, and muskrat. It is an excellent place to observe dragonflies and damselflies throughout the summer months. In the fall and winter, look for flocks of Canada Geese and dabbling ducks on Moonlight Bay.

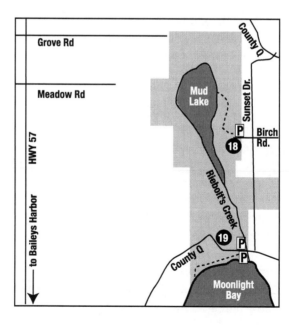

Because access by foot is limited, it is best visited by canoe or kayak (see P8 Paddling Route).

TRAILS, ACCESS, AND FACILITIES

Depending on lake levels, there are two foot trails. One (a half-mile long or less) is south of the County Q parking area and heads through the marsh down to Moonlight Bay; the other starts on the north side of County Q (look for the yellow State Natural Area signs) and heads north along the creek through the wetlands. When conditions are dry, you can follow the trail along the creek for quite a way, but typically much of the trail is under water, so appropriate footwear is essential. Though not well marked, the trails should be obvious from the parking areas on both sides of County Q. There are no facilities.

CONTACT INFORMATION AND DIRECTIONS

Wisconsin Department of Natural Resources, 101 S. Webster St., P.O. Box 7921, Madison, WI 53707, (608) 266-2621, http://www.dnr.wi.gov/. From the intersection of Highway 57 and County F in Baileys Harbor, head north on Highway 57 for 0.6 mile to County Q. Turn right and go northeast on County Q for about 2.75 miles to the point where Riebolt's Creek crosses County Q. Look for yellow State Natural Area signs indicating parking on both sides of the road where Riebolt's Creek crosses under County Q (if you cross the creek and reach Sunset Drive, you've gone too far). There is a small parking area for about ten cars on the south (Lake Michigan) side of County Q, and an additional pullout for one or two cars across the road. No fee.

20. Baileys Harbor Boreal Forest and Wetlands State Natural Area—Spike Horn Bay

This State Natural Area, managed by the Wisconsin Department of Natural Resources (WDNR), includes a complex of parcels on the peninsula east of Highway Q near Baileys Harbor and along Cana Island Road, between Moonlight Bay to the south and North Bay to the north. This general area has various local names, including Moonlight Bay, Cana

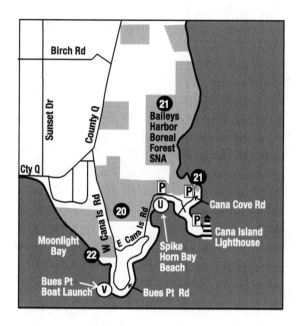

Point, Baileys Harbor Point, Bues Point, and Bues Point Landing, among others. The parcel along East Cana Island Road that includes Spike Horn Bay Beach has a wide sandy beach with a characteristic Great Lakes beach and dune community. It provides direct access to the lake and great views of the Cana Island Lighthouse, in an area otherwise restricted to property owners along a small bay called Spike Horn Bay. The area around Spike Horn Bay has a cold microclimate that allows boreal forest communities to coexist with northern wet-mesic forest communities. In summer, watch for uncommon breeding Blackburnian and Yellow-rumped Warblers, and ducks such as tree-nesting Common Goldeneye, along with ermine, porcupine, and hoary bat, all of which thrive here at latitudes far south of their core Canadian breeding range. In spring and summer this is a good spot to look for rare dwarf lake iris and pink and yellow ladyslipper orchids.

TRAILS, ACCESS, AND FACILITIES

WDNR owns the land generally bounded by the homes along Bues Point Road to the south and Lake Michigan, though some private gravel operations and homes are interspersed within the WDNR's land portfolio. To reach the WDNR parcels from East and West Cana Island Roads, look for yellow WDNR State Natural Area signs. Respect the rights of those adjacent private property owners and do not block driveways or park on the road.

There are several miles of trails through this area, including those that reach the Lake Michigan shoreline. Trails may be confusing at times and are best suited to those with good map and compass skills. There are no facilities.

CONTACT INFORMATION AND DIRECTIONS

Wisconsin Department of Natural Resources, 101 S. Webster St., P.O. Box 7921, Madison, WI 53707, (608) 266-2621, http://www.dnr.wi.gov/. From Highway 57 and County F in Baileys Harbor, go north on Highway 57 for 0.6 mile to County Q. Head northeast on County Q for 3.4 miles to West Cana Island Road. Turn right and follow West Cana Island Road for 1.1 miles to the intersection with East Cana Island Road. Turn left and follow East Cana Island Road for about 0.6 mile to an off-shoulder parking area, located between the private residences at 8635 and 8739 East Cana Island Road. For access to sandy beaches, park off East Cana Island Road near signage for the State Natural Area. The path to the beach goes directly across the dunes. Several residences are across from this beach, and parking on the road is prohibited. Private property rights should be respected at all times. Consult the WDNR website for more detailed maps of the area. No fee.

21. Baileys Harbor Boreal Forest and Wetlands State Natural Area—Cana Cove

Those with a sense of adventure and a penchant for getting way off the beaten track will want to investigate Baileys Harbor Boreal Forest and Wetlands State Natural Area, a complex of parcels on the peninsula east of Highway Q near Baileys Harbor, and along Cana Island Road between Moonlight Bay to the south and North Bay to the north. Managed by the Wisconsin Department of Natural Resources (WDNR), the parcels form

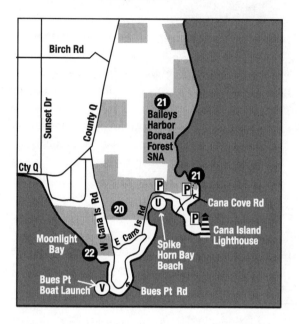

a checkerboard with private lands, and to access them you need to be an experienced hiker with good map and compass skills and a willingness to explore. One accessible WDNR parcel, located at the end of Cana Cove Road, offers sweeping views of a rocky dolomite ledge along the lake. Once you're at the lakeshore, you can walk along the shoreline to reach additional WDNR parcels to the north and west. This area has a cold microclimate influenced by Lake Michigan. You'll find both boreal forest and northern wet-mesic forest communities. In the summer, listen for the songs of breeding birds like Black-throated Green Warbler, Yellow-rumped Warbler, and Common Goldeneye, and watch for ermine, porcupine, and hoary bat, all of which generally breed much farther north. This is also a good spot in spring and summer to look for rare dwarf lake iris and pink and yellow ladyslipper orchids. During migration, the rocky parts of the shoreline may host migratory shorebirds, including large flocks of Whimbrel and Greater Yellowlegs.

Trails, Access, and Facilities

There is a good short trail at the end of Cana Cove Road, which heads through some scrubby shrub carr plants for about 0.1 mile to the rocky ledges along Lake Michigan. From here you can head in either direction along the shoreline. To the north and west along the lake, most of the contiguous woodlands are open to the public as WDNR property until you reach the private gated residential community south of Gordon Lodge Resort. There are several miles of trails through this area, including those that reach the Lake Michigan shoreline. Look for WDNR signage. The parcels are not contiguous and hikers should be respectful of the rights of adjacent property owners. Trails may be confusing at times and are suitable only for serious hikers with good maps. There are no facilities.

CONTACT INFORMATION AND DIRECTIONS

Wisconsin Department of Natural Resources, 101 S. Webster St., P.O. Box 7921, Madison, WI 53707, (608) 266-2621, http://www.dnr.wi.gov/. To access the Cana Cove Road site, follow the signs to the Cana Island Lighthouse. From the intersection of Highway 57 and County F in Baileys Harbor, head north on Highway 57 for 0.6 mile to County Q. Go northeast on County Q for 3.4 miles to West Cana Island Road. Turn right and follow West Cana Island Road for 1.1 miles to the intersection with East Cana Island Road. Turn left and follow East Cana Island Road for 1.2 miles to Cana Cove Road, a cul-de-sac. Turn left onto Cana Cove Road and proceed 0.2 mile to the end, past 8910 Cana Cove Road. Consult the WDNR website for more detailed maps of the area. No fee.

22. Moonlight Bay Bedrock Beach State Natural Area

Moonlight Bay Bedrock Beach State Natural Area is a five-acre parcel, owned by the Wisconsin Department of Natural Resources (WDNR), adjacent to Baileys Harbor Boreal Forest State Natural Area on the east side of Moonlight Bay. It is not a sand beach but a dolomite ledge, or flat rock, that you can walk out on when lake levels are low. While there are no official hiking trails, the exposed rock ledges are a good place to stretch your legs and look at Toft Point across the bay. Fed by Rieboldt's Creek, the areas inland from Moonlight Bay are characterized by a northern wet-mesic forest community dominated by white cedar swamp and some smaller tamarack swamp remnants, with a few paper birch, white pine, and some northern hardwood swamp pockets of black ash mixed in. Birds like Winter Wren, Northern Parula, and Mourning Warbler can be heard on the edges of the bay during the breeding season. Along the lake, forest gives way to shrub carr and then northern sedge meadows, ultimately dropping off to a Great Lakes alkaline rockshore community—the flat ledges you'll see when the water levels are low. The bay provides spawning habitat for whitefish, and is often a stopover site in spring and fall for migratory birds, including Whimbrel and Tundra Swan. Moonlight Bay also hosts Bald Eagle and Osprey for much of the year, and large rafts of Greater Scaup and Long-tailed Ducks during winter.

Trails, Access, and Facilities

There are no facilities. From the intersection of East and West Cana Island Roads and Bues Point Road, park off the shoulder on the southeast side of the intersection, look for the sign and trailhead, and then walk west along the trail leading toward Moonlight Bay. You will reach the shoreline in less than 0.1 mile.

Contact Information and Directions

Wisconsin Department of Natural Resources, 101 S. Webster St., P.O. Box 7921, Madison, WI 53707, (608) 266-2621, http://www.dnr.wi.gov/. From the intersection of Highway 57 and County F in Baileys Harbor, go north on Highway 57 for 0.6 mile to County Q. Head northeast on County Q for 3.4 miles to West Cana Island Road. Proceed south on West Cana Island Road for about 1.0 mile to the three-way (stop sign) intersection of West and East Cana Island and Bues Point Roads. Proceed straight ahead on Bues Point Road about 50 feet to the sign on the right. Park off Bues Point Road on the southeast side of the intersection. No fee.

23. The Ridges Sanctuary

It takes a visit to The Ridges Sanctuary to fully appreciate its cultlike following and worldwide reputation. Countless books and articles have been written about its scenic beauty, wildlife, plant life, and history. It has hosted naturalists from around the world and served as a living laboratory for

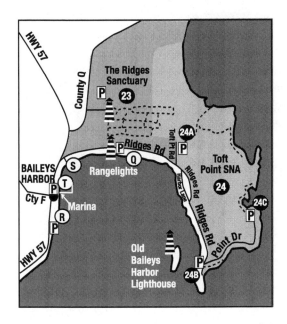

decades of ecological studies. Its historic wooden range lights have attracted lighthouse enthusiasts from around the world.

The conservation values of the area have long been recognized. Through the efforts of local preservationists and landowners, it was established in 1937 and became a Wisconsin State Natural Area in 1953. Today, The Ridges Sanctuary is operated as a nonprofit environmental center, with a cadre of devoted volunteers who put in tens of thousands of hours every year to clear its trails, maintain its buildings, and spread its conservation message to visitors. To visit is to understand.

The Ridges Sanctuary, also known as Baileys Harbor Ridges Sanctuary, looks like a big green area on a map of Door County. That's because the Ridges–Toft Point–Mud Lake area is the largest contiguous undeveloped tract of land on Door County, one that is so biologically significant that it's been designated by the federal government as a National Natural Landmark. The Ridges Sanctuary includes a 1,600-acre preserve situated atop a series of 30 Great Lakes ridges and swales just north of Baileys Harbor along Lake Michigan. These ridges and swales first formed about 1,400 years ago—each ridge took about 30 to 50 years to form, as Lake

Michigan's water levels changed over time. The Ridges is one of the best places for wildlife observation in Door County because it contains a diversity of forest types, including boreal and northern mesic forests. The localized microclimate here is highly influenced by the cooling and precipitation effects of Lake Michigan, and many of the plants and animals found here are northern boreal forest specialists.

The Ridges is home to a host of rare plants and animals; more than 20 types of native orchids, including the showy ladyslipper and yellow ladyslipper; the rare dwarf lake iris; the endangered Hine's emerald dragonfly; and 17 species of nesting warblers. The Ridges also boasts a long list of mammals, including coyote, river otter, fisher, gray fox, and black bear. Listen for Winter Wren, White-throated Sparrow, Northern Parula, Red-eyed Vireo, and Black-throated Green Warbler singing from the white spruce and balsam fir trees along the trails, or walk through the marshy Great Lakes ridge and swale communities to the lakefront to observe Caspian Terns and Double-crested Cormorants moving along Lake Michigan. Raptors, including Merlin, Bald Eagle, and Osprey, can also be found throughout much of the year.

Trails, Access, and Facilities

The sanctuary contains several miles of well-marked interpretive trails with small bridges that pass over the swales. The Red Loop (Winter Wren Trail, Woodfrog Swale, and Labrador Trail) is 1.2 miles. The Green Loop (Spruce, Deerlick, Wintergreen, and Sandy Trails) is 0.8 mile. The Blue Loop (Cowslip, Sandy Swale, Cedar, and Fir Trails) is 1.3 miles. The sanctuary has well-marked interpretive trails, restrooms, a visitor center and store, guided naturalist hikes, guided tours of the historic range lights, special events, nature programs, and volunteer opportunities. The Ridges is also well known for its environmental education programs for both adults and children. It is open subject to daily and seasonal hours.

Contact Information and Directions

The Ridges Sanctuary, P.O. Box 152, Baileys Harbor, WI 54202, (920) 839-2802 or (920) 839-1101, http://www.ridgessanctuary.org/. The Ridges Sanctuary is located just north of the intersection of Highway 57 and County Q in Baileys Harbor. Fee area.

24. Toft Point State Natural Area

Toft Point State Natural Area is a local favorite for naturalists, artists, and hikers. Originally settled by the Toft family in the 1870s, the property has a rich heritage that reflects early settlement and industry in Door County. A hundred years later, Emma Toft, the last of the family to live at Toft Point, was devoted to seeing that the area would be preserved. Toft Point is part of a larger contiguous block of undisturbed woodlands, spanning Mud Lake and The Ridges Sanctuary, that has been designated a National Natural Landmark, for its scenic beauty and ecological values. Located just to the east of Baileys Harbor, the 740-acre site is owned and operated by University of Wisconsin–Green Bay as a research and natural area. More than 440 species of plants have been found here, and recent research projects have surveyed mammals, fish, birds, plants, erosion, and the impact of deer populations.

Located along a peninsula that stretches into Lake Michigan, Toft Point State Natural Area contains pockets of mature boreal forest, with plenty

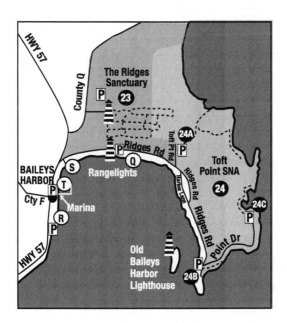

of balsam fir and spruce trees, and northern wet-mesic forest interspersed with white pines. Toft Point also contains a shore fen community with round-leaved sundew and spike rush, rare in Door County. Look for Ovenbird, Black-and-white Warbler, Winter Wren, Northern Parula, Mourning Warbler, Chestnut-sided Warbler, American Redstart, Blackburnian Warbler, Magnolia Warbler, Yellow-rumped Warbler, red squirrel, hoary bat, woodland jumping mouse, and porcupine. This site can also be excellent for butterflies during the summer and fall, particularly around the meadows.

The two main access points are off Toft Point Road and Ridges Road. The Toft Point Road access has an easy trail that heads past grassy meadows, historic cabins, and a historic kiln, ending at a rocky ledge at Lake Michigan. On warm summer afternoons, these dolomite outcrops along Lake Michigan are an ideal place for napping, sunbathing, and watching gulls, Caspian Terns, and Double-Crested Cormorants hunting for fish. The Ridges Road access provides more direct access to the lakeshore, kayak launching, and views of the Old Baileys Harbor Lighthouse (private property), within easy walking distance of the parking area.

Trails, Access, and Facilities

You can access trails into Toft Point at Toft Point Road and Point Drive. The Toft Point Road access has an easy trail less than a mile long to Lake Michigan. The trail is well maintained and suitable for all ages and abilities. For launching kayaks or viewing the lake and Old Baileys Harbor Lighthouse, there is a parking area just past the private residence at 7949 Ridges Road that provides excellent views of the lighthouse and Lake Michigan. (Note that the small peninsula out to the Old Baileys Harbor Lighthouse, and the lighthouse itself, is private property and there is no public access.) There are also several mostly overgrown trails to Lake Michigan and across the interior of Toft Point located off pullouts toward the end of Point Drive (no road sign), for those interested in scrambling along the rocky shoreline. There are no facilities.

Contact Information and Directions

Cofrin Center for Biodiversity, University of Wisconsin–Green Bay, Department of Natural and Applied Sciences, Green Bay, WI 54311-7001, (920) 465-5032, http://www.uwgb.edu/biodiversity. No fee.

A. To the Toft Point Road trailhead: From the intersection of Highway 57 and County F in Baileys Harbor, head north on Highway 57 for 0.1 mile to Ridges Road. Go east on Ridges Road (bear left when Ridges Road and Harbor Lane split off) and turn left onto Toft Point Road. (If you reach Baileys Harbor Yacht Club, you've gone too far.) Follow Toft Point Road north for about 0.2 mile until the road dead-ends into a parking lot and trailhead.

B. To the Ridges Road parking/kayak launching area: From the intersection of Highway 57 and County F in Baileys Harbor, head north on Highway 57 for 0.1 mile to Ridges Road. Go east on Ridges Road, past the yacht club, about 1.5 mile, until it ends near the private residence at 7949 Ridges Road.

C. To the Point Drive trailhead: From the intersection of Highway 57 and County F in Baileys Harbor, head north on Highway 57 for 0.1 mile to Ridges Road. Go east on Ridges Road, past the yacht club, until it ends and you can bear left onto a gravel road (Point Drive, no sign). Follow Point Drive about 1.0 mile to the end.

BEACHES AND OVERLOOKS
Q. Baileys Harbor Ridges Park Beach

This beach is one of several sandy patches along the otherwise rocky or muddy Baileys Harbor. It is located off Ridges Road on a narrow strip of sand between The Ridges Sanctuary and Lake Michigan. The park has restrooms, parking, access to a sandy beach, and views of the historic range lights on the grounds of The Ridges Sanctuary.

CONTACT INFORMATION AND DIRECTIONS

Town of Baileys Harbor, 2392 County Road F, P.O. Box 308, Baileys Harbor, WI 54202, (920) 839-9509, http://townofbaileysharbor.com/. From the intersection of Highway 57 and County F in Baileys Harbor, head north on Highway 57 for 0.1 mile to Ridges Road. Follow Ridges Road along the bay for 0.4 mile to a small parking lot. The park is free; The Ridges Sanctuary has an entrance fee.

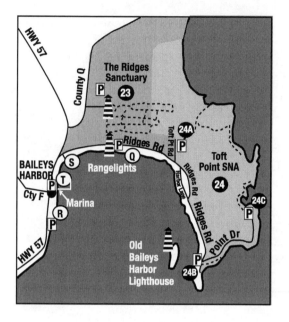

R. Anclam Park and Beach

Anclam Park has a wide, protected sand beach, with some rocky areas. The park has a picnic area with grills and restrooms. This is a popular spot for windsurfing, kite boarding, and swimming. There is a path out along a breakwater that stretches about 300 feet into the lake and provides excellent views of the beach.

CONTACT INFORMATION AND DIRECTIONS

Town of Baileys Harbor, 2392 County Road F, P.O. Box 308, Baileys Harbor, WI 54202, (920) 839-9509, http://townofbailesharbor.com/. From the intersection of Highway 57 and County F in Baileys Harbor, go south on Highway 57 for 0.5 mile to Church Street. Look for the entrance to the park just south of the intersection with Church Street. You will see the beach and a large parking area. No fee.

S. Baileys Harbor Lake View

Here you can walk out about 300 feet to the lake and view Baileys Harbor, the marina, Toft Point, and the Old Baileys Harbor Lighthouse. Park only in designated spaces.

CONTACT INFORMATION AND DIRECTIONS

Town of Baileys Harbor, 2392 County Road F, P.O. Box 308, Baileys Harbor, WI 54202, (920) 839-9509, http://townofbaileysharbor.com/. From the intersection of Highway 57 and County F in Baileys Harbor, go north on Highway 57 less than 0.1 mile. The overlook is located on the northern end of Baileys Harbor at the corner of Highway 57 and Ridges Road, next to Harbor Sands Condominiums. No facilities. No fee.

T. Baileys Harbor Marina

The marina breakwater provides a nice 0.5-mile walk, round-trip, out into the harbor. A paved walkway extends along the breakwater with benches and a viewing platform at the end. This spot has great views of the harbor, Anclam Park, Toft Point, and the Old Baileys Harbor Lighthouse.

CONTACT INFORMATION AND DIRECTIONS

Town of Baileys Harbor, 2392 County Road F, P.O. Box 308, Baileys Harbor, WI 54202, (920) 839-9509, http://townofbaileysharbor.com/. The marina is in downtown Baileys Harbor on Lake Michigan at 8132 Highway 57. Restrooms and parking. No fee.

U. Spike Horn Bay Beach

This beach is one of the parcels owned by the Wisconsin Department of Natural Resources (WDNR) as part of the Baileys Harbor Boreal Forest and Wetlands State Natural Area. It is tucked away in a small cove, Spike

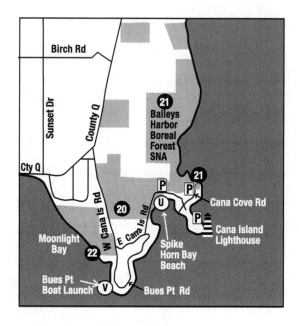

Horn Bay, in an area otherwise restricted to private property owners along the road to the Cana Island Lighthouse. The sandy beach has great views of Lake Michigan and Cana Island Lighthouse, and is a good spot for experienced kayakers to launch.

CONTACT INFORMATION AND DIRECTIONS

Wisconsin Department of Natural Resources, 101 S. Webster St., P.O. Box 7921, Madison, WI 53707, (608) 266-2621, http://www.dnr.wi.gov/. From the intersection of Highway 57 and County F in Baileys Harbor, go north on Highway 57 to County Q. Head northeast on County Q for 3.4 miles to West Cana Island Road. Turn right and follow West Cana Island Road for 1.1 miles to the intersection with East Cana Island Road. Turn left and follow East Cana Island Road for about 0.6 mile to an off-shoulder parking area, located between the private residences at 8635 and 8739 East Cana Island Road. Watch for yellow signage for the State Natural Area. Several private residences are along this bay, and parking on the road is prohibited, so park only in designated areas. No fee.

V. Bues Point Boat Launch

This boat launch provides easy access to Moonlight Bay and Cana Island for kayaking. Its parking area provides views of Toft Point across Moonlight Bay.

CONTACT INFORMATION AND DIRECTIONS

Town of Baileys Harbor, 2392 County Road F, P.O. Box 308, Baileys Harbor, WI 54202, (920) 839-9509, http://townofbaileysharbor.com/. No facilities. From the intersection of Highway 57 and County F in Baileys Harbor, go north on Highway 57 for 0.6 mile to County Q. Head northeast on County Q for 3.4 miles to West Cana Island Road. Turn right and proceed south on West Cana Island Road for about 1.1 miles to the three-way intersection of West Cana Island, East Cana Island, and Bues Point Roads. Proceed straight on Bues Point Road about 0.1 mile down the road to the sign and small parking lot on the right. No fee to park; fee to use the boat launch.

LIGHTHOUSES

L4. Upper and Lower Range Lights

Built in 1869 and no longer used for navigation, these two range lights were configured to help mariners find safe passage into Baileys Harbor. They are located on the grounds of The Ridges Sanctuary. The upper range light serves as summer staff quarters for naturalists at The Ridges and should be treated as you would any private residence. The Door County Maritime Museum hosts an annual guided tour of the range lights.

CONTACT INFORMATION AND DIRECTIONS

The Ridges Sanctuary, P.O. Box 152, Baileys Harbor, WI 54202, (920) 839-2802 or (920) 839-1101, http://www.ridgessanctuary.org/. Door County Maritime Museum, 120 N. Madison Ave., Sturgeon Bay, WI 54235, (920) 743-5958, http://www.dcmm.org/. From the intersection of Highway 57

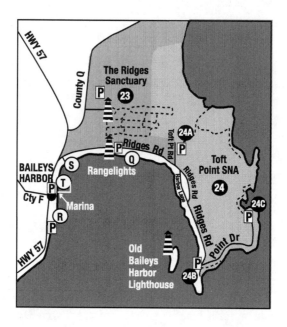

and County F in Baileys Harbor, head north on Highway 57 for 0.1 mile to Ridges Road. Go east on Ridges Road along the bay for about 0.4 mile to a small parking lot (this is the same parking lot as the one for Baileys Harbor Ridges Park Beach.) The lot provides access to a sandy beach, as well as views of the range lights. The Ridges Sanctuary charges an entrance fee.

L5. Old Baileys Harbor Lighthouse

This inactive lighthouse is located on tiny Lighthouse Island off Toft Point on the north side of Baileys Harbor. The distinctive stone tower with a birdcage lantern was built in 1852 with stones from a local quarry. The island and the lighthouse building are now private property and off limits to the public, but you can view the lighthouse from Toft Point. The best views are from Ridges Road.

DIRECTIONS

From the intersection of Highway 57 and County F, head north on Highway 57 for 0.1 mile to Ridges Road. Go east on Ridges Road for 1.5 miles, past the Baileys Harbor Yacht Club, until it ends near 7949 Ridges Road, a private residence. Park in the lot just past the residence for excellent views of the lighthouse and Lake Michigan. Do not enter the private property. No fee.

L6. Cana Island Lighthouse

Built in 1869, Cana Island Lighthouse, widely considered one of the most beautiful on the Great Lakes, is still an active navigational structure for Great Lakes shipping. The grounds and buildings have been restored and are maintained as a museum by Door County Maritime Museum and the Door County Parks System. Unless water levels in Lake Michigan are very high, Cana Island is joined to the mainland by a rocky causeway. The island includes pockets of remnant boreal forest and northern wet-mesic

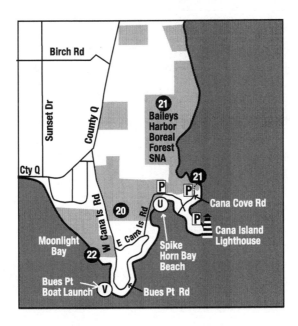

forest, along with open areas that provide scenic views of Lake Michigan along Moonlight Bay. In the summer, listen for singing Black-throated Green Warblers from the treetops around the grounds of the light-house, and watch for Caspian Terns, Double-crested Cormorants, and gulls soaring along the lake. Cana Island is open seasonally, subject to daily hours. There are restrooms and well-marked short trails around the island and lighthouse grounds. The lighthouse itself is open for guided tours on a limited basis in association with Door County Maritime Museum.

CONTACT INFORMATION AND DIRECTIONS

Door County Maritime Museum, 120 N. Madison Ave., Sturgeon Bay, WI 54235, (920) 743-5958, http://www.dcmm.org/canaisland.html/. Door County Parks System, 3528 Park Dr., Sturgeon Bay, WI 54235, (920) 746-9959, http://map.co.door.wi.us/parks/. From the intersection of Highway 57 and County F in Baileys Harbor, go north on Highway 57 for 0.6 mile to County Q. Head northeast on County Q for 3.4 miles to West Cana Island Road. Turn right and follow West Cana Island Road for 1.1 miles to East Cana Island Road. Turn left and follow East Cana Island Road for 1.5 miles to the lighthouse parking area. Fee area.

BIKE ROUTES

B8. Baileys Harbor to Kangaroo Lake Causeway
(4.8 miles round-trip—easy)

This flat route on mostly quiet roads is good for beginning cyclists of all ages. The route goes past a mix of farm fields, orchards, northern mesic forests, and wetlands. Overall this trip provides scenic views of Kangaroo Lake on relatively low-traffic roads.

ROUTE

From the intersection of Highway 57 and County F in Baileys Harbor, take Highway 57 south for 0.2 mile to Bluff Road. Go west on Bluff Road for 1.1 miles to Red Cherry Road. Turn left on Red Cherry Road and pro-ceed for 1.0 mile to County E. Turn right and follow County E 0.9 mile across the Kangaroo Lake Causeway. Once you are across the causeway,

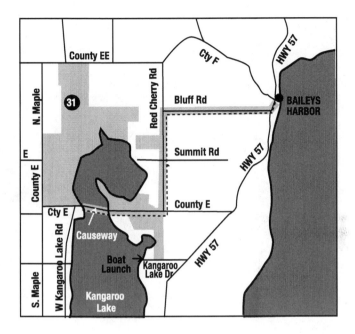

turn around at the Coyote Roadhouse Bar and Restaurant, and retrace your route back to Baileys Harbor. No fee.

B9. Baileys Harbor to Ephraim and North Bay

(18.0 miles round-trip—moderate)

This route is appropriate for intermediate and experienced road cyclists. It runs mostly through farmland, with a few northern wet-mesic and northern mesic forested areas and small rolling hills. It is highly recommended in October and early November when the fall colors in this part of the interior of the Door Peninsula can be outstanding. Use caution biking on Highway 57 and County Q.

ROUTE

From the intersection of Highway 57 and County F in Baileys Harbor, go south on Highway 57 for 0.2 mile to Bluff Road. Head west on Bluff Road

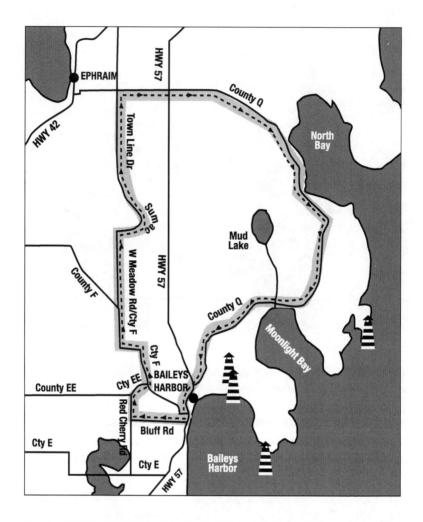

for 1.1 Miles to Red Cherry Road. Turn right and follow Red Cherry Road for 0.5 mile to County EE. Turn right and follow County EE for 0.5 mile to County F. Turn left and follow County F for 2.0 miles to West Meadow Road. Follow West Meadow Road for 1.6 miles and stay on it as it jogs right, for an additional 0.5 mile, until you come to Sumac Road. Turn left and follow Sumac Road for 0.6 mile until you reach Town Line Drive. Follow Town Line Drive for 2.1 miles until you reach County Q. Turn right and follow County Q for 10.6 miles to Highway 57 in Baileys

Harbor. Follow Highway 57 south about 0.6 mile to the intersection with County F. No fee.

PADDLING ROUTES
P8. Riebolt's Creek to Mud Lake State Natural Area
(4.0 miles round-trip—moderate)

Riebolt's Creek is one of Door County's premier kayaking destinations for wildlife-watching, and should be on the list for any Door County paddler. The trip begins at the mouth of Riebolt's Creek at Moonlight Bay and passes through the Mud Lake State Natural Area, an area rich in rare plants and animals. Riebolt's Creek is generally protected from the wind, and the trip is suitable for intermediate paddlers, provided water levels are sufficient. If you're an experienced paddler you can take a canoe under most conditions, though a sea kayak is the best vehicle for the trip, particularly if the wind picks up. It is very rare that you will

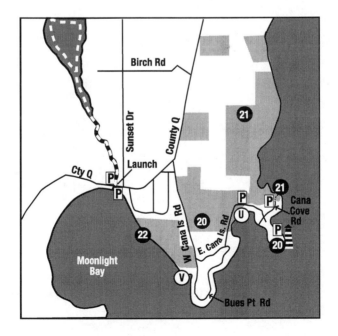

encounter anyone else along the route. When the water levels are low, the creek can be muddy at points and portaging may be required, but for most of the year, you can paddle right up the creek with no problems. It is generally protected and calm. The lake itself is generally navigable depending on water levels, but be aware that on windy days the lake can have rough water and make an open canoe somewhat of a challenge to navigate. You don't want to end up on the bottom stuck in the namesake mud! Intermediate paddlers will do fine on calm days, but should think twice and check the weather forecast before venturing out. Note also that several of the local kayaking outfitters offer day trips to this spot—which might be a good idea if you're unsure about the conditions.

ROUTE

From the parking areas, you can see up Riebolt's Creek, which flows under Highway Q, through a large culvert, as the creek empties into Lake Michigan at Moonlight Bay. You'll want to launch inland off Highway Q, beyond the culvert, which involves either parking in one of two small spots on the west side of the road, or parking in the larger lot and carrying your boat across the road. Where water levels are sufficient, follow the creek until you reach Mud Lake.

CONTACT INFORMATION AND DIRECTIONS TO LAUNCH SITE

Wisconsin Department of Natural Resources, 101 S. Webster St., P.O. Box 7921, Madison, WI 53707, (608) 266-2621, http://www.dnr.wi.gov/. From the intersection of Highway 57 and County F in Baileys Harbor, go north on Highway 57 for 0.6 miles to County Q. Head north on County Q for about 2.75 miles to the point where Riebolt's Creek crosses County Q. Look for yellow State Natural Area signs indicating parking on both sides of the road. If you cross the creek and reach Sunset Drive, you've gone too far. There is a parking area for about ten cars on the south (Lake Michigan) side of County Q, and an additional pullout for one or two cars across the road. Look for yellow WDNR State Natural Area signs at the parking where Riebolt's Creek passes under County Q. The launch has no facilities. No fee.

P9. Moonlight Bay to Cana Island

(6.0 miles round-trip—difficult)

The trip from Moonlight Bay provides views of Bues Point, Spike Horn Bay, Baileys Harbor Boreal Forest and Wetlands State Natural Area, and Cana Island Lighthouse. While the scenery is spectacular, this trip is suitable only for experienced kayakers. Conditions can quickly become extremely rough and windy, and this area of Lake Michigan has claimed the lives of several boaters from hypothermia in recent years. Check the weather and take appropriate safety precautions, including packing foul weather gear, wearing a dry suit, and taking food and water.

ROUTE

Put in from the parking area on Moonlight Bay and head along the north shore of Moonlight Bay toward Bues Point. You can stop at the Bues Point Boat Launch if you need a break. Head north around Bues Point,

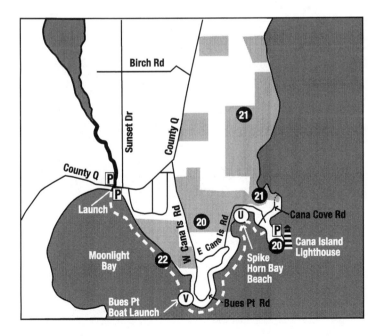

past the southern parcels of the Baileys Harbor Boreal Forest, to Spike Horn Bay. This wide sandy beach offers another stopping point. As soon as you round Bues Point you will see Cana Island and the Cana Island Lighthouse in the distance. Continue on to the area around the lighthouse. You can also land at the causeway to the Cana Island Lighthouse if you wish to stop. Retrace your route to return to Moonlight Bay.

CONTACT INFORMATION AND DIRECTIONS TO LAUNCH SITE

Wisconsin Department of Natural Resources, 101 S. Webster St., P.O. Box 7921, Madison, WI 53707, (608) 266-2621, http://www.dnr.wi.gov/. From the intersection of Highway 57 and County F in Baileys Harbor, go north on Highway 57 for 0.6 mile to County Q. Head north on County Q for about 2.75 miles to the point where Riebolt's Creek crosses County Q. Look for yellow State Natural Area signs indicating parking on both sides of the road. If you cross the creek and reach Sunset Drive, you've gone too far. There is a small parking area for about ten cars on the Lake Michigan side of County Q, and an additional pullout for one or two cars across the road. The launch has no facilities. No fee.

4

Peninsula State Park Area

Sister Bay, Ephraim, and Fish Creek

Archaeologists believe that the area around Nicolet Bay, now part of Peninsula State Park, has the oldest human occupation in Door County, with use estimated to date back more than eleven thousand years. Native American artifacts collected from sites here show at least a thousand years of occupation by various groups along Nicolet Bay.

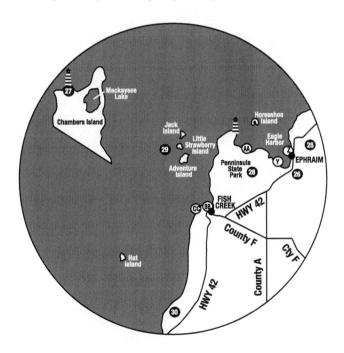

Today, many visitors to this region come to Ephraim, a village settled in the 1850s by Moravian pioneers from Norway. Ephraim is a favorite with art and nature lovers and history buffs. Places like Eagle Harbor, Old Ephraim Firehouse, Anderson Dock, and Ephraim's busy shops and restaurants attract crowds all summer. To the north, bustling Sister Bay, a former logging town also settled by Norwegian immigrants in the 1850s, has grown into the commercial hub for this part of Door County. Nearby Fish Creek, first settled in the 1840s–1850s as a shipping dock, has been a popular summer tourist destination for more than 100 years. Both Fish Creek and Sister Bay draw thousands of summer visitors in search of fine dining, shops, art galleries, and festivals. Peninsula State Park itself also attracts its share of crowds in the summer, including to its outdoor American Folklore Theatre.

The area is well known to boaters. Opportunities for sailing, offshore fishing, and kayaking abound. There are plenty of marinas, boat launches, and boat ramps and lots of offshore islands to visit. If you're more interested in exploring the area on foot, places like Ephraim Preserve at Anderson Pond, right near downtown Ephraim, and White Cliff Fen and Forest State Natural Area are not to be missed. Within the state park, you can find everything from a quiet family bike ride to wildlife-watching at Weborg Marsh. Peninsula State Park's beaches, golf course, camping, and accessible trails make it very popular, but you can still find peace and quiet on the trails even in the busiest months if you look hard enough. The birch groves along the shoreline, warm breezes off Green Bay, and towering limestone cliffs make the scenery around Peninsula State Park tough to beat.

MAJOR POINTS OF INTEREST

25. Ephraim Preserve at Anderson Pond

Ephraim Preserve at Anderson Pond is a quiet, scenic 27-acre Door County Land Trust preserve near downtown Ephraim. Though located near an urban center, this spot makes it easy to forget that you are right in the middle of town, and this easy-to-moderate hike is highly recommended for anyone seeking a peaceful walk in the woods. The trails are also popular for jogging and dog-walking.

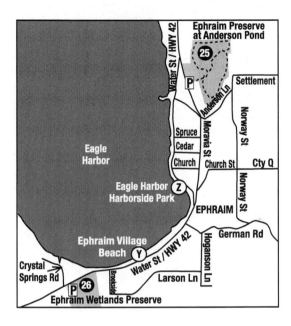

The 1.0-mile Davis Trail works around the perimeter of the property through gorgeous open northern mesic woodlands, making the property seem far larger than 27 acres. Less than half as long, the interior trail to the preserve's namesake ephemeral, or seasonal, Anderson Pond has excellent wildlife-watching potential, particularly at dawn and dusk. In the summer, look for breeding Black-throated Green Warbler, Common Yellowthroat, Wood Duck, and American Redstart, as well as for resident species like Wild Turkey, Brown Creeper, White-breasted Nuthatch, Pileated Woodpecker, and Black-capped Chickadee. At dusk, watch for little brown bat, raccoon, red fox, and Virginia opossum.

TRAILS, ACCESS, AND FACILITIES

At the trailhead choose among 1.5 miles of easy-to-moderate hiking trails. Trails are well marked and easy to follow. Leashed dogs are permitted. Bikes, horses, and motorized vehicles are prohibited. This site has no facilities.

CONTACT INFORMATION AND DIRECTIONS

Door County Land Trust, P.O. Box 65, Sturgeon Bay, WI 54235, (920) 746-1359, http://www.doorcountylandtrust.org/. From the intersection of Highway 42/Water Street and Cedar Street in downtown Ephraim, go east on Cedar Street about 0.1 mile until it ends at Moravia Street. Turn left on Moravia and proceed 0.2 mile to Anderson Lane. As soon as you cross Anderson Lane, look for the rustic fencing and the trailhead. Interpretive signage is located a short distance down the path. Note that the Village of Ephraim does not officially allow on-street parking in this area, so park in one of the public lots and walk in. No fee.

26. Ephraim Wetlands Preserve

Located along Highway 42 in downtown Ephraim, this tiny seven-acre site, managed by the Village of Ephraim, contains a series of trails and boardwalks. The preserve is organized in two short loops, which provide views of forested wetlands. While primarily of interest for its spring

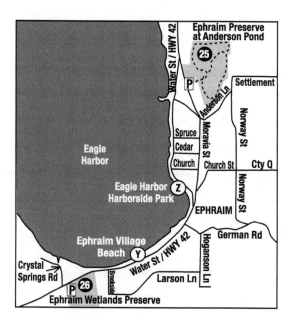

wildflowers, it is a good place to observe transitioning plant communities and provides a short walk for those who have trouble walking long distances or are walking with small children. Formerly cleared for development, this area is predominantly regenerating as a northern wet-mesic forest, with some northern hardwood swamp pockets. The preserve is noteworthy for its Hine's emerald dragonfly population. In the spring and summer, watch for northern spring peepers, eastern chipmunk, gray squirrel, American Robin, American Redstart, Chestnut-sided Warbler, and Rose-breasted Grosbeak.

TRAILS, ACCESS, AND FACILITIES

The preserve has 0.3 mile of very easy trails, boardwalks, benches, and parking for about fifteen cars. No facilities.

CONTACT INFORMATION AND DIRECTIONS

Village of Ephraim, P.O. Box 138, Ephraim, WI 54211, (920) 854-5501, http://www.ephraim-wisconsin.com/. From Highway 42/Water Street in downtown Ephraim (at Wilson's), head south about 0.9 mile. Look for signage and trailheads off the parking lot at 9820 Water Street (Highway 42). No fee.

27. Chambers Island

Chambers Island is located five miles offshore, northwest of Peninsula State Park, in the Green Bay. Its historic lighthouse makes this 2,834-acre island an enticing destination for visitors. It harbors a mixed northern mesic forest, dominated by red maple, red oak, and American beech, and a highly productive understory, due in no small part to the recent extirpation, or removal, of its white-tailed deer population. Chambers Island contains a large freshwater lake, Mackaysee Lake; a small pond called Mud Lake; and small pockets of northern dry-mesic forest pine barrens with wild sarsaparilla and Canada mayflower understory.

Largely undeveloped, with the exception of a small summer home community, a private airstrip, and a Catholic retreat center, Chambers Island is an excellent place to find breeding wood warblers, including Black-throated Green, Black-and-white, Blackburnian, Chestnut-sided,

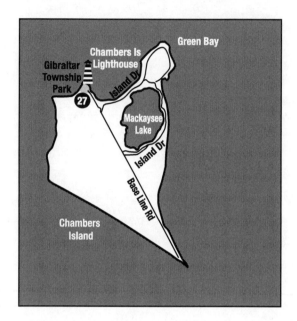

Ovenbird, and American Redstart during the summer months. Other breeders include American Woodcock, Ruby-throated Hummingbird, and Sharp-shinned Hawk. From the shoreline, watch for Common Merganser, Osprey, Bald Eagle, American White Pelican, and Caspian Tern.

Aside from the small public marina and lighthouse area managed by the Town of Gibraltar, the island is private and organized under the Chambers Island Association. Access to the island is by private boat or plane. A number of local boat captains offer tours and transportation out to the island. Kayaking to the island makes a challenging day trip for experienced paddlers.

TRAILS, ACCESS, AND FACILITIES

The lighthouse site, managed by the Town of Gibraltar as a town park, is open to the public. Door County Maritime Museum offers an annual tour.

CONTACT INFO

Contact: Town of Gibraltar, 4097 Hwy 42, P.O. Box 850, Fish Creek, WI 54212, (920)868-1714, http://www.townofgibraltar.com/. Door County

Maritime Museum, 120 N. Madison Ave., Sturgeon Bay, WI 54235, (920) 743-5958, http://www.dcmm.org/. No fee to visit the town park.

28. Peninsula State Park

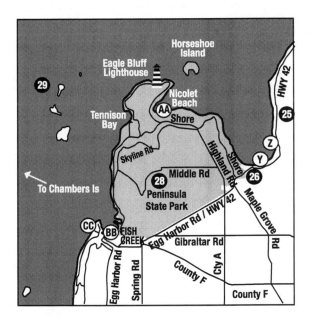

Established as one of Wisconsin's first state parks more than a hundred years ago, Peninsula State Park is a favorite for visitors and residents alike. The park protects more than seven miles of shoreline and 3,770 acres of wetlands, meadows, and forests. It gets heavy use in summer months by campers, boaters, hikers, bikers, golfers, and sightseers, but you can still find quiet and solitude on the trails on an early morning or off-season visit. Visitors should make a point of seeking out the towering, rugged limestone cliffs of Sven's Bluff, the scenic vistas and birch forests of Upper Skyline Trail, the dense cathedral-like white cedar forests of Sunset Trail, the 75-foot observation tower with panoramic views of Green Bay, and the picturesque wetlands and meadows at Weborg Marsh. These special places attract many visitors, but their natural splendor will make the summer crowds bearable. Come in the off-season, and you'll have much of the park to yourself. A kayak or canoe day trip out to Horseshoe Island can also provide a great break from the crowds.

Peninsula State Park has excellent diversity of forest ecosystems and microclimates. The predominantly northern wet-mesic and northern mesic forest communities support a large number of forest bird species, small mammals, and amphibians. Though white-tailed deer are present in large numbers, understory defoliation has not reached levels seen in some other parts of the county. As such, the park remains home to a diverse group of forest floor plants and ground-nesting birds and animals. Look for Wild Turkey, raccoon, wood frog, red-backed salamander, and Mourning Warbler. Weborg Marsh and Weborg Point have emergent marsh vegetation and sweeping views of Green Bay, and are home to Marsh Wren, Sandhill Crane, Virginia Rail, Sora, Bald Eagle, Common Yellowthroat, Osprey, and painted turtle. Watch for migrating songbirds and raptors during the spring and fall migrations along the bluffs. These same overlooks and wet marshy areas just inland are also great places to look for migrating and wintering ducks and geese.

Trails, Access, and Facilities

The park has well-maintained hiking, biking, and mountain-biking trails. Trails include Eagle Trail, a moderate 2.0-mile loop with some rocky sections and views of 150-foot cliffs and Eagle Harbor; Hemlock Trail, a moderate 3.6-mile round-trip with some rocky sections and views of Green Bay; Hidden Bluff, an easy 0.75-mile gravel connector for hiking and biking; Lone Pine Trail, a 1.0-mile round-trip, moderate connector trail; Minnehaha Trail, an easy 1.4-mile round-trip with Green Bay views; Nicolet Bay Trail, a moderate 4.4-mile round-trip that connects to a beach access trail; Sentinel Trail, a 2.0-mile loop interpretive trail; Skyline Trail, a 3.0-mile moderate loop with some hills; Sunset Bike Trail, an easy-to-moderate 9.6-mile gravel bike trail with some hills and access to Weborg Marsh and Nicolet Beach; Tramper's Delight, an easy 0.5-mile access trail to Nicolet Bay and Eagle Bluff Lighthouse; and White Cedar Nature Trail, an easy 0.5-mile interpretive loop. Trail maps are available throughout the park and at the visitors' center. The park also has camping, a visitor/nature center, an observation tower, picnic areas, golf course, a lighthouse, boating, swimming beaches, fishing, and American Folklore Theatre. Concessions and kayak and small boat rentals are available during the summer months. Campsites can be reserved through the Wisconsin State Park System.

CONTACT INFORMATION AND DIRECTIONS

Peninsula State Park, Wisconsin Department of Natural Resources, 9462 Shore Rd., Fish Creek, WI 54212, (920) 868-3258, http://www.dnr.wi.gov/. From downtown Fish Creek at the intersection of Highway 42/Egg Harbor Road and Spruce Street, proceed north on Highway 42/Egg Harbor Road for 0.5 miles to Shore Drive, the main entrance of Peninsula State Park. Fee area.

29. Offshore Islands: Horseshoe, Strawberry, Hat, and Sister Islands

A number of small islands lie off the Door Peninsula and the Grand Traverse Islands. Some are federally protected as sanctuaries for breeding birds, as part of the Green Bay and Gravel Island National Wildlife Refuges (see chapter 1). This section describes the rest of these islands—those that are privately owned and state owned. They are primarily low-lying sand and gravel bars that provide nesting habitat for

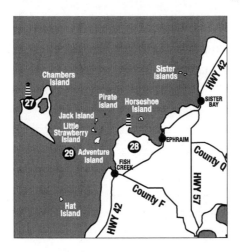

Double-crested Cormorants and Herring and Ring-billed gulls and roosting and occasional nesting sites for Caspian and Common Terns, Red-breasted Mergansers, and Great Blue Herons. Also look for American White Pelican, Bonaparte's Gull, American Black Duck, and Common Merganser. A trip out to these islands (the only way to see them is from a boat) makes a nice day trip for power boat owners or experienced kayakers. Local kayaking outfitters and charter boat captains offer day trips to many of them. Note that access is limited and nesting colonies should not be closely approached during waterbird nesting seasons (late spring through August).

Horseshoe Island

Legend has it that the seventeenth-century explorer Jean Nicolet landed on Horseshoe Island. Today you can still see the foundations of a private estate, which was purportedly traded in the 1800s for a shipment of tobacco.

Located less than 1.0 mile offshore from the mainland portion of Peninsula State Park, in Nicolet Bay, and managed by the Wisconsin Department of Natural Resources (WDNR) as part of the park, Horseshoe Island is highly recommended as a destination for a day trip. Unlike other islands featured in this section, it is well wooded and not a bird colony. The island features a hiking trail 1.0 mile in circumference. (Note that while the short hike is worthwhile, the trails are full of garlic mustard, so you'll want to brush off your clothes and shoes before coming back to the mainland.)

On calm days, it is an easy day trip by canoe or kayak from Peninsula State Park's Tennison Harbor or Nicolet Beach. Several kayak outfitters offer guided day trips. See Paddling Route P11.

Strawberry Islands

Pirate, Jack, Adventure, and Little Strawberry Islands are all small islands located east of Chambers Island, about 1.5 miles off Peninsula State Park, and known collectively as the Strawberry Islands. The group can be seen in the distance from Chambers Island and from the Eagle Bluff Lighthouse area in the park. These islands are basically sand and gravel bars that provide nesting habitat for Double-crested Cormorants and Herring and Ring-billed Gulls, and provide roosting and occasional nesting sites for Caspian and Common Terns, Red-breasted Mergansers, and Great Blue Herons. Little Strawberry Island and Jack Island in particular have seen massive increases in the number of nesting Double-crested Cormorants in the last few decades. Population control efforts have been underway on Jack Island in recent years.

All of these islands are privately owned and uninhabited, and access is restricted. A trip around them is an excellent excursion for experienced kayakers, launching from Tennison Bay in Peninsula State Park or from Fish Creek Beach or Sunset Beach in Fish Creek. See Paddling Route P12.

Hat Island

Hat Island, about three miles offshore and just west of Peninsula State Park, was named for its shape. Privately owned, it is generally gravel and sand, with some red osier dogwood and stinging nettles. In recent years, the number of nesting Double-crested Cormorants has increased exponentially, and population control efforts are underway. Access to Hat Island is restricted, so if the bird colonies aren't enough to convince you not to go ashore, the stinging nettles should. A shipwreck here makes the area popular with scuba divers.

Sister Islands

The Sister Islands, sometimes referred to as Big Sister and Little Sister, are a pair of islands located in Sister Bay and visible from the Village of Sister Bay. They total about 15 acres but vary depending on lake levels. Currently, each island is surrounded by shallow submerged ledges, but as lake levels drop, more is exposed. When Lake Michigan water levels are very low, the islands are connected to one another. These uninhabited islands are owned by the Wisconsin Department of Natural Resources (WDNR) and designated as a State Natural Area. Access to them requires special permission from WDNR.

The Sister Islands have historically been important nesting colonies for gulls and Common Terns. As lake levels have receded in recent decades, understory vegetation has been restored, and recent WDNR surveys have turned up a variety of nesting marsh birds and ducks. The islands continue to regenerate as a northern mesic forest. These islands are an excellent day trip for experienced kayakers, launching out of Sister Bay Beach. Be aware that the islands are full of stinging nettles and active bird colonies, so landing on them, especially during summer months, is inadvisable and prohibited except by special permission of the WDNR. See Paddling Route P10.

Trails, Access, and Facilities

Horseshoe Island has a 1.0-mile loop trail. Other islands generally lack trails. Except for Horseshoe Island, they should be considered wildlife refuges, and nesting birds should not be closely approached or disturbed during nesting season (late April through August).

Contact Information

Peninsula State Park, Wisconsin Department of Natural Resources, 9462 Shore Rd., Fish Creek, WI 54212, (920) 868-3258, http://www.dnr.wi.gov/. Horseshoe Island is part of Peninsula State Park, and is considered a fee area.

30. White Cliff Fen and Forest State Natural Area

Preserved by the Door County Land Trust (DCLT), White Cliff Fen and Forest State Natural Area is a 100-acre tract north of Egg Harbor along Juddville Bay. The fen has several short scenic loop trails, totaling about 1.0 mile, that allow visitors to walk among the wetlands. This is a lovely walk in all seasons and easy enough for hikers of all abilities. A hidden gem, it sees few visitors, so if you're looking for a nice, quiet walk in a beautiful area, White Cliff Fen should be at the top of your list. This area is predominantly northern wet-mesic and northern mesic forest bordering a northern sedge meadow community. The most noteworthy feature of the site is a spring-fed shore fen community, located along the Niagara Escarpment. Fen plants, including common bog arrow-grass, occur here, along with less rare plants like marsh milkweed, northern bog goldenrod, marsh marigold, and northern bog aster. This is an excellent spot for Hine's emerald dragonfly, and butterflies like Aphrodite fritillary and monarch.

TRAILS, ACCESS, AND FACILITIES

From the trailhead across from 8247 White Cliff Road, there is approximately 1.0 mile of trails, including two loop trails. There are no facilities. Leashed dogs are permitted. Bikes, horses, and motorized vehicles are prohibited. Hunting is authorized pursuant to DCLT guidelines and permission.

CONTACT INFORMATION AND DIRECTIONS

Door County Land Trust, P.O. Box 65, Sturgeon Bay, WI 54235, (920) 746-1359, http://www.doorcountylandtrust.org/. From the intersection of Highway 42 and County G in Egg Harbor, take Highway 42 north 200 feet to White Cliff Road. Take a left on White Cliff Road and follow it about 2.2 miles to the preserve sign across from 8247 White Cliff Road. Alternatively, from the intersection of Main Street/Highway 42 and Egg Harbor Road/Highway 42 in Fish Creek, proceed south on Egg Harbor Road/Highway 42 about 3.2 miles to Juddville Road. Turn right and proceed about 0.6 mile until Juddville Road ends at White Cliff Road. Turn left and follow White Cliff Road for about 1.0 mile to the preserve sign.

The sign and trailhead are across from 8247 White Cliff Road. Additional parking is available at the nearby public boat ramp. No fee.

BEACHES AND OVERLOOKS

W. Sister Bay Beach and Waterfront Park

Sister Bay Beach is a small, narrow sand and rock beach at Sister Bay Waterfront Park. Both the park and the beach have great views of the Sister Islands. The park has a marina, restrooms, a pavilion, a large playground, a picnic area with grills, and a kayak and canoe launch area. This is a good place for experienced paddlers to put in kayaks for trips out to the Sister Islands.

CONTACT INFORMATION AND DIRECTIONS

Village of Sister Bay, 2383 Maple Dr., P.O. Box 769, Sister Bay, WI 54234, (920) 854-4118, http://www.sisterbay.com/. The park is located in downtown Sister Bay on the west side of Highway 42 behind the post office. No fee.

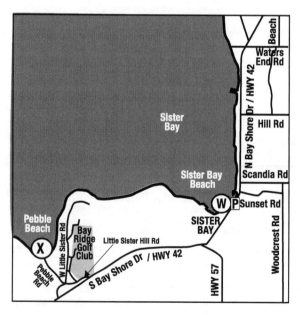

X. Pebble Beach Road Beach

This local favorite is an impressive, wide cobble beach—one of the nicest in Door County—in a protected cove surrounded by private homes. It is an excellent launching point for kayaking out around Peninsula State Park, past Eagle Bluff Lighthouse. There is parking along the road for about fifteen cars. There are no facilities. Removing cobbles is prohibited.

CONTACT INFORMATION AND DIRECTIONS

Village of Sister Bay, 2383 Maple Dr., P.O. Box 769, Sister Bay, WI 54234, (920) 854-4118, http://www.sisterbay.com/. From Sunset Road in downtown Sister Bay, head south on Highway 42 for 1.5 miles. At Bay Ridge Golf Course, turn right on Little Sister Road and proceed (parallel to Highway 42) about 0.2 mile to Pebble Beach Road. Follow Pebble Beach Road about 0.2 mile (past the cemetery and the turnoff to Fred and Fuzzy's) to the end, at the beach. Park on the shoulder of the road and walk to the beach. No fee.

Y. Ephraim Village Beach

This small sand beach is located in protected Eagle Harbor, in the heart of downtown Ephraim. Village visitor information, drinking fountains, and restroom facilities are adjacent to the beach. Parking is available along Highway 42 around Wilson's and in the public Spruce Street parking lot.

CONTACT INFORMATION AND DIRECTIONS

Village of Ephraim, Administration Offices, Hwy Q and Norway St., Ephraim, WI 54211, (920) 854-5501, http://www.ephraim-doorcounty .com/. The beach is at 9877 Water Street in downtown Ephraim. No fee.

Z. Eagle Harbor and Harborside Park

Located in the heart of downtown Ephraim, this harbor has a grassy open space, a marina and boat launch, restrooms, drinking fountains, a fishing pier, and picnic areas. The park provides stunning views of Lake Michigan, Horseshoe Island, and the cliffs of nearby Peninsula State Park. In the summer, look for foraging Caspian Terns, Double-crested Cormorants, and gulls, Purple Martins, Tree and Northern Rough-winged Swallows, and occasionally Osprey. During the busy season this park is popular for fishing, boating, and picnicking, and can be crowded at times. Eagle Harbor is a good launching spot for kayaking.

CONTACT INFORMATION AND DIRECTIONS

Village of Ephraim, Administration Offices, Hwy Q and Norway St., Ephraim, WI 54211, (920) 854-5501, http://www.ephraim-doorcounty .com/. The park and harbor are in downtown Ephraim at 9986 Water Street (Highway 42). Park in the public lot on Spruce Street off Highway

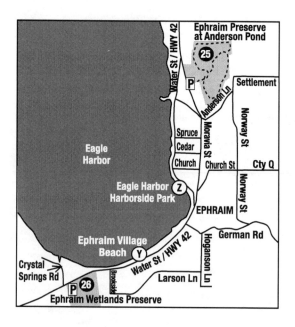

42, along Highway 42 near Wilson's, or other public spaces at the marina. No fee to use the park or beach.

AA. Nicolet Beach—Peninsula State Park

Nicolet Beach is a sand and cobble beach off Shore Road within Peninsula State Park. It has a large parking area, restrooms, drinking fountains, changing facilities, and boat rentals and concessions during the summer months. Nearby Tennison Bay is an ideal launching spot for kayakers setting out for trips to the Strawberry Islands, Chambers Island, Horseshoe Island, or offshore to view the bluffs.

CONTACT INFORMATION AND DIRECTIONS

Peninsula State Park, Wisconsin Department of Natural Resources, 9462 Shore Rd., Fish Creek, WI 54212, (920) 868-3258, http://www.dnr.wi.gov/. From the intersection of Highway 42/Egg Harbor Road and Spruce Street in downtown Fish Creek, proceed north on Highway 42/Egg Harbor

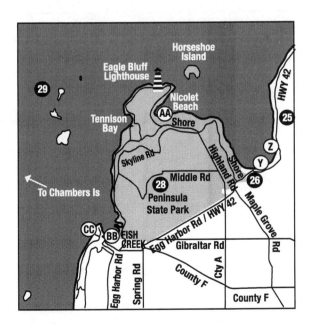

Road for 0.5 miles to Shore Drive, the main entrance of Peninsula State Park. Follow Shore Road past the lookout tower to the beach. Fee area.

BB. Fish Creek Beach

This small sand beach in a protected harbor area is popular with families with young children or those looking for a quick dip in the lake. The town maintains a parking lot and portable toilets during the summer months. There is also a very small playground.

CONTACT INFORMATION AND DIRECTIONS

Town of Gibraltar, 4097 Highway 42, P.O. Box 850, Fish Creek, WI 54212-0850, (920) 868-1714, http://www.townofgibraltar.com/. The park is located in downtown Fish Creek on the west side of Highway 42. No fee.

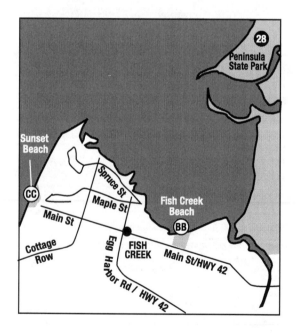

CC. Sunset Beach

This small, rocky beach, at the end of Main Street in Fish Creek west of the White Gull Inn, provides an ideal place to set up beach chairs and watch the sun set. This is more of an overlook spot than a place for swimming. There are no facilities.

CONTACT INFORMATION AND DIRECTIONS

Town of Gibraltar, 4097 Highway 42, P.O. Box 850, Fish Creek, WI 54212-0850, (920) 868-1714, http://www.townofgibraltar.com/. Park in Fish Creek's town parking lots or on-street parking and walk down to the end of Main Street. No fee.

LIGHTHOUSES

L7. Chambers Island Lighthouse

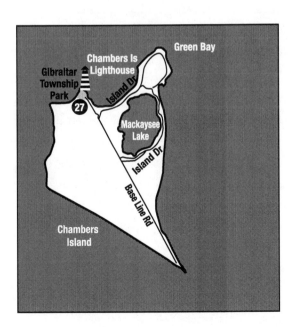

Chambers Island Lighthouse is located on Chambers Island about five miles offshore from Peninsula State Park. Construction on octagonal Cream City brick tower and lightkeeper's quarters began in 1868. Today, the light is inactive and has been replaced by an automated tower nearby. The lighthouse and 40-acre grounds are owned and operated by the Town of Gibraltar as a town park. Volunteers staff the park and open it to the public on summer weekends. There is no public boat service, but many local boat captains run charter services out to the island. This also makes a great day trip for experienced kayakers. The Door County Maritime Museum hosts an annual guided boat tour and can provide information on hours and dates of seasonal operation.

CONTACT INFO

Town of Gibraltar, 4097 Hwy 42, P.O. Box 850, Fish Creek, WI 54212, (920) 868-1714, http://www.townofgibraltar.com/. Door County Maritime Museum, 120 N. Madison Ave., Sturgeon Bay, WI 54235, (920) 743-5958, http://www.dcmm.org/. No fee to visit the park.

L8. Eagle Bluff Lighthouse

Eagle Bluff Lighthouse is on a high bluff within Peninsula State Park. The picturesque four-sided lighthouse tower and residence were built of Cream City brick in 1868. The lighthouse and lightkeeper's residence have been restored and are now a historical museum, open for daily tours during the summer season. Contact the park for specific hours of operation and tour schedules.

CONTACT INFORMATION AND DIRECTIONS

Peninsula State Park, Wisconsin Department of Natural Resources, 9462 Shore Rd., Fish Creek, WI 54212, (920) 868-3258, http://www.dnr.wi.gov/ and http://www.eagleblufflighthouse.org/. From the intersection of Highway 42/Egg Harbor Road and Spruce Street in downtown Fish Creek, proceed north on Highway 42/Egg Harbor Road for 0.5 mile to Shore Drive, the main entrance of Peninsula State Park. Fee area.

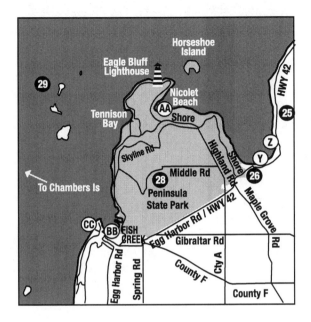

BIKE ROUTES

B10. Sister Bay to Three Springs Preserve
(5.0 miles round-trip—easy)

This easy ride, suitable for cyclists of all ages and ability levels, starts in downtown Sister Bay, travels across some of the peninsula's prime agricultural areas on County ZZ, and ends at Harold C. Wilson Three Springs Preserve, a Door County Land Trust (DCLT) conservation area that includes Three Springs Creek. Combining this bike ride with a short hike at Three Springs Preserve (see Major Point of Interest 15, chapter 2) makes an excellent half-day excursion. There are no facilities at the preserve, but the Village of Sister Bay maintains public restrooms in the town center.

ROUTE

From the intersection of Highway 42/57 and Maple Drive/County ZZ in Sister Bay, go east on Maple Drive/County ZZ for 2.0 miles to Three

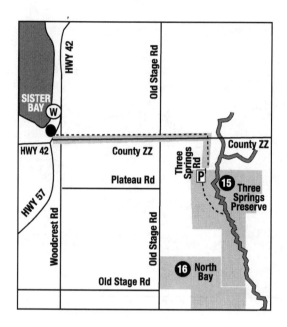

Springs Road. Turn right and follow Three Springs Road to the end, about 0.5 mile, and the DCLT trailhead. Retrace your route back to Sister Bay.

CONTACT INFORMATION

Door County Land Trust, P.O. Box 65, Sturgeon Bay, WI 54235, (920) 746-1359, http://www.doorcountylandtrust.org/. No fee.

B11. Sister Bay to Rowleys Bay

(10.2 miles round-trip—easy to moderate)

This mostly flat route traverses a patchwork of farmland and northern wet-mesic and northern mesic forests until it ends at Lake Michigan. It is moderate in length, but the biking is easy, and the route is suitable for beginners of all ages. The Village of Sister Bay maintains public restrooms in the town center, and there are restrooms at Sand Bay Town Park.

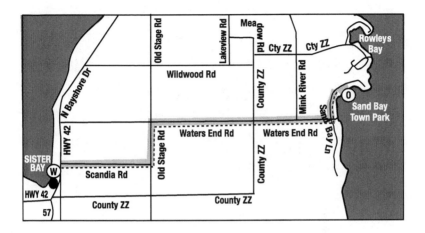

ROUTE

From the intersection of Highway 42/57 and Scandia Road in Sister Bay, go east on Scandia Road for 1.3 miles to Old Stage Road. Turn left and follow Old Stage Road for 1.0 mile to Waters End Road. Turn right and follow Waters End Road until it ends at Rowleys Bay on Lake Michigan, about 2.5 miles. From there you could follow Sand Bay Lane north for about 0.2 mile to Sand Bay Town Park.

CONTACT INFORMATION

Town of Liberty Grove, 11161 Old Stage Rd., Sister Bay, WI 54234, (920) 854-2934, http://libertygrove.org/. No fee.

B12. Fish Creek to Peninsula State Park Sunset Trail

(9.6 miles round-trip—easy)

The Sunset Trail is Peninsula State Park's main groomed bike trail. Mostly flat, it does have some small hills as it winds up the bluffs. This trail is easy enough for beginners of all ages, but can be crowded, so it is important to ride single file and follow the park rules. Public restrooms are available in downtown Fish Creek and in Peninsula State Park.

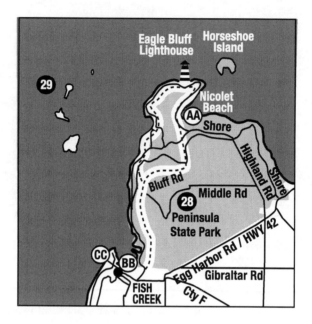

ROUTE

From downtown Fish Creek, proceed north on Highway 42 for 0.3 mile to the main entrance of Peninsula State Park. Just past the first parking area, pick up the Sunset Trail, a well-graded gravel bike trail. The trail winds past White Cedar Forest State Natural Area, Tennison Bay, and Weborg Marsh. The trail then loops around Nicolet Bay, heads back south, providing glimpses of Green Bay, and links up with the road to the park entrance.

CONTACT INFORMATION

Peninsula State Park, Wisconsin Department of Natural Resources, 9462 Shore Rd., Fish Creek, WI 54212, (920) 868-3258, http://www.dnr.wi.gov/. Peninsula State Park is a fee area.

B13. Ephraim to Mink River Estuary

(22 miles round-trip—moderate)

This mostly flat route runs through a mix of farmlands and northern wet-mesic and northern mesic forests, over roads with generally light traffic. It traverses some of the most scenic farming areas along the interior of the Door Peninsula and is generally excellent for fall colors during October. The route is designated as moderate for its distance, but is otherwise mostly flat, easy road cycling.

ROUTE

From the intersection of Highway 42 and County Q in downtown Ephraim, head north on Highway 42 for 0.8 mile to Anderson Lane. Turn

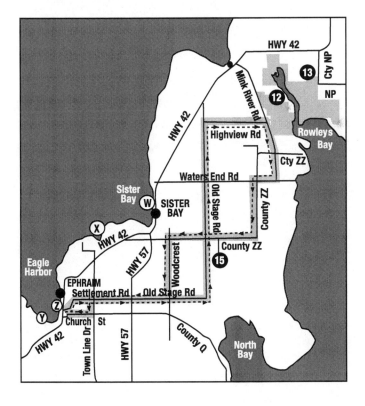

right and follow Anderson Lane 0.4 mile to Norway Street. Turn left and follow Norway Street until it turns into Settlement Road, about 0.1 mile. Continue on Settlement Road for 1.6 miles until it turns into Old Stage Road. Continue on Old Stage Road for 6.5 miles to Highview Road. Turn right and follow Highview Road for 1.8 miles to Mink River Road. Turn right and follow Mink River Road south for 1.5 miles to Waters End Road. Turn right and follow Waters End Road for 0.5 mile to County ZZ. Turn left and follow County ZZ south for 1.5 miles and then west for 2.5 miles to Woodcrest Road. Turn left and head south on Woodcrest Road for 1.5 miles to Old Stage Road. Turn right and follow Old Stage Road west as it turns into Settlement Road and continue 2.0 miles to Town Line Drive. Turn left and follow Town Line Drive for 0.5 mile to Church Street. Turn right and follow Church Street 0.8 mile to downtown Ephraim.

B14. Fish Creek to Peninsula Players Road to Spring Road

(7.6 miles round-trip—moderate with some challenging hills)

This moderately challenging route winds through Cottage Row, a high point atop the Niagara Escarpment overlooking Fish Creek, and then heads south through farmlands and northern mesic and northern wet-mesic forests. The route then returns through a wooded stretch of Spring Road to downtown Fish Creek. The route is best suited to experienced cyclists. Public restrooms are available in downtown Fish Creek.

ROUTE

From downtown Fish Creek, head west on Main Street for 0.1 mile to Cottage Row. Turn left and go about 400 feet, then take a right to stay on Cottage Row. Follow Cottage Row for 1.2 miles, and then as it turns left (east) for 0.3 mile to Gibralter Bluff Road. Turn right (south) and follow Gibralter Bluff Road for 1.5 miles to Peninsula Players Road. Turn left and follow Peninsula Players Road for 1.3 miles to Spring Road. Turn left and follow Spring Road north for 2.4 miles to Highway 42/Main Street. Turn left and return to downtown Fish Creek, about 0.8 mile.

PADDLING ROUTES

P10. Sister Bay to the Sister Islands
(5.0 miles round-trip—difficult)

The Sister Islands are an excellent destination for experienced kayakers (see 29D in this chapter for details). Take adequate safety precautions, take warm clothes, wear foul weather gear or a dry suit, and take plenty of food and water, as these islands are about 2.2 miles offshore and waters can be rough.

ROUTE

Launch from Sister Bay Beach, a narrow sand and cobble beach downtown at Sister Bay Waterfront Park. From the launching spot, head north from Sister Bay. North of the harbor, you will pass a buoy that marks the *Meridian*, a schooner wrecked in a storm in 1873. The site is popular with divers, and while the wreck sits in about 35 feet of water, it is not easily visible from the surface. Continue about 2.0 miles out to the

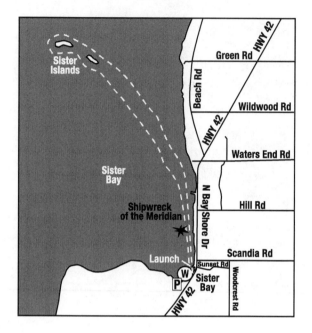

islands, and make a loop around them, retracing your route to return to
Sister Bay.

CONTACT INFORMATION AND DIRECTIONS TO LAUNCH SITE

Village of Sister Bay, 2383 Maple Dr., P.O. Box 769, Sister Bay, WI 54234,
(920) 854-4118, http://www.sisterbay.com/. Sister Bay Waterfront Park is
located in downtown Sister Bay on the west side of Highway 42 behind
the post office. The park has restrooms and other facilities. No fee.

P11. Nicolet Bay to Horseshoe Island

(2.0 miles round-trip—easy)

On calm days, Horseshoe Island is an easy day trip by canoe or kayak
from Peninsula State Park's Nicolet Beach. This extremely popular trip is
appropriate for paddlers of all abilities, though beginners might consider

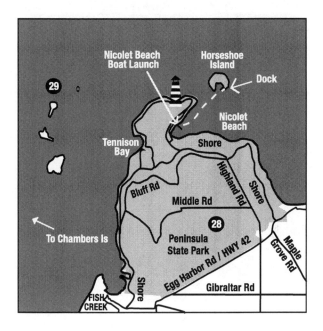

taking a guided tour offered by one of the local kayaking outfitters. Horseshoe Island is less than 1.0 mile offshore from the mainland portion of Peninsula State Park, in Nicolet Bay (see 29A in this chapter for details).

ROUTE

Paddlers can launch kayaks or canoes from the park's Nicolet Beach boat launch, or directly from rocky Nicolet Beach, and then paddle across to Horseshoe Island's dock. Watch out for power boats in this area, particularly on summer weekends.

CONTACT INFORMATION AND DIRECTIONS TO LAUNCH SITE

Peninsula State Park, Wisconsin Department of Natural Resources, 9462 Shore Rd., Fish Creek, WI 54212, (920) 868-3258, http://www.dnr.wi.gov/. Entrances to Peninsula State Park are located off Highway 42 in Fish Creek and several miles south of Ephraim. Fee area.

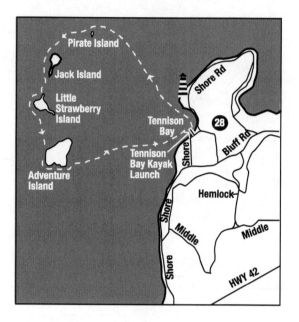

P12. Tennison Bay to the Strawberry Islands

(4.0 miles round-trip—difficult)

Experienced kayakers should definitely consider a trip out around the Strawberry Islands, about 1.5 miles from Peninsula State Park (see 29D in this chapter for details). This route provides great offshore views of the Eagle Bluff Lighthouse and the bluffs and sea caves of Peninsula State Park. The route is generally protected and suitable for well-prepared paddlers under most weather conditions. Take appropriate safety precautions, and take good maps, food, and water. Wearing a wet or dry suit no matter the season is also advisable.

Access to these private islands is restricted, and should not be attempted. Paddlers should also avoid disturbing nesting birds during the spring and summer. Note that the water may be shallow; underwater rocks are visible when lake levels are low. Experienced paddlers might combine this trip with a visit to Chambers Island, about 5.25 miles from the Strawberry Islands chain.

ROUTE

The chain of islands is easy to spot on the horizon from the launching site on Tennison Bay in Peninsula State Park. Head northwest to the northernmost island in the chain, Pirate Island, about 1.5 miles from Tennison Bay. Paddle around Pirate Island and down past Jack Island and Little Strawberry Island, and then around the southernmost, and largest, of the chain, Adventure Island, an additional 1.0 mile. Return to the Tennison Bay launch, about 1.5 miles back across the bay.

CONTACT INFORMATION AND DIRECTIONS TO LAUNCH SITE

Peninsula State Park, Wisconsin Department of Natural Resources, 9462 Shore Rd., Fish Creek, WI 54212, (920) 868-3258, http://www.dnr.wi.gov/. Entrances to the park are off Highway 42 just north of Fish Creek and several miles south of Ephraim. Fee area.

5

Kangaroo Lake to Whitefish Dunes
Jacksonport, Valmy, and Sevastopol

It's easy to see the effects of ancient glaciers on this region of Door County, situated along Lake Michigan between Baileys Harbor and Shivering Sands. Five to ten thousand years ago, the last of the glaciers receded, leaving behind massive sand dunes and separating Clark and Kangaroo Lakes from Lake Michigan. Over time, stately northern wet-mesic forests

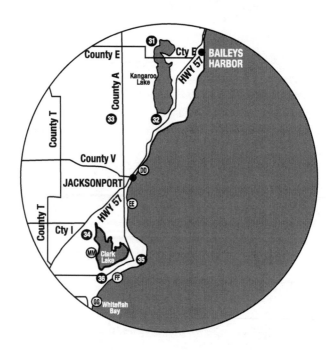

grew atop these sand dunes, and the woods and spring-fed lakes in the region became home to a number of Native American settlements, some around Kangaroo Lake and at Whitefish Dunes. From the 1840s to the 1880s, land around Kangaroo Lake was cleared for agriculture, and Whitefish Dunes became a commercial center for fishing, logging, shipping, and trading. By the late 1880s, as nearby Baileys Harbor grew, Kangaroo Lake became a thriving community, and summer resort development soon followed. Summer visitors from points south began to flock to the resorts and build cottages along the lakeshores. Today this area is still a popular summer destination for visitors. Boaters, sailors, and anglers come to Kangaroo Lake in search of panfish, bass, and walleye, while Clark Lake provides a quieter setting. This part of Door County, known as "the quiet side," is a relaxed summer alternative to the hustle and bustle of the larger towns, and provides a multitude of outdoor adventures for the intrepid visitor.

MAJOR POINTS OF INTEREST

31. Kangaroo Lake

The shape of this glacial lake is thought to resemble the Australian marsupial. While private cottages and resorts line most of the lakeshore, several large parcels at the north end of the lake have been protected by The Nature Conservancy (TNC) and the Door County Land Trust (DCLT). The DCLT lands have a well-maintained and extremely scenic hiking trail. Though very few visitors know about this corner of Kangaroo Lake, locals consider it to offer some of the most beautiful hiking in all of Door County. The area includes northern sedge meadow and emergent marshes, fed by Piel Creek, which form a large wetlands complex along the spring-fed headwaters of the lake. These wetlands comprise the core habitat for the endangered Hine's emerald dragonfly in Door County. Look for water lily, cattails, and bulrush in the shallower parts of the lake. Careful observers may also find beaver, muskrat, northern leopard frog, wood frog, *Dorcas* copper butterfly, Sandhill Crane, Common Goldeneye, Osprey, and Bald Eagle. Though there has been major impact from grazing by deer in recent years, the northern and western

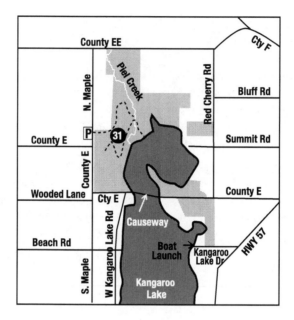

shores of Kangaroo Lake still include pockets of northern wet-mesic forest with a diverse understory, with rare plants such as Canada yew and
dwarf lake iris, and a willow-alder community.

A causeway, today part of County E, was built in the 1800s and divides
the northern and southern parts of the lake. It provides easy access for
those who only have a few minutes to stop and admire the lake (note that
parking is not allowed on the causeway).

There are three main public access points on the lake: the Door
County Land Trust trail, the Kangaroo Lake causeway, and the Kangaroo
Lake public boat launch.

Door County Land Trust Trail (northwest side of Kangaroo Lake)

This well-maintained trail can be accessed by parking along the east side
of Maple Road, just north of County E. The trail is moderate, starting at
one of the higher points in the county, and traverses down through an
open northern mesic forest, past old stone walls from the area's agricultural past, and down to an extensive cattail marsh along the lakeshore.

TRAILS, ACCESS, AND FACILITIES

The trail is about 1.5 miles round-trip and is relatively steep in places. Note that the trail is cleared by volunteers regularly, and the path downhill to the lake should be obvious. Bikes, horses, and motorized vehicles are prohibited on the DCLT preserve. Hunting is authorized on DCLT parcels and subject to DCLT guidelines and permission.

CONTACT INFORMATION AND DIRECTIONS

Door County Land Trust, P.O. Box 65, Sturgeon Bay, WI 54235, (920) 746-1359, http://www.doorcountylandtrust.org/. From the intersection of Highway 57 and County F in Baileys Harbor, head west on County F for about 0.9 mile to County EE. Take a left and follow County EE west for 1.8 miles to North Maple Road. Turn left and head south on North Maple Road for about 0.75 mile. Watch for the trail signage on the east side of North Maple Road, just north of County E. If you reach County E, you've gone too far. Park off the shoulder of North Maple Road and head east from the trailhead. No fee.

Kangaroo Lake Causeway (County E)

The Kangaroo Lake Causeway is an ideal launching point for a relaxed canoe or kayak trip around Kangaroo Lake.

DIRECTIONS

From the intersection of Highway 57 and County F in Baileys Harbor, head south on Highway 57 for about 1.4 miles to County E. Turn right and head west on County E for 1.5 miles across Kangaroo Lake. You'll see parking along the road near the bar/restaurant on the west end of the causeway. Cross the causeway to view the lake or launch canoes or kayaks. For more details on paddling, see Paddling Route P13. Parking is not allowed on the causeway. No fee.

Kangaroo Lake Public Boat Launch (East Side of Kangaroo Lake)

The Town of Baileys Harbor, working with the Kangaroo Lake Property Owners Association, maintains a small public boat launch on the east side of the lake.

DIRECTIONS

From the intersection of Highway 57 and County F in Baileys Harbor, head south on Highway 57 for about 2.1 miles to Kangaroo Lake Drive. Turn right and proceed west 0.6 mile until you see the lake and the boat ramp. No fee.

32. Meridian County Park

Meridian County Park is named for its location at the 45th parallel, halfway between the North Pole and the equator. Over the years, The Nature Conservancy, Door County Land Trust, local landowner families, and other partners have worked to preserve adjacent parcels known as Lyle-Harter-Matter Sanctuary. Despite the various names used to identify the parcels, this area (hereafter, "the park") is now a contiguous unit, managed by the county and designated as a State Natural Area. The park is located along an isthmus between Lake Michigan and the south end of Kangaroo Lake, interspersed with adjacent privately owned parcels. It is

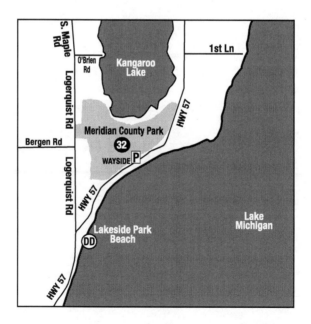

very scenic, and, despite some road noise from Highway 57, a hike is highly recommended. Trails are not developed or marked, but the area is small enough that visitors won't get lost.

The 200-acre park is well wooded, with forests growing atop an ancient Great Lakes beach and dune community and well-worn glacial Great Lakes ridge and swale. It is dominated by a northern mesic forest with some northern wet-mesic forest, with substantial stands of American beech. As in many other parts of Door County, prior to overgrazing by white-tailed deer, the park had a well-developed understory of wood fern, Canada yew, and Canada mayflower, but now many of the plants along the forest floor are gone. This has effectively eliminated the presence of understory-nesting birds, like Black-throated Blue Warbler, which formerly bred in the park. The original Meridian County Park section is noteworthy for its clay seepage bluff communities—damp, mossy, and dramatic 15-foot dolomite rock outcrops, characteristic of the Niagara Escarpment, which provide habitat for a variety of plants and such animals as wood frog, blue-spotted salamander, and Northern Waterthrush. The sanctuary sections of the park include several areas of emergent marsh, the springs that feed Kangaroo Lake, and 60-foot forested ancient sand dunes.

TRAILS, ACCESS AND FACILITIES

The easiest way to access the trails is to park at the wayside located at 6799 Highway 57 between Jacksonport and Baileys Harbor and follow the path behind the restrooms. There is no trail signage and trails are not marked, but they are easy to follow. There are several miles of trails throughout the property.

CONTACT INFORMATION AND DIRECTIONS

Door County Parks System, 3528 Park Dr., Sturgeon Bay, WI 54235, (920) 746-9959, http://map.co.door.wi.us/parks/. Door County Land Trust, P.O. Box 65, Sturgeon Bay, WI 54235, (920) 746-1359, http://www.door countylandtrust.org/. The wayside at 6799 Highway 57 is about 2.5 miles north of Jacksonport. No fee.

33. Hibbard Creek Preserve

This 80-acre parcel includes a significant wetlands complex along Hibbard Creek. The preserve has about 0.5 mile, round-trip, of rustic trails, which are not well marked and may not always be well maintained. In addition, where Junction Road crosses Hibbard Creek, you will see creek on both sides of the road and can launch canoes and kayaks, or wade in to fish.

Hibbard Creek is a well-known trout stream, stocked annually by the Wisconsin Department of Natural Resources with rainbow trout, brook trout, and steelhead. The preserve includes a number of emergent marsh areas and springs, and is home to Red-winged Blackbird, Song Sparrow, and muskrat. In addition to wetlands, the preserve includes northern wet-mesic and northern dry-mesic forest communities, with breeding Rose-breasted Grosbeak, American Robin, Eastern Kingbird, Scarlet Tanager, and Red-eyed Vireo. In addition to fish habitat, the preserve provides habitat for a variety of riparian plants, including marsh horsetail and slender bog-arrowgrass.

TRAILS, ACCESS, AND FACILITIES

The preserve contains a rustic, occasionally maintained trail of about 0.25 mile to the wetlands area near the creek. It begins at the border of the property with the neighboring farm field and ends at the creek. Areas near the creek may be wet, and visitors should wear appropriate footwear. There are no facilities. Leashed dogs are permitted. Bikes, horses, and motorized vehicles are prohibited. Hunting is authorized and subject to DCLT guidelines and permission.

CONTACT INFORMATION AND DIRECTIONS

Door County Land Trust, P.O. Box 65, Sturgeon Bay, WI 54235, (920) 746-1359, http://www.doorcountylandtrust.org/. From the intersection of Highway 57 and County V in Jacksonport, go west on County V for 0.3 mile to County A. Turn right and go north on County A about 1.7 miles to North Junction Road. Turn left and go west for about 0.35 mile. Park off the shoulder of North Junction Road just past the intersection with the creek, and proceed northeast on foot to the trailhead. As you're coming in on County A, you will also see an access point for fishing and boat launching where North Junction Road crosses the creek. No fee.

34. Logan Creek Preserve

The Logan Creek Preserve, operated by The Ridges Sanctuary and designated as a State Natural Area, is the perfect place for a quiet walk or for cross-country skiing. The property is located along the northwest shore of Clark Lake and includes namesake Logan Creek, a small trout stream that feeds the lake. The trails wind through a diversity of northern wet-mesic and hardwood swamp forest habitats, with towering stands of old growth hemlocks and beech and maple groves. The site also features wetlands and ephemeral, or seasonal, wetlands, and a well-developed understory of plants, including Canada mayflower, wild sarsaparilla, and wood fern. Except for spring wildflower seekers and photographers, rarely will you see others on the trails.

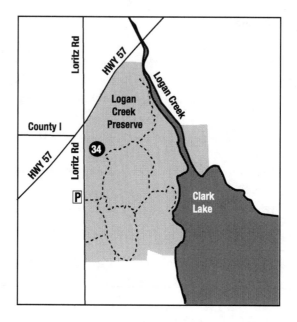

Logan Creek is widely considered one of the premier places in Door County to visit in April, May, and June for orchids and other spring wildflowers, such as trout lily, spring beauty, Dutchman's-breeches, large-flowered trillium, and a number of native wood violets. During a morning walk during the second and third weeks of May, you can expect to see twenty or more species of migrant wood warblers, including Canada, Cape May, Blackburnian, Blackpoll, and Bay-breasted, along with several species of vireo, and all of the more common breeding species, such as Ovenbird, Rose-breasted Grosbeak, and American Redstart.

TRAILS, ACCESS, AND FACILITIES

The property has about 1.5 miles of trails, from the trailhead to the edge of the property at Clark Lake and to Logan Creek. They are wide and well maintained, with some boardwalks. At the trailhead is a kiosk with a trail map. There are no facilities. Deer hunting is authorized and subject to rules and permission of The Ridges Sanctuary.

Contact Information and Directions

The Ridges Sanctuary, P.O. Box 152, Baileys Harbor, WI 54202, (920) 839-2802, http://www.ridgessanctuary.org/. From the intersection of Highway 57 and County V in Jacksonport, go south on Highway 57 for 2.6 miles, then south on Loritz Road for 0.25 miles to 5724 Loritz Road. Park in the small parking lot and walk to the kiosk and trailhead. Fee area.

35. Cave Point County Park

Cave Point County Park, owned and operated by the Door County Parks System, occupies only 19 acres, but it packs a lot into that small area. It is well worth a visit for the scenic overlooks alone: sweeping views of Lake Michigan, several sections of an underwater cave along the shoreline, and limestone bluffs.

Along Lake Michigan, trails pass through northern wet-mesic forest. Elsewhere, look for northern mesic forests, with well-developed native fern understory. It's a good place to look for wood frog, red-backed salamander, and spotted salamander, as well as breeding Mourning Warbler, particularly in areas with extensive fern understory along the main road into the park. Chestnut-sided Warbler, Red-eyed Vireo, and Great Crested Flycatcher also breed here. In the winter, look for the tracks of snowshoe hare, raccoon, ermine, and porcupine.

Trails, Access, and Facilities

Surrounded on three sides by Whitefish Dunes State Park, Cave Point County Park has hiking access to the state park via an easy 0.5-mile loop that links up with hiking trails at Whitefish Dunes. It has parking, restrooms, and a picnic area.

Contact Information and Directions

Door County Parks System, 3528 Park Dr., Sturgeon Bay, WI 54235, (920) 746-9959, http://map.co.door.wi.us/parks/. From the intersection of Highway 57 and County V in Jacksonport, travel south on Highway 57 about 0.7 mile to North Cave Point Drive. Turn left and follow Cave Point

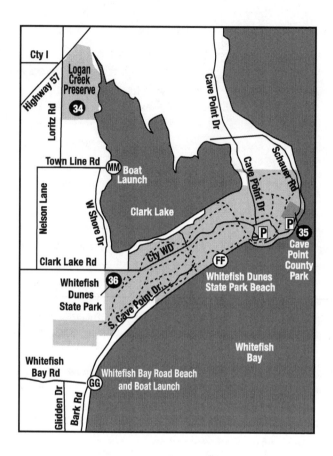

Drive about 1.9 miles to Clark Lake Road/County WD (you will be enter-ing Whitefish Dunes State Park). Turn left, follow Clark Lake Road/County WD for 0.3 mile, and bear left at Schauer Road. Follow Schauer Road to the park entrance at 5360 Schauer Road, Sevastopol Township. No fee.

36. Whitefish Dunes State Park

Whitefish Dunes State Park is very popular during the summer months, and with good reason. The 865-acre park has hiking and biking trails, a nature center, picnic areas, interpretive programs, archaeological sites, and great beaches. It is home to the largest sand dunes on the western shore of Lake Michigan, and its wide sandy beaches and the relatively shallow waters of Whitefish Bay make it ideal for swimming. Inland, the bike paths, picnic areas, and visitors' center are also popular with vacationers. However, there are still some relatively quiet areas, particularly along the Old Baldy dune, early in the morning, and during the off-season.

The park encompasses a great diversity of ecological communities, including some of Wisconsin's premier examples of Great Lakes beach and dune, wetlands and northern sedge meadow near Clark Lake, northern wet-mesic forest, and northern mesic forest. Many of these forests are growing atop old stabilized dunes and have an understory of native ferns and Canada yew. Wildlife viewing in any season can be exceptional, as the park boasts a large list of mammals, including black bear, river otter, mink, and ermine. In the summer, look for breeding Red-shouldered Hawk, Blue-headed Vireo, Chestnut-sided Warbler, Black-and-white Warbler, Ruffed Grouse, Indigo Bunting, and American Redstart. Along the shores of Clark Lake, scan for the occasional families of breeding Mallard, Blue-winged Teal, Common Goldeneye, and Common Merganser.

TRAILS

Whitefish Dunes State Park has a network of well-developed trails, primarily for hiking, but some are mixed-use hiking and biking. In winter the park grooms about eight miles of trails for cross-country skiing and leaves other trails open for snowshoeing. Trails include Black Trail (2.5-mile loop), Green Trail (1.8-mile loop), Clark Lake Spur Trail (0.7-mile connector), Yellow Trail (4.2-mile loop), Whitefish Creek Spur (1.0-mile connector), Red Trail (2.8-mile hike and bike trail, which connects to a less-than-0.5-mile boardwalk loop around Old Baldy sand dune and provides beach access), Brachiopod Trail (1.5-mile connector and interpretive trail, which includes a boardwalk area), and Red Pine Trail (easy 0.25-mile interpretive loop). The Red Trail is highly recommended for views of the lake and of the massive ancient dunes.

CONTACT INFORMATION AND DIRECTIONS

Whitefish Dunes State Park, Wisconsin Department of Natural Resources, 3275 Clark Lake Rd., Sturgeon Bay, WI 54235, (920) 823-2400, http://

dnr.wi.gov/. From the intersection of Highway 57 and County V in Jacksonport, go south on Highway 57 for 0.7 mile to North Cave Point Drive. Turn left and follow North Cave Point Drive for 3.1 miles and bear left onto Clark Lake Road/County WD. Turn left and follow Clark Lake Road/County WD for 0.7 mile to the entrance to the park. Fee area.

BEACHES AND OVERLOOKS

DD. Lakeside Park Beach

Lakeside Park Beach is a 50-foot stretch of sand on windswept Lake Michigan shores that can be accessed from Lakeside Park in downtown Jacksonport. The quality of this beach depends on lake levels. In high water, this beach is very narrow and may have rough waves and strong currents. The park has restrooms, a picnic area with grills and covered pavilions, and a playground.

CONTACT INFORMATION AND DIRECTIONS

Town of Jacksonport, 3733 Bagnall Rd., Sturgeon Bay, WI 54235, (920) 823-2954, http://www.jacksonport.org/. The beach is in downtown Jacksonport, near the intersection of Highway 57 and County V. No fee.

EE. Lakeshore Drive Beach

Lakeshore Drive Beach is a small access point to a hidden beach with great views, but you must climb down a rocky outcrop to the beach below. Note that this stretch of shoreline can be windy and water is often rough with strong currents, so climbing down to the beach should be considered only in calm weather. From the beach you can see Whitefish Dunes State Park to the south.

CONTACT INFORMATION AND DIRECTIONS

Town of Jacksonport, 3733 Bagnall Rd., Sturgeon Bay, WI 54235, (920) 823-2954, http://www.jacksonport.org/. From Lakeside Park in downtown Jacksonport, head south on Highway 57 for 0.4 mile to Lake Shore

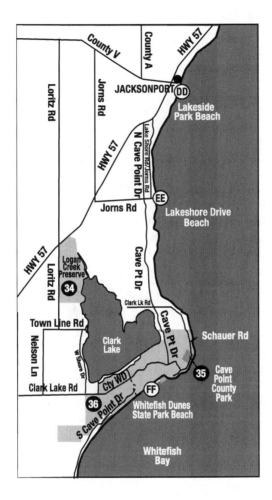

Road/Jorns Road. Turn left and follow Lake Shore Road south along the lake for 0.8 mile to the intersection with Jorns Road. There is parking for one or two cars. No fee.

FF. Whitefish Dunes State Park Beach

Whitefish Dunes is perhaps the best known beach in Door County, famous for its massive sand dunes, wide, white sand beaches, and excellent

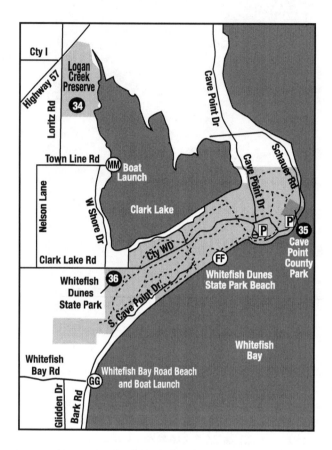

swimming conditions. It also has such amenities as restrooms, changing areas, and shower facilities. This popular beach can be very crowded during the summer months, so get there early to ensure a parking spot. Other features include a nature center with interpretive programs and hiking trails.

CONTACT INFORMATION AND DIRECTIONS

Whitefish Dunes State Park, Wisconsin Department of Natural Resources, 3275 Clark Lake Rd., Sturgeon Bay, WI 54235, (920) 823-2400, http://dnr.wi.gov/. From the intersection of Highway 57 and County V in Jacksonport, go south on Highway 57 for 0.7 mile to North Cave Point Drive. Turn left and follow Cave Point Drive for 3.1 miles and bear left onto

Clark Lake Road/County WD. Turn left and follow Clark Lake Road/ County WD for 0.7 mile to the entrance to the park. Once inside the park, follow signs to parking for beach access. Fee area.

GG. Whitefish Bay Road Beach and Boat Launch

This wide, scenic, white sand Lake Michigan beach, just south of White-fish Dunes State Park, is generally much quieter than the state park, although it lacks facilities. It is a popular launching point for experienced paddlers kayaking to the sea caves at nearby Cave Point County Park. Caution is advised, however, as this stretch of Lake Michigan coast-line can be very treacherous, particularly during the colder months. Swimming is not advised. This area has strong rip tides. This beach has a parking lot, boat launch, and dock.

CONTACT INFORMATION AND DIRECTIONS

Town of Sevastopol, P.O. Box 135, Sturgeon Bay, WI 54235, (920) 746-1230, http://www.townofsevastopol.com/. This beach can be accessed from the town boat ramp at the end of Whitefish Bay Road. From the intersection of Highway 57 and County V in Jacksonport, go south on Highway 57 for 6.4 miles to the crossroads town of Valmy. At the inter-section of Highway 57 and Whitefish Bay Road/County T, turn left and go east on Whitefish Bay Road/County T for about 2.3 miles, until it ends at a large sandy parking area at the intersection of Whitefish Bay Road, Bark Road, and South Cave Point Drive. No fee for use of the beach; small fee to launch boats.

HH. White Pine Lane Beach

This 50-foot-wide beach access point, located between private residences, provides access to extensive sandy beaches, part of the Shivering Sands State Natural Area. There is one parking space. Remember to respect the rights of adjacent property owners when visiting this beach and the fol-lowing ones near private residences.

Contact Information and Directions

Town of Sevastopol, P.O. Box 135, Sturgeon Bay, WI 54235, (920) 746-1230, http://www.townofsevastopol.com/. From the Bayview Bridge in downtown Sturgeon Bay, head north on Highway 42/57 for 1.9 miles to County T. Turn right and follow County T east for 4.0 miles until it intersects with Glidden Drive (still County T). Follow Glidden Drive northeast for 2.5 miles to White Pine Lane, a short driveway across from 4083 Glidden Drive. No fee.

II. Goldenrod Lane Beach

This 50-foot-wide beach access point, located between private residences, provides access to extensive sandy beaches, part of the Shivering Sands State Natural Area. It often has some algae and is rocky in parts. There is one parking space.

CONTACT INFORMATION AND DIRECTIONS

Town of Sevastopol, P.O. Box 135, Sturgeon Bay, WI 54235, (920) 746-1230, http://www.townofsevastopol.com/. From the Bayview Bridge in downtown Sturgeon Bay, head north on Highway 42/57 for 1.9 miles to County T. Turn right and follow County T east for 4.0 miles until it intersects with Glidden Drive (still County T). Follow Glidden Drive northeast for 2.1 miles to Goldenrod Lane, a short driveway between 4030 and 4016 Glidden Drive. No fee.

JJ. Hemlock Lane Beach

This 50-foot-wide beach access point, located between private residences, provides access to extensive sandy beaches, part of the Shivering Sands State Natural Area. There is one parking space.

CONTACT INFORMATION AND DIRECTIONS

Town of Sevastopol, P.O. Box 135, Sturgeon Bay, WI 54235, (920) 746-1230, http://www.townofsevastopol.com/. From the Bayview Bridge in downtown Sturgeon Bay, head north on Highway 42/57 for 1.9 miles to County T. Turn right and follow County T east for 4.0 miles until it intersects with Glidden Drive (still County T). Follow Glidden Drive northeast for about 1.0 mile to Hemlock Lane, a short driveway across from 3845 Glidden Drive. No fee.

KK. Deer Path Lane Beach

This 50-foot-wide beach access point, located between private residences, provides access to extensive sandy beaches, part of the Shivering Sands State Natural Area. There is room for two cars.

CONTACT INFORMATION AND DIRECTIONS

Town of Sevastopol, P.O. Box 135, Sturgeon Bay, WI 54235, (920) 746-1230, http://www.townofsevastopol.com/. From the Bayview Bridge in downtown Sturgeon Bay, head north on Highway 42/57 for 1.9 miles to County T. Turn right and follow County T east for 4.0 miles until it intersects with Glidden Drive (still County T). Follow Glidden Drive northeast for 0.7 mile to Deer Path Lane, a short driveway across from 3797 Glidden Drive. No fee.

LL. Evergreen Lane Beach

This 50-foot-wide beach access point, located between private residences, provides access to extensive sandy beaches, part of the Shivering Sands State Natural Area. It has room for two or three cars and stairs down to the beach.

CONTACT INFORMATION AND DIRECTIONS

Town of Sevastopol, P.O. Box 135, Sturgeon Bay, WI 54235, (920) 746-1230, http://www.townofsevastopol.com/. From the Bayview Bridge in downtown Sturgeon Bay, head north on Highway 42/57 for 1.9 miles to

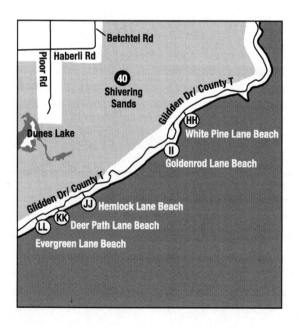

County T. Turn right and follow County T east for 4.0 miles until it intersects with Glidden Drive (still County T). Follow Glidden Drive northeast for 0.4 mile to Evergreen Lane, a short driveway across from 3757 Glidden Drive. No fee.

MM. Clark Lake Boat Launch

The Town of Sevastopol, in conjunction with volunteers from the Clark Lake Advancement Association, a property owners group, maintains a small boat launch on the west shore of Clark Lake. It provides the easiest public access for kayaking or canoeing on the lake. (There is additional

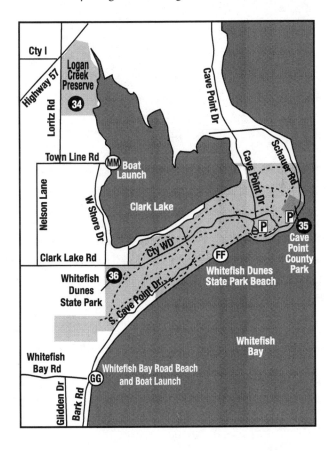

public access from Whitefish Dunes State Park on the southeast side of the lake, which requires portaging boats a significant distance.)

CONTACT INFORMATION AND DIRECTIONS

Town of Sevastopol, P.O. Box 135, Sturgeon Bay, WI 54235, (920) 746-1230, http://www.townofsevastopol.com/. From the intersection of Highway 57 and County V in Jacksonport, go south on Highway 57 for 2.6 miles to Loritz Road. Turn left and follow Loritz Road for 1.1 miles to East Town Line Road. Turn left and proceed about 0.5 mile. The boat ramp is at the intersection of Town Line Road and West Shore Drive, where Town Line Road meets the lake. Fee to launch boats.

BIKE ROUTES

B15. Jacksonport and North Cave Point Drive
(8.2 miles round-trip—easy)

This easy route from Jacksonport to Cave Point County Park is suitable for beginners of all ages. Cave Point Drive is relatively quiet traffic-wise and mostly flat. The route passes through northern wet-mesic and northern mesic woodlands, and offers glimpses of Lake Michigan, beginning at Lakeside Park in downtown Jacksonport.

ROUTE

From Lakeside Park in downtown Jacksonport, turn left onto Highway 57 and proceed south for about 0.7 mile to North Cave Point Drive. (Note that traffic can be heavy in this stretch of Highway 57, and cyclists should stay on the shoulder.) Turn left and follow North Cave Point Drive for about 3.1 miles to Clark Lake Road/County WD. Turn left and follow Clark Lake Road/County WD for 0.3 mile, and then bear left on Schauer Road. Cave Point County Park is on the right. Retrace your route to return to Jacksonport. Cave Point County Park and Lakeside Park have restrooms.

CONTACT INFORMATION

Town of Jacksonport, 3733 Bagnall Rd., Sturgeon Bay, WI 54235, (920) 823-8136, http://www.jacksonport.org/. No fee.

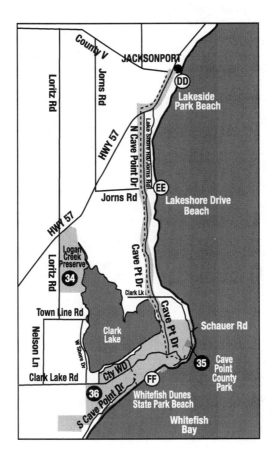

B16. Whitefish Dunes Trails

(2.8 miles—easy to moderate)

Whitefish Dunes State Park has about 2.8 miles of trails open to biking. You can pick up the Red Trail, which runs roughly parallel to the beach, from the main parking area for the beach. The trails run through a scenic mix of Great Lakes beach and dune and northern mesic forest communities. Note that the trails can be sandy and soft, making biking tough in spots along the beach.

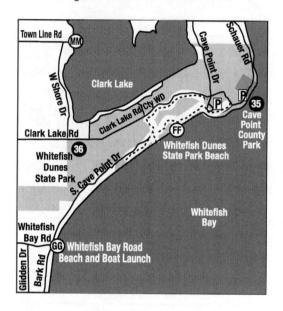

ROUTE

From the visitors' center, head southwest on the Red Trail along the beach. You can follow it to the boardwalk/beach steps and then retrace your path back to the Third Beach access point. At the Third Beach access, pick up the short connector path that takes you inland to Clark Lake Road. Turn right on Clark Lake Road, which has generally slow-moving car traffic, and follow it back to the visitors' center. Whitefish Dunes State Park has restrooms.

CONTACT INFORMATION

Whitefish Dunes State Park, Wisconsin Department of Natural Resources, 3275 Clark Lake Rd., Sturgeon Bay, WI 54235, (920) 823-2400, http:// dnr.wi.gov/. Fee area.

B17. Whitefish Dunes to Lily Bay County Park

(20.2 miles round-trip—moderate)

This winding route begins from the main parking lot for the beaches at Whitefish Dunes State Park, heads slightly inland, and then veers back to Lake Michigan, hugging the wooded Shivering Sands State Natural Area and the Lake Michigan lakeshore along Glidden Drive. Note that while Glidden Drive has minimal traffic, the road has many turns, blind curves, and numerous hidden driveways, so cyclists should use caution on this road.

ROUTE

From the parking area at Whitefish Dunes State Park, head west on Clark Lake Road/County WD for 2.6 miles to Nelson Lane. Turn left and follow Nelson Lane for 1.1 miles to Whitefish Bay Road/County T. Turn left and follow Whitefish Bay Road/County T for 0.3 mile to Glidden Drive/County T. Turn right and follow Glidden Drive/County T for about 6

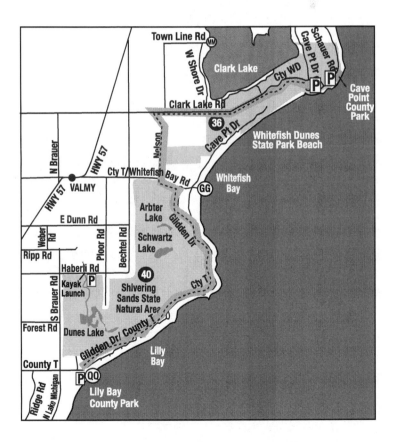

miles through the Shivering Sands State Natural Area to Lily Bay County Park. Retrace your route to return to Whitefish Dunes State Park. Whitefish Dunes State Park has restrooms. Lily Bay County Park on the south end of the bike route has a small parking lot but no facilities.

CONTACT INFORMATION

Whitefish Dunes State Park, Wisconsin Department of Natural Resources, 3275 Clark Lake Rd., Sturgeon Bay, WI 54235, (920) 823-2400, http://dnr.wi.gov/. Whitefish Dunes is a fee area. For free parking, you can leave your car at Cave Point County Park.

B18. Jacksonport to Carlsville

(20.6 miles round-trip—moderate)

This route from Jacksonport to the tiny crossroads of Carlsville traverses some of Door County's most productive agricultural areas. On mostly flat and quiet roads, it passes through a patchwork of farm fields and orchards. There are a few very gently rolling hills.

ROUTE

From the intersection of Highway 57 and County V in Jacksonport, go northwest on County V for 3.1 miles to County T. Turn left and follow County T for 0.5 mile to Sunny Slope Road. Turn right and follow Sunny Slope Road for 2.7 miles (past the Oak Road wetlands) to Oak Road. Turn left and proceed for 2.5 miles to County I. Turn right and follow County I for 1.5 miles to Carlsville. Retrace your route to return to Jacksonport. Lakeside Park in downtown Jacksonport has restrooms.

CONTACT INFO

Town of Jacksonport, 3733 Bagnall Rd., Sturgeon Bay, WI 54235, (920) 823-8136, http://www.jacksonport.org/. No fee.

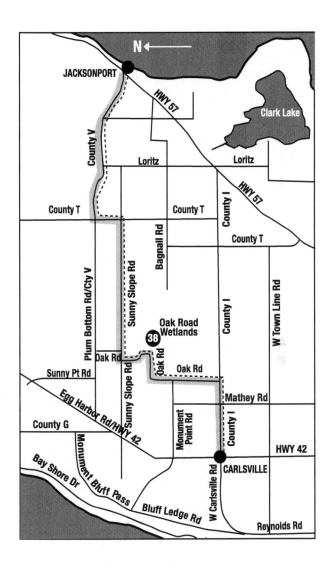

PADDLING ROUTES
P13. Kangaroo Lake
(1.0–8.5 miles round-trip—easy)

Kangaroo Lake is the largest inland lake—1,123 acres—in Door County, and should be at the top of the list for any Door County paddler. It is a great spot to learn to kayak or canoe, and an easy paddle around the lake can be a great way to spend part of a day. But experienced kayakers will also find plenty to hold their interest. While private cottages and resorts line most of the lakeshore, there are several large parcels at the north end of the lake that have been protected by The Nature Conservancy and the Door County Land Trust. The section of the lake north of the causeway that intersects the lake provides paddlers with exceptional wildlife-watching opportunities.

The north end includes northern sedge meadow and emergent marshes, fed by Piel Creek, which form a large wetlands complex along the spring-fed headwaters of the lake. These wetlands comprise the core habitat

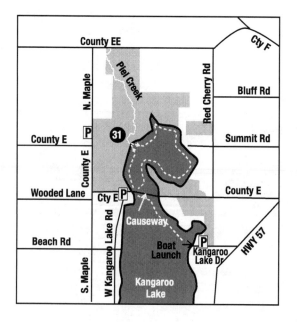

for the endangered Hine's emerald dragonfly in Door County. Careful observers may also find beaver, muskrat, northern leopard frog, wood frog, *Dorcas* copper butterfly, Sandhill Crane, Common Goldeneye, Osprey, and Bald Eagle. The area around the causeway is shallow and has extensive submergent marsh vegetation, primarily yellow pond lily, attracting painted turtles, Caspian Terns, Pied-billed Grebes and Common Mergansers.

ROUTE

You can spend half a day poking around the entire lake, but the northern end is the most interesting area for wildlife-watching. Launching from the causeway will put you at the north end of the lake right away, but those in search of a longer paddle can launch from the town boat ramp. When water levels are sufficient, head up Piel Creek and go as far as you can paddle. Depending on water levels, this can be a mile or so. A trip around the whole lake is about 7.5 miles, not including Piel Creek.

DIRECTIONS TO LAUNCH

The Kangaroo Lake causeway and the Kangaroo Lake boat launch are both good launching points. To launch from the causeway, park along the road near the Coyote Roadhouse restaurant on the west end of the causeway and walk your boat around the end of the causeway to the "head" of the Kangaroo. Heading north along the western shore of the lake, proceed about 1,000 feet to the entrance to Piel Creek. If you're interested in paddling up Piel Creek, the causeway is the best place to launch.

To reach the causeway from Baileys Harbor, head south on Highway 57 for about 1.4 miles, turn right at County E, and follow it west for 1.5 miles across Kangaroo Lake. Parking is not allowed on the causeway, but you may park on the road near the restaurant. There are no facilities, except at the restaurant.

To launch from the Town of Baileys Harbor boat launch on the east side of the lake, from Highway 57 and County F in Baileys Harbor, head south on Highway 57 for about 2.1 miles to Kangaroo Lake Drive, turn right, and proceed 0.6 mile until you see the lake and the boat ramp. There are no facilities.

Town of Baileys Harbor, 2392 County Road F, P.O. Box 308, Baileys Harbor, WI 54202, (920) 839-9509, http://townofbaileysharbor.com/. No fee.

P14. Clark Lake

(3.0 miles round-trip—easy)

Clark Lake, adjacent to Whitefish Dunes State Park, is suitable for beginning kayakers and canoers. The 868-acre lake is protected and generally quiet and becomes rough only in windy weather. The lake is bordered by the state park, by Logan Creek Preserve, and a few private cottages. You can put in boats at the Town of Jacksonport's public boat ramp. There are no facilities at the boat ramp, but you can walk into Whitefish Dunes State Park (fee area) or Cave Point County Park to find restrooms.

Clark Lake is relatively shallow, with an average depth of just seven feet. As a result, it has a significant amount of emergent and submergent marsh vegetation, primarily bulrush and a few invasive species like giant

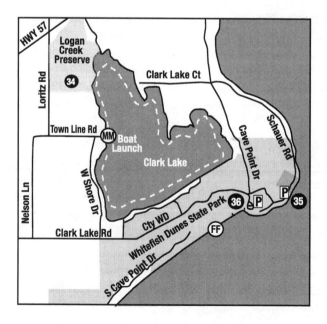

reed (phragmites). This adds up to great wildlife-viewing opportunities and easy kayaking and canoeing for paddlers of all ability levels. The lake is typically quiet, and you can scan the shorelines for families of breeding Mallard, Blue-winged Teal, Common Goldeneye, and Common Merganser. Look for the occasional beaver, or even river otter, foraging in the early morning hours or around dusk.

ROUTE

A complete paddle around the shores of Clark Lake is about 3.0 miles.

CONTACT INFORMATION AND DIRECTIONS TO LAUNCH SITE

Town of Jacksonport, 3733 Bagnall Rd., Sturgeon Bay, WI 54235, (920) 823-8136, http://www.jacksonport.org/. From the intersection of Highway 57 and County V in Jacksonport, go south on Highway 57 for 2.6 miles to Loritz Road. Turn left on Loritz Road and proceed for 1.1 miles to East Town Line Road. Turn left and head east for 0.5 mile. You will see the lake and the boat launch at the end of Town Line Road. Small fee to launch boats.

P15. Lakeside Park to Cave Point

(2.0–5.0 miles round-trip—difficult)

A trip to Cave Point County Park, part of the Door County Parks System, and its spectacular sea caves is a highlight for any Great Lakes kayaker. On calm days the stretch from Jacksonport's Lakeside Park to Cave Point County Park is fine for kayakers of intermediate ability levels, but when the winds come up, it can become downright dangerous, with crashing waves and rip currents. On a windy day, this area rivals the Porte des Morts crossing for the title of most dangerous stretch of water in Door County. Conditions can be unpredictable, and kayaking around Cave Point should be attempted only by well-prepared, experienced paddlers, after taking a look at the weather. Less experienced paddlers shouldn't be scared off entirely—several local outfitters run trips to this area, and beginners and intermediate paddlers should definitely consider going out with a guide on a calm day. Cave Point County Park has several large sea

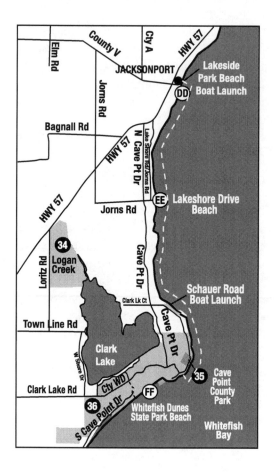

caves, which you can paddle into and listen to the echoes of the waves crashing. On calm days you can paddle into a cave and then lie flat on your kayak to enter a second hidden cave deeper into the limestone cliffs. Launch from Lakeside Park in Jacksonport to get the full experience of paddling this stretch of scenic coastline, which consists primarily of residential homes set on low cliffs. Lakeside Park has restrooms and other facilities. For a shorter paddle and direct access to the sea caves, try a route that the kayaking outfitters use, launching from the small beach at the end of Schauer Road.

ROUTE

Launching from Lakeside Park in Jacksonport, paddle due south along the Lake Michigan shoreline for about 2.2 miles to Cave Point County Park. Retrace your route to return to Lakeside Park. Launching from Schauer Road, head due south around Cave Point for less than 1.0 mile. Retrace your route to return to the beach at Schauer Road.

CONTACT INFORMATION AND DIRECTIONS TO LAUNCH SITES

Town of Jacksonport, 3733 Bagnall Rd., Sturgeon Bay, WI 54235, (920) 823-8136, http://www.jacksonport.org/. Lakeside Park is in downtown Jacksonport near the intersection of Highway 57 and County V. To reach the Schauer Road launch site, from the intersection of Highway 57 and County V in Jacksonport, take Highway 57 for 0.7 mile south to Cave Point Drive. Take a left and follow Cave Point Drive due south about 1.8 miles to Schauer Road. Turn left on Schauer Road and look for the town boat launch, a concrete pier area, at 5648 Schauer Road. You can park in the gravel areas off the shoulder of the road and carry your boat in at the sandy beach area next to the old dock. No fee.

6

Egg Harbor Area

The dynamic region along the shores of Green Bay is one of the most scenic, and one of the most popular, in all of Door County. Along the lake, you'll find gorgeous mixed deciduous forests atop towering bluffs, snug harbors, and warm water beaches. Inland, 150 years of agricultural history continues, with family farms and orchards dominating the landscape.

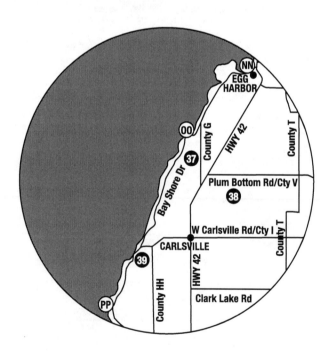

Founder Asa Thorp established nearby Fish Creek in the early 1880s, when the area was little more than a stopping off point for fur traders. The area quickly grew, first attracting English settlers, who were soon followed by French Canadian fur traders and trappers and German farmers. By the early 1860s, the enterprising Thorp family had constructed docks at both Fish Creek and Egg Harbor, and this area had grown into a busy logging, farming, fishing, and trading center. By the turn of the century, a number of summer resorts were thriving, drawing tourists from Chicago, St. Louis, and Milwaukee, many of whom built summer cottages of their own. Today, more than a century later, the beaches, vistas, towering bluffs, and extensive forests continue to make this area one of the most popular tourist destinations in Door County. It offers a varied assortment of outdoor activities, including some of the premier hiking in Door County.

MAJOR POINTS OF INTEREST

37. Lautenbach Woods Preserve

Quiet and picturesque Lautenbach Woods Preserve includes 140 acres conserved by the Door County Land Trust (DCLT). Not only is this site beautiful, but it also provides important protection of local watersheds (the underground water reserves that feed local wetlands and creeks). Visitors can stroll through scenic forests and wetlands and traverse some rocky outcrops along the Niagara Escarpment.

Lautenbach Woods Preserve is predominantly northern mesic forest community, with a substantial component of mature white pine and hemlock, as well as pockets of northern hardwood swamp community. Hikers can explore Niagara Escarpment outcrops and watch for Hermit Thrush, American Redstart, Black-capped Chickadee, Red-breasted Nuthatch, Least Flycatcher, and Indigo Bunting. At dusk, keep an eye out for big brown and red bats.

Trails, Access, and Facilities

The preserve contains a well-maintained 1.25-mile loop trail. Moderate overall, the trail may be steep and rocky in some areas. There are no facilities. Leashed dogs are permitted. Bikes, horses, and motorized vehicles

are prohibited. Hunting is authorized subject to DCLT guidelines and permission.

CONTACT INFORMATION AND DIRECTIONS

Door County Land Trust, P.O. Box 65, Sturgeon Bay, WI 54235, (920) 746-1359, http://www.doorcountylandtrust.org/. From the intersection of Horseshoe Bay Road/County G and Highway 42 in Egg Harbor, head south about 5.2 miles to County G (at Schartner's Farm Market), turn right, and follow County G for 0.7 mile to a small parking lot on the west side of County G, across from the art gallery at 6746 County G. No fee.

38. Oak Road Wetlands Preserve

Oak Road Wetlands Preserve, conserved by the Door County Land Trust (DCLT), includes 155 acres of restored prairie and woodlands along Oak Road and Sunnyslope Road, just south of Egg Harbor. While this site has

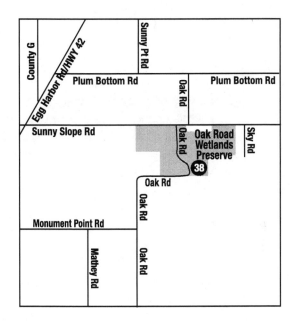

no trails, it is easily viewed by pulling off to the side of the road. Birding and wildlife-viewing are the primary attractions. This is also a perfect starting point for a bike ride, past bucolic farms with red barns and rolling hills. Fall colors in this area can be excellent. The preserve protects the headwaters, or underground water source, of the west branch of Whitefish Bay Creek.

The preserve includes an excellent example of a prairie restoration project as well as ephemeral wetlands that flood with the spring rains. Where water conditions are right, these wetlands provide significant habitat for amphibians and migrant shorebirds like Dunlin, Short-billed Dowitcher, and Wilson's Phalarope. In the summer and fall, in the drier upland areas, look for Sandhill Crane; Clay-colored, Vesper, and Savannah Sparrows; Bobolink; Eastern Kingbird; and Eastern Meadowlark. DCLT has installed nest boxes for Eastern Bluebirds and Tree Swallows.

TRAILS, ACCESS, AND FACILITIES

There are no trails or facilities at the site. Check with Door County Land Trust for access information. Hunting is authorized subject to DCLT guidelines and permission.

Door County Land Trust, P.O. Box 65, Sturgeon Bay, WI 54235, (920) 746-1359, http://www.doorcountylandtrust.org/. From the intersection of Horseshoe Bay Road/County G and Highway 42 in Egg Harbor, head south on Highway 42 for about 5.5 miles to Sunnyslope Road. Turn left and proceed east about 1.5 miles to the intersection with Oak Road. The preserve is primarily on the south side of Sunnyslope Road and along the portion of Oak Road that heads south and curves around the wetlands. Visitors can view the preserve by parking along the shoulder of Oak Road or the south side of Sunnyslope Road. No fee.

39. Bayshore Blufflands Preserve

Bayshore Blufflands Preserve includes some of the tallest bluffs in Door County, some rising up to 200 feet above the Green Bay shoreline. The preserve itself is a hidden gem and contains some of the best hiking in

Door County. It includes parcels owned and managed by the Door County Land Trust (DCLT), The Nature Conservancy, and other landowners. DCLT maintains about 2.5 miles of hiking trails on a 150-acre parcel roughly bounded by Reynolds Road and Bay Shore Drive.

This complex of parcels includes several distinct ecological communities associated with a three-mile swath of the Niagara Escarpment. The talus-covered bluffs of the escarpment create a cool microclimate that supports pockets of moist cliff community, characterized by native ferns and wild sarsaparilla. This preserve also has massive ancient white cedars typical of the surrounding northern wet-mesic forest community, and other hardwood trees typical of the surrounding northern mesic forest community. There are seeps and ephemeral wetlands that flood annually below and near the bottom of the escarpment, supporting a clay seepage bluff community along with wetter pockets of northern hardwood swamp, including silver maple, green ash, and swamp white oak. Along the bay is a small wetlands area with northern sedge meadow and emergent marsh communities, and an ephemeral creek. Near the top of the escarpment, a northern mesic forest community gradually gives way to a drier pine-dominated northern dry-mesic forest, with an understory of ferns, goldenrod, and dogwood. This can be an exceptional place to look for spring wildflowers, including orchids. Bayshore Blufflands Preserve also supports a community of uncommon understory plants and animals, including dwarf lake iris and northern ring-necked snake.

Trails, Access, and Facilities

There are 2.5 miles of hiking trails on the Door County Land Trust parcels, including a combination of a loop trail and return access. There are two trailheads, one on each side of the preserve. You can park your car at either the east or west trailhead and retrace your steps to return, or leave a car at each side and complete a through-hike from end to end. Trails are moderate but may be steep or rocky along the escarpment. Leashed dogs are permitted. Bikes, horses, and motorized vehicles are prohibited. Hunting is authorized subject to DCLT guidelines and permission.

Contact Information and Directions

Door County Land Trust, P.O. Box 65, Sturgeon Bay, WI 54235, (920) 746-1359, http://www.doorcountylandtrust.org/. The Nature Conservancy,

242 Michigan St., Ste. B103, Sturgeon Bay, WI 54235, (920) 743-8695, http://www.nature.org/. To reach the east trailhead, from the intersection of Horseshoe Bay Road/County G and East Shore Drive in downtown Egg Harbor, head west on Horseshoe Bay Road/County G for 2.9 miles. The road will become Bay Shore Drive/County B. Continue on Bay Shore Drive/County B for 5.8 miles to West Carlsville Road. Turn left and proceed 0.7 mile to Reynolds Road. Go about 0.7 mile on Reynolds Road to the parking area, trailhead, and DCLT kiosk on your right. To reach the west trailhead, from the intersection of Horseshoe Bay Road/County G and East Shore Drive in downtown Egg Harbor, head west on Horseshoe Bay Road/County G for 2.9 miles. The road will become Bay Shore Drive/County B. Continue on Bay Shore Drive/County B for 6.8 miles to the parking area and trailhead on the east side of the road. The trail runs between these two parking areas. No fee.

BEACHES AND OVERLOOKS
NN. Egg Harbor Beach

Egg Harbor Beach is a narrow sand and gravel beach with a view of Hat Island and can be a good launching point for experienced kayakers interested in a trip around the island. The beach and adjoining park were

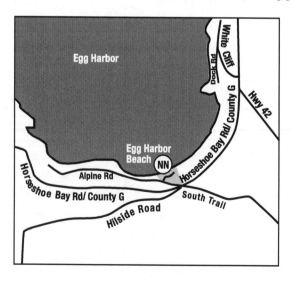

recently renovated. The park has restrooms and parking, along with beach access and nice lake views.

CONTACT INFORMATION AND DIRECTIONS

Village of Egg Harbor, P.O. Box 175, Egg Harbor, WI 54209, (920) 868-3334, http://www.villageofeggharbor.org/. From Egg Harbor, at the intersection of Highway 42 and County G/Horseshoe Bay Road follow County G/Horseshoe Bay Road south about 0.5 mile to the five-points intersection (South Trail/County G/Alpine Road/Hillside Road) and follow signs directing you to the Alpine Resort. From the intersection, bear right on Alpine Road (the road closest to the lake) and go about 300 feet to your first right on Beach Road. Turn right and follow Beach Road to the parking area. If you reach the Alpine Resort, you've gone too far. No fee.

OO. Frank E. Murphy County Park

Frank E. Murphy County Park, a well-developed 14-acre county-managed park, has a wide sandy beach, dock, boat launch, restrooms, playground, volleyball court, picnic area, and pavilion. While there isn't much of natural interest or scenic beauty, this is a fine spot for having a family picnic, launching a kayak, or just taking in the view of Green Bay.

CONTACT INFORMATION AND DIRECTIONS

Door County Parks System, 3528 Park Dr., Sturgeon Bay, WI 54235, (920) 746-9959, http://map.co.door.wi.us/parks/. From the intersection of Horseshoe Bay Road/County G and Highway 42 in Egg Harbor, head southwest on Horseshoe Bay Road/County G for 3.9 miles until it becomes Bay Shore Drive/County B. Follow Bay Shore Drive/County B another 0.3 mile to the park entrance at 7119 Bay Shore Drive. No fee.

PP. Olde Stone Quarry County Park

Olde Stone Quarry County Park has a dock, boat launch, extensive parking, restrooms, a picnic area, and a pavilion. The main attraction is the marina, but you can also take in the scenery and check out the graffiti-covered abandoned quarry across Bay Shore Drive. This is an excellent spot for views of Green Bay and Potawatomi State Park across the bay, particularly in the off-season, but there is no real beach or much natural beauty in the park itself.

CONTACT INFORMATION AND DIRECTIONS

Door County Parks System, 3528 Park Dr., Sturgeon Bay, WI 54235, (920) 746-9959, http://map.co.door.wi.us/parks/. From the intersection of Horseshoe Bay Road/County G and Highway 42 in Egg Harbor, head south on Highway 42 for 7.7 miles to West Carlsville Road. Turn right and go west on West Carlsville Road for 2.2 miles, where it ends at Bay Shore Drive/County B. Take a slight left and follow Bay Shore Drive/County B south for 3.4 miles to the park entrance, 4879 Bay Shore Drive/County B, Sturgeon Bay. No fee.

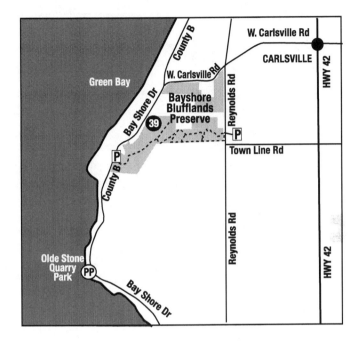

BIKE ROUTES
B19. Egg Harbor to Frank E. Murphy County Park
(7.0 miles round-trip—moderate)

This short route from Egg Harbor along Green Bay passes by the Alpine Resort golf course and a mix of farm fields and forests, with dramatic views of Green Bay to the west. This route is short, but the road gains some elevation, garnering it a moderate rating.

ROUTE

From the five-points intersection (Horseshoe Bay Road/County G/South Trail/Alpine Road/Hillside Road) in Egg Harbor, follow Horseshoe Bay Road/County G south for 3.5 miles. Near the entrance to Frank E. Murphy County Park, Horseshoe Bay Road/County G turns into Bay Shore Drive/County B. Continue to the entrance to the park, and retrace your route to return to Egg Harbor. The park has restrooms.

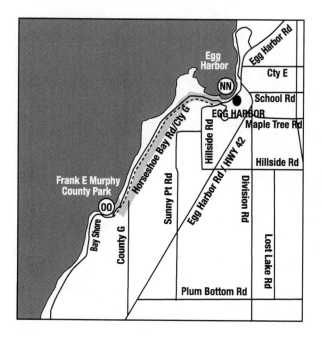

CONTACT INFORMATION

Door County Parks System, 3528 Park Dr., Sturgeon Bay, WI 54235, (920) 746-9959, http://map.co.door.wi.us/parks/. No fee.

B20. Egg Harbor–Peninsula Center–Juddville Loop

(17.3 miles round-trip—moderate)

This route passes through a mix of residential and urban areas, northern mesic and northern wet-mesic forests, and agricultural areas, as well as through the crossroads settlements of Juddville and Peninsula Center. Though rated moderate for its length, the route is generally flat and the roads have wide shoulders and relatively light traffic.

ROUTE

From the intersection of Horseshoe Bay Road/County G and Highway 42 in Egg Harbor, head north on Highway 42 for 3.4 miles to Peninsula

Players Road. Turn right and follow Peninsula Players Road 0.9 mile to Spring Road. Turn left and follow Spring Road for 2.4 miles to County F. Turn right and follow County F for 1.9 miles to County A. Turn right and follow County A for 4.0 miles to County E. Turn right and follow County E for 4.2 miles to Highway 42. Turn left and head south on Highway 42 for 0.3 mile to the intersection with Horseshoe Bay Road/County G.

B21. Egg Harbor–Kangaroo Lake Causeway Loop

(26 miles round-trip—moderate)

This longer route is best suited for road cyclists. It goes from Egg Harbor through Door County's interior agricultural region and ends at the Kangaroo Lake causeway, with excellent views of Kangaroo Lake. It is rated moderate for its length, but the cycling is generally flat and the roads have wide shoulders. This route covers some of the best road cycling in the county, on quiet roads with relatively light traffic, past scenic hay pastures on Logerquist Road, a patchwork of cherry orchards, and views of northern wet-mesic forests on County A and County E.

ROUTE

From the five-points intersection (Horseshoe Bay Road/County G/South Trail/Alpine Road/Hillside Road) in Egg Harbor, head east on Horseshoe Bay Road/County G for 1.1 miles to Highway 42. Turn left and follow Highway 42 north for 0.3 mile to County E. Turn right and follow County E for 4.2 miles to County A. Turn right and follow County A south for 3.0 miles to Berger Road. Turn left and head east on Berger Road for 1.0 miles to Logerquist Road. Turn left and head north on Logerquist Road for 2.6 miles to County E. Turn right and follow County E for 0.7 mile across the Kangaroo Lake causeway. Retrace your route to return to Egg Harbor. No fee.

PADDLING ROUTES

P16. Frank E. Murphy County Park and Horseshoe Bay
(7.6 miles round-trip—moderate to difficult)

Intermediate and advanced kayakers will find challenge in a trip along the shores of Horseshoe Bay. While the area lacks any truly noteworthy

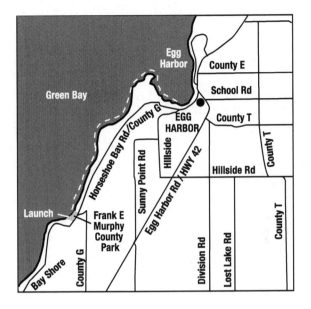

features, the scenery is lovely and there are some underwater wrecks that make it popular with divers. Frank E. Murphy County Park has both a beach and a boat launch for putting in boats. It also has restroom facilities.

ROUTE

From Frank E. Murphy County Park, you can paddle north 3.8 miles along the shore to downtown Egg Harbor, along the relatively protected waters of Horseshoe Bay. Retrace your route to return. Watch for power-boats around Murphy Park, which is popular with anglers.

CONTACT INFORMATION AND DIRECTIONS TO LAUNCH SITE

Door County Parks System, 3528 Park Dr., Sturgeon Bay, WI 54235, (920) 746-9959, http://map.co.door.wi.us/parks/. To reach the launch site, from the intersection of Horseshoe Bay Road/County G and High-way 42 in Egg Harbor, take Horseshoe Bay Road/County G heading southwest. Follow Horseshoe Bay Road/County G for 3.9 miles until it becomes Bay Shore Drive/County B. Follow Bay Shore Drive/County B another 0.3 mile to the park entrance at 7119 Bay Shore Drive, Egg Harbor. No fee.

P17. Olde Stone Quarry County Park and Sherwood Point
(6.0 miles round-trip—moderate)

Olde Stone Quarry County Park has a large dock and you can launch kayaks here for a trip around Sturgeon Bay. This launching point is suitable for intermediate and experienced kayakers only. In addition to Great Lakes shipping traffic in this area, Olde Stone Quarry Park is also popular for fishing and wreck diving, so watch out for other boat traffic in the area, particularly during the busy summer months. This area can have rough water when the winds are coming off Green Bay. Take appropriate safety precautions, as you would when paddling anywhere on Lake Michigan. The park has restrooms and parking.

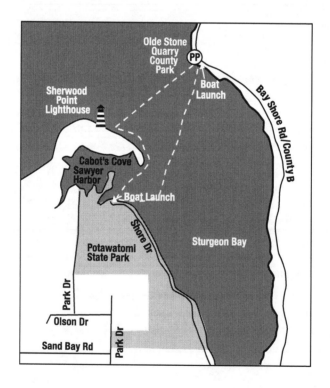

ROUTE

From the dock at Olde Stone Quarry County Park, you can paddle across to Sawyer Harbor or, for experienced kayakers, out around the tip of Sherwood Point to the Sherwood Point Lighthouse, about 1.0 mile across the mouth of Sturgeon Bay. If you need a break, you can come ashore at Sherwood Point near Cabot's Cove, a wreck-diving site. You can also paddle directly across Sturgeon Bay to Potawatomi State Park (see Major Point of Interest 46, chapter 8), about 2.0 miles, and access the boat launch there.

CONTACT INFORMATION AND DIRECTIONS TO LAUNCH SITE

Door County Parks System, 3528 Park Dr., Sturgeon Bay, WI 54235, (920) 746-9959, http://map.co.door.wi.us/parks/. To reach Olde Stone Quarry County Park, from the intersection of Highway 42 and County T (just west of Egg Harbor), head south on Highway 42 for 7.1 miles to West Carlsville Road. Take a right heading west on West Carlsville Road for 2.2 miles. West Carlsville Road will end at Bay Shore Drive/County B. Take a slight left and follow Bay Shore Drive/County B south for 3.4 miles to the park entrance, 4879 Bay Shore Drive/County B. No fee.

7

Shivering Sands

Sturgeon Bay to Whitefish Dunes

The Shivering Sands region, running along Lake Michigan from the Sturgeon Bay Ship Canal in the south to Whitefish Dunes in the north, is one of the most ecologically important areas in all of Door County. It is home to a large number of threatened and endangered species, and some of the most impressive landscapes in all of the upper Midwest.

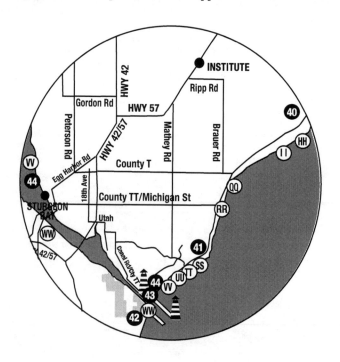

This area was the site of a number of different Native American settlements over a period of about a thousand years. By the late nineteenth century, it was a bustling port. In the 1880s the Sturgeon Bay Ship Canal was built, and, though there is little trace today, Lily Bay was a commercial center for logging, trading, and shipping. By the 1920s, a local would-be developer named Oram Glidden had purchased most of the land between what is now Whitefish Dunes State Park and the present-day Sturgeon Bay Ship Canal.

Perhaps it was lucky that Glidden lost most of his fortune and died without realizing his dream of large-scale development. During the period from the 1930s through the 1990s, Glidden Lodge and a handful of homes along Glidden Drive were built, but the area has retained much of its conservation value and character, due in large part to preservation efforts in the last few decades by The Nature Conservancy, the Door County Land Trust, and other landowners. Today, Glidden Drive, recognized by the state as a Wisconsin Rustic Road, winds through the area, offering up glimpses of the forests and wetlands inland, and the Lake Michigan dunes and beaches along the shore. For those interested in solitary walks on empty beaches, or exploring the truly wild areas of Door County, look no further than the Shivering Sands.

MAJOR POINTS OF INTEREST

40. Shivering Sands State Natural Area

Shivering Sands State Natural Area, a unit of Cave Point–Clay Banks State Natural Area, is one of the most ecologically significant sites in Door County, comprising dozens of community types over more than six thousand acres. Shivering Sands is a large wetland complex, which includes Geisel Creek to the north, Dunes Lake, Lower Dunes Lake, and Shivering Sands Creek to the south, along with several other adjacent smaller ponds, bogs, fens, and lakes with peat, marl, loam, and dolomite bottoms. The area has a very complex hydrology, with the wetlands and lakes fed by multiple springs and creeks. These springs also drain the complex through fissures in the underlying dolomite bedrock. A large section of this area is protected by The Nature Conservancy, along with

the Door County Land Trust and other partners. Wetlands breeding birds, including Sandhill Crane, Virginia Rail, Sora, Bald Eagle, and Osprey can be found, along with Hine's emerald dragonfly, muskrat, striped skunk, pygmy shrew, beaver, and occasionally river otter. The diverse wetlands include northern sedge meadows, emergent and submergent marsh, shrub carr, and fen communities. Closer to Lake Michigan, the adjacent northern wet-mesic and northern mesic forests cover a substantial Great Lakes ridge and swale complex. In the spring and summer, look for wildflowers, including showy ladyslipper orchid and dwarf lake iris. The area also includes some significant sand dunes, as its name suggests.

Trails, Access, and Facilities

This area along Lake Michigan, primarily west of Glidden Drive, is maintained as a natural area and lacks well-developed trail systems. There are no facilities. The lakes, creek, and wetlands areas can be explored by kayak or canoe (see, for example, Paddling Route P19). Foot access is restricted and interested visitors should contact the Door County Land Trust or The Nature Conservancy for information on access.

CONTACT INFORMATION
Door County Land Trust, P.O. Box 65, Sturgeon Bay, WI 54235, (920) 746-1359, http://www.doorcountylandtrust.org/. The Nature Conservancy, 242 Michigan St., Ste. B103, Sturgeon Bay, WI 54235, (920) 743-8695, http://www.nature.org/. No fee.

41. Kellner Fen

Kellner Fen is an ecologically significant shore fen wetland complex that includes a floating peat mat with a number of interconnected areas of open water, surrounded by northern sedge meadow, northern wet-mesic forest, and northern mesic forest communities, situated atop dolomite bedrock. It is a unit of Cave Point–Clay Banks State Natural Area, and parcels within this complex are owned and managed by Door County Land Trust (DCLT), along with the Wisconsin Department of Natural

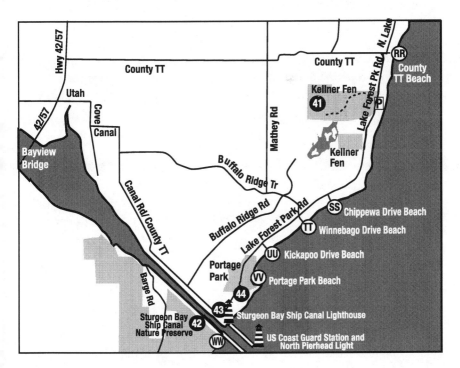

Resources and The Nature Conservancy. DCLT maintains a short trail that crosses over several ridges and swales. The fen itself has been designated as a Critical Habitat area and is federally protected.

The fen is just inland of the major Great Lakes ridge and swale complex, which is situated between the fen and Lake Michigan. Though the fen has no natural outlet to Lake Michigan, several manmade canals were excavated during agricultural use of the property in the mid-1900s. Along Lake Michigan, across Lake Forest Park Road, the fen is bordered by 30-foot-high natural sand dunes and a rocky cobble and bedrock beach (not accessible from the trails).

Kellner Fen contains a number of uncommon and rare plants, including spring orchids, coast sedge, northern bog sedge, and slender bog arrow-grass. Its diversity of wildlife includes Ruffed Grouse, Canada Warbler, Hine's emerald dragonfly, Blanchard's cricket frog, black bear, striped skunk, fisher, snowshoe hare, and porcupine. As a key wetland situated along the lake, it provides an important stopover site for migrating birds, such as raptors in the spring and fall, when conditions are right.

TRAILS, ACCESS AND FACILITIES

The fen has no facilities. There is about 1.0 mile, round-trip, of maintained trails on the upland portions of the DCLT parcels. Bikes, horses, and motorized vehicles are prohibited. Hunting is authorized and subject to DCLT guidelines and permission.

CONTACT INFORMATION AND DIRECTIONS

Door County Land Trust, P.O. Box 65, Sturgeon Bay, WI 54235, (920) 746-1359, http://www.doorcountylandtrust.org/. The Nature Conservancy, 242 Michigan St., Ste. B103, Sturgeon Bay, WI 54235, (920) 743-8695, http://www.nature.org/. From the Michigan Street Bridge in downtown Sturgeon Bay, go northeast on Michigan Street past Third Avenue. Michigan Street will become County B. Continue on County B for about 1.9 miles. When County B turns into County TT, continue east for 2.9 miles (almost to the end of County TT) until it meets Lake Forest Park Road. Turn right and head south on Lake Forest Road for about 0.6 mile. Look for the DCLT signs and trailhead across the road from 3220 Lake Forest Park Road. Park off Lake Forest Park Road. No fee.

42. Sturgeon Bay Ship Canal Nature Preserve

The Sturgeon Bay Ship Canal Nature Preserve is a local favorite, with a network of trails, beaches, and views of Lake Michigan, the ship canal, and two lighthouses. The recreation area generally includes the areas south of the ship canal that are open to the public. Considered part of the Cave Point–Clay Banks State Natural Area, parcels on either side of the Sturgeon Bay Ship Canal contain a significant Great Lakes ridge and swale formation, just inland of a large Great Lakes beach and dune community. The Great Lakes ridge and swale formation was bisected by the construction of the Sturgeon Bay Ship Canal in the late 1800s, in an effort to create a faster and less dangerous route between the port of Green Bay and Lake Michigan. In later years, this area was extensively farmed. Today, these parcels are protected by the Door County Land Trust (DCLT), in cooperation with The Nature Conservancy, the City of Sturgeon Bay, Sturgeon Bay Utilities, and other partners.

The Great Lakes ridge and swale area on both sides of the present-day canal is forested with bands of northern mesic and northern dry-mesic forests, interspersed with wet swales and dry ridges that contain a number of rare plants, including dwarf lake iris, dune thistle, and dune goldenrod. Further inland, the canal passes through an ancient lakebed that was once part of Lake Michigan. This is an excellent area for sighting migrant birds during late spring. A network of trails and a great sandy beach are best accessed from two parking areas along Lake Lane on the south side of the Ship Canal. From the beach there are also excellent views of the Sturgeon Bay Ship Canal Lighthouse and the North Pierhead Light, the U.S. Coast Guard facility, and the canal itself.

TRAILS, ACCESS, AND FACILITIES

There are about 2.0 miles of easy hiking trails throughout the site, including those along the edges of the canal. DCLT has recently acquired additional property in this area and new trails are being developed. Contact DCLT for more specific trail information. There are no facilities.

CONTACT INFORMATION AND DIRECTIONS

Door County Land Trust, P.O. Box 65, Sturgeon Bay, WI 54235, (920) 746-1359, http://www.doorcountylandtrust.org/. The Nature Conservancy, 242 Michigan St., Ste. B103, Sturgeon Bay, WI 54235, (920) 743-8695, http://www.nature.org/. From the Bayview Bridge in Sturgeon Bay, go south on Highway 42/57 about 0.4 mile to County U/Clay Banks Road. Turn left on County U/Clay Banks Road and follow it southeast for 1.8 miles to Lake Lane. Turn left and follow Lake Lane about 1.7 miles to the end, at South Lake Michigan Drive. The nature preserve lies north of Lake Lane. There are two parking areas along Lake Lane. No fee.

43. U.S. Coast Guard Station and North Pierhead Light

For a truly unusual hike, not for the faint of heart, visitors can walk out to the end of 1,200-foot North Pierhead Light into Lake Michigan at the mouth of the Sturgeon Bay Ship Canal. The North Pierhead is about 10 feet wide, with an arching metal infrastructure overhead, and should be

attempted only in calm weather. At the very end is the striking red North Pierhead Light (closed to the public).

This site has long been used as a navigation point and landmark in Door County. After the Sturgeon Bay Ship Canal was completed in 1881 as an alternative to the dangerous Porte des Morts, construction began on the original lighthouse, pierheads, and U.S. Coast Guard buildings. The canal is still used for shipping, under authority of the U.S. Army Corps of Engineers, and today there are two lighthouses, the North Pierhead Light and the Sturgeon Bay Ship Canal Lighthouse. A small U.S. Coast Guard station sits at the mouth of the ship canal. The station is staffed year-round, and operations focus on search and rescue, law enforcement, and cold-water rescue missions. The public is allowed access to the North Pierhead but not to Coast Guard buildings and lighthouses, except for special occasions such as the annual Door County Maritime Museum lighthouse tour.

The end of the North Pierhead offers panoramic views of Lake Michigan, from Lily Bay and Whitefish Point to the north to Kewaunee County to the south, and excellent views of both lighthouses, the ship canal, and the Coast Guard station. Though rarely crowded, this is a popular spot for lighthouse aficionados and maritime history buffs.

TRAILS, ACCESS, AND FACILITIES

The round-trip walk along the North Pierhead is about 0.4 mile. Access and closures are subject to U.S. Coast Guard rules and regulations. Park only in designated areas. There are no facilities.

CONTACT INFORMATION AND DIRECTIONS

United States Coast Guard Station–Sturgeon Bay, 2501 Canal Rd., Sturgeon Bay, WI 54235-9103, (920) 743-3366, http://www.uscg.mil. From the Bayview Bridge in Sturgeon Bay, go north on Highway 42/57 for about 0.4 mile to Utah Street. Turn right and follow Utah Street 0.4 mile to Cove Road. Turn right and follow Cove Road 0.2 mile to County TT/Canal Road. Turn left, heading east, for 0.2 miles on County TT/Canal Road and follow County TT/Canal Road as it turns south for 2.4 miles along the ship canal to the U.S. Coast Guard Station visitors' parking lot on the south side of Canal Road. No fee.

44. Portage Park

Portage Town Park, operated by the Township of Sturgeon Bay, is just north of the Sturgeon Bay Ship Canal and the U.S. Coast Guard Station. Even during the busiest months, it is generally empty, unknown to all but a few locals, and you may have the sandy, expansive beaches to yourself. The park forms a natural point into Lake Michigan, and during migration is a good place to watch for migrant raptors and songbirds as they follow the shoreline. In winter this can be an excellent spot for Redhead, Greater Scaup, Long-tailed Duck, Common Goldeneye, and Common and Red-breasted Mergansers. Swimmers and boaters should use caution in the water, as this stretch of Lake Michigan can have strong rip tides and unpredictable currents.

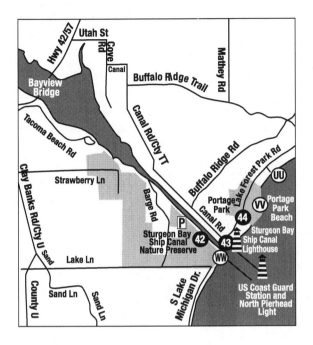

Trails, Access, and Facilities

Portage Park offers access to other beaches to the north (Kickapoo Drive Beach, Winnebago Drive Beach, Chippewa Drive Beach) below the high water mark. Watch carefully for the sign to the park, as it is easy to miss.

Directions

From the Bayview Bridge in Sturgeon Bay, go north on Highway 42/57 for 0.4 mile to Utah Street. Turn right and follow Utah Street for about 0.2 mile to Cove Road. Turn right, heading south on Cove Road for about 0.2 mile to County TT/Canal Road. Turn left and follow County TT/Canal Road east for 0.2 mile. Take a right to stay on County TT/Canal Road and proceed southeast for 2.4 miles along the Ship Canal toward the Coast Guard station at Lake Forest Park Road/County TT. Turn left at the Coast Guard station onto County TT/Lake Forest Park Road and go about 0.3 mile to the entrance road for the park, which is marked with a large boulder with a plaque that says Portage Park, 2650 Lake Forest Park Road. (Note that this marker is very easy to miss.) No fee.

BEACHES AND OVERLOOKS
QQ. Lily Bay County Park

Lily Bay County Park, on Glidden Drive/County T, occupies about one acre and is distinguished only by the fact that it was the site of a major commercial port in the 1880s. In this part of the county beaches are generally empty, even during the high season. Private vacation homes predominate, but areas below the high water mark are open to the public. This park offers access to miles of quiet, sandy Lake Michigan beaches to the north, including Arrowhead Lane Beach, Deer Path Beach, Hemlock Lane Beach, Goldenrod Lane Beach, and White Pine Lane Beach, all accessible from Glidden Drive through public easements between private residences in these areas. Remember to respect private property rights at all times. Lily Bay Park has a small parking lot, but no facilities.

CONTACT INFORMATION AND DIRECTIONS

Door County Parks System, 3528 Park Dr., Sturgeon Bay, WI 54235, (920) 746-9959, http://map.co.door.wi.us/parks/. From the Bayview Bridge in

Sturgeon Bay, head north on Highway 42/57 for 2.1 miles to County T. Turn right and follow County T east for 4.0 miles until it meets Glidden Drive (still County T) at Lake Michigan. The parking area and boat ramp is located at the point where County T meets/continues past Glidden Drive at the lake, on the Sturgeon Bay–Sevastopol Township line. No fee.

RR. County TT Beach

This narrow, sandy beach is located at the end of County TT, in a residential area. There are no facilities.

DIRECTIONS

From the Bayview Bridge in Sturgeon Bay, head north on Highway 42/57 for 0.9 mile to Michigan Street. Turn right and follow Michigan Street/ County TT east about 3.5 miles to a sandy parking area at North Lake Michigan Drive, 4602 County TT. Park off the shoulder and respect private property rights of neighboring landowners. No fee.

SS. Chippewa Drive Beach

This 50-foot-wide strip of public beach offers access to sandy Great Lakes beach and dune areas. There is space for three or four cars. It is accessible from Glidden Drive through public easements between private residences. Remember to respect private property rights at all times. There are no facilities.

DIRECTIONS

From the Bayview Bridge in Sturgeon Bay, head north on Highway 42/57 for 0.9 mile to Michigan Street/County TT. Turn right and follow Michigan Street/County TT east for 1.6 miles to Mathey Road. Turn right and follow Mathey Road south for 1.2 miles to Buffalo Ridge Trail. Turn left and follow Buffalo Ridge Trail east for 1.2 miles to Lake Forest Park Road. Turn left and head north on Lake Forest Park Road for 0.4 miles to Chippewa Drive. Turn right and follow Chippewa Drive 400 feet to the

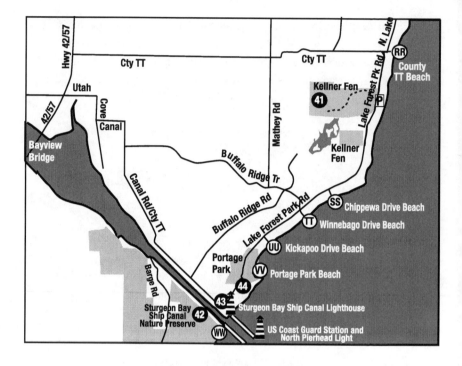

end of the road. The access point is on Chippewa Drive between two private residences, 2914 and 2912 Lake Forest Park Road. No fee.

TT. Winnebago Drive Beach

This sliver of public beach offers access to sandy, remote Great Lakes beach and dune areas and scenic views of the North Pierhead Light. There are no facilities. It is accessible from Glidden Drive through public easements between private residences in these areas. Remember to respect private property rights at all times.

DIRECTIONS

From the Bayview Bridge in Sturgeon Bay, head north on Highway 42/57 for 0.9 mile to Michigan Street/County TT. Turn right and follow Michigan Street/County TT east for 1.6 miles to Mathey Road. Turn right and follow Mathey Road south for 1.2 miles to Buffalo Ridge Trail. Turn left and follow Buffalo Ridge Trail east for 1.2 miles to Lake Forest Park Road. Park on the shoulder of Lake Forest Park Road and walk down Winnebago Drive. No fee.

UU. Kickapoo Drive Beach

This 50-foot-wide strip of beach allows the public access to high quality, extensive, sandy Great Lakes beach and dune areas and scenic views of the North Pierhead Light. The beach is accessible from Glidden Drive through public easements between private residences in these areas. Remember to respect private property rights at all times.

DIRECTIONS

From the Bayview Bridge in Sturgeon Bay, head north on Highway 42/57 0.9 mile to Michigan Street/County TT. Turn right and follow Michigan Street/County TT east for 1.6 miles to Mathey Road. Turn right and follow Mathey Road south for 1.2 miles to Buffalo Ridge Trail. Turn left and follow Buffalo Ridge Trail southeast for 1.2 miles to Lake Forest Park Road/County TT. Turn right and follow Lake Forest Park Road/County TT southwest along the lake for 0.5 mile to Kickapoo Drive. Turn left and follow Kickapoo Drive 300 feet to the end of the road. The access is on Kickapoo Drive between two private residences, across the street from 2713 Lake Forest Park Road. There is space for one or two cars. No facilities. No fee.

VV. Portage Park Beach

This sand and rock Lake Michigan beach adjacent to Portage Park is remote and rarely traveled. With great views of the lake and nearby lighthouses, it is a popular spot for locals and artists, and is generally considered one of the most scenic beaches in the county. It has no facilities except a picnic table. This area often has strong rip tides and swimmers should use caution.

DIRECTIONS

From the Bayview Bridge in Sturgeon Bay, go north on Highway 42/57 for 0.4 mile to Utah Street. Turn right and follow Utah Street for about 0.2 mile to Cove Road. Turn right, heading south on Cove Road for about 0.2 mile to County TT/Canal Road. Turn left and follow County TT/Canal Road east for 0.2 mile. Take a right to stay on County TT/Canal Road and proceed southeast for 2.4 miles along the ship canal toward the Coast Guard station at Lake Forest Park Road/County TT. Turn left at the Coast Guard station onto County TT/ Lake Forest Park Road and go about 0.3 mile to the entrance road for the park, which is marked with a large boulder with a plaque that says Portage Park, 2650 Lake Forest Park Road. (Note that this maker is very easy to miss.) No fee.

WW. Sturgeon Bay Ship Canal Nature Preserve Beach

This fantastic, protected beach, with sand dunes, is a local favorite. Located south of the Sturgeon Bay Ship Canal, at the breakwater at the entrance to the canal, it has great views of the North Pierhead Light, the North and South Pierheads, the U.S. Coast Guard Station, and the ship canal entrance. Ownership of the property has changed hands over the last few years, and the Door County Land Trust recently acquired 330 acres of property south of the ship canal, so public access to the beach from Lake Lane will continue. This is also a great place to launch kayaks on calm days, to paddle around the pierheads of the ship canal. Note that this area can have strong rip tides and boat traffic, so swimmers and boaters should exercise caution. There are no facilities.

DIRECTIONS

From the Bayview Bridge in Sturgeon Bay, go south on Highway 42/57 0.4 mile to County U/Clay Banks Road. Turn left and follow County U/Clay Banks Road south for 1.8 miles to Lake Lane. Turn left and follow Lake Lane east about 1.7 miles to the end. Park off the road in designated parking areas and walk to the beach. No fee.

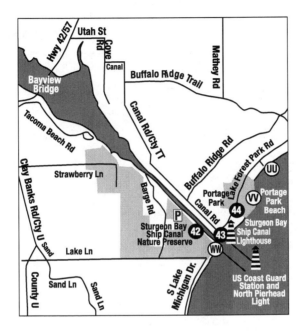

LIGHTHOUSES

L9. Sturgeon Bay Ship Canal Lighthouse

The Sturgeon Bay Ship Canal Lighthouse is located on Canal Road at the U.S. Coast Guard Station. Construction was completed in 1899, and this lighthouse remains an important aid for ships navigating the Sturgeon Bay Ship Canal. Noted for its unique exterior steel skeleton, this classic white lighthouse is complemented by the nearby red and white buildings of the U.S. Coast Guard Station. The grounds are off limits to the public, except for an annual summer tour hosted by the Door County Maritime Museum. The North Pierhead is open to the public, however, and it provides excellent views of the lighthouse at any time of the year.

CONTACT INFORMATION AND DIRECTIONS

United States Coast Guard Station–Sturgeon Bay, 2501 Canal Rd., Sturgeon Bay, WI 54235-9103, (920) 743-3366, http://www.uscg.mil/d9/sect

LakeMichigan/STASturgeonBay.asp. From the Bayview Bridge in Sturgeon Bay, go north on Highway 42/57 to Utah Street. Turn right and follow Utah Street 0.4 mile to Cove Road. Turn right and follow Cove Road 0.3 mile to Canal Road. Turn left follow Canal Road for 2.5 miles to the U.S. Coast Guard Station visitors' parking lot on the south side of Canal Road. No fee.

L10. Sturgeon Bay Ship Canal North Pierhead Light

This light is located about 1,200 feet out into Lake Michigan at the end of the North Pierhead of the ship canal. Built in 1881, this distinctive red lighthouse remains an important aid for ships navigating the Sturgeon Bay Ship Canal. While the public is not allowed inside the North Pierhead Light, there is public access to the North Pierhead itself. By walking to the end of the North Pierhead, you can get excellent and surprising up-close views of the lighthouse at any time of the year (see Major Point of Interest 43 for more information).

CONTACT INFORMATION AND DIRECTIONS

United States Coast Guard Station–Sturgeon Bay, 2501 Canal Rd., Sturgeon Bay, WI 54235-9103, (920) 743-3366, http://www.uscg.mil/d9/sect LakeMichigan/STASturgeonBay.asp. From the Bayview Bridge in Sturgeon Bay, go north on Highway 42/57 to Utah Street. Turn right and follow Utah Street 0.4 mile as it goes right onto Cove Road. Follow Cove Road for 0.3 mile to Canal Road. Turn left and follow Canal Road for 2.5 miles to the U.S. Coast Guard Station visitors' parking lot on the south side of Canal Road. No fee.

BIKE ROUTES

B22. Portage Park to Lily Bay County Park
(9.2 miles round-trip—easy)

This easy route mainly traverses a flat, lightly traveled stretch along the Lake Michigan shoreline, primarily through northern wet-mesic-forested residential areas, and is suitable for cyclists of all ages and ability levels. The road has some blind curves, so cycle defensively.

ROUTE

From the parking lot at Portage Park, head northeast on Lake Forest Park Road/County TT for 3.0 miles. The road will jog slightly, intersecting with County TT. Turn right and follow County TT for about 200 feet, and then take a left and continue heading north on North Lake Forest Drive/North Lake Michigan Drive. After 1.1 miles, North Lake Forest Drive/North Lake Michigan Drive will intersect County T. Turn right and proceed east on County T for 0.5 mile to the Lily Bay County Park. Retrace your route to return to Portage Park.

CONTACT INFORMATION

Door County Parks System, 3528 Park Dr., Sturgeon Bay, WI 54235, (920) 746-9959, http://map.co.door.wi.us/parks/. No fee.

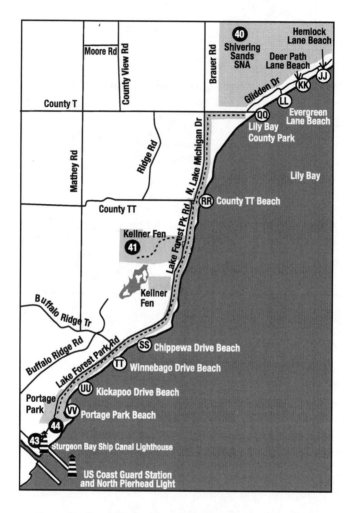

B23. Lily Bay County Park to South Cave Point Drive

(15.6 miles round-trip—moderate)

This winding route hugs the Lake Michigan shoreline along Glidden Drive and ends at a small beach. While Glidden Drive has minimal traffic, traffic tends to move fast and the road has many turns, curves, and hidden driveways, so cyclists should use appropriate caution on this road.

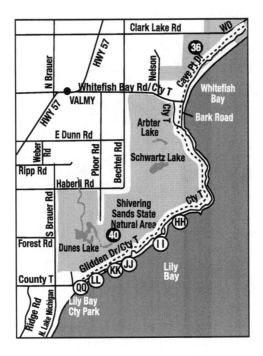

ROUTE

From Lily Bay County Park at the intersection of County T and Glidden Drive, head northeast on Glidden Drive/County T for 5.5 miles to Bark Road. Turn right and follow Bark Road for 0.6 mile to the intersection with Whitefish Bay Road. Cross Whitefish Bay Road and continue to follow the same road, now called South Cave Point Drive. Follow South Cave Point Drive for 1.2 miles to the end. There is a small public beach here. Retrace your route to return to Lily Bay County Park. No fee.

B24. U.S. Coast Guard Station to County TT Beach

(8.5 miles round-trip—easy)

This wooded route, suitable for cyclists of all ages, skirts the southern edges of one of Door County's largest Great Lakes ridge and swale communities, the Shivering Sands complex. While residential areas are along the route, The Nature Conservancy, the Door County Land Trust, and other private landowners have conserved significant wetlands in this area. This route begins with views of Lake Michigan, two lighthouses, and the U.S. Coast Guard Station; heads along the Sturgeon Bay Ship Canal and then inland, with some slight hills as the road traverses the ancient ridges and swales; heads north and then east through agricultural areas; and then works its way south along Lake Michigan past forested wetlands areas. While the roads are generally flat, there are a number of small hills and hidden curves, and traffic tends to go above the posted speed limit in this area. Cyclists should use caution accordingly.

ROUTE

From the visitor parking lot at the U.S. Coast Guard Station, head northwest on Canal Road/County TT (along the ship canal and away from Lake Michigan) for 2.1 miles to Buffalo Ridge Trail. Turn right and follow

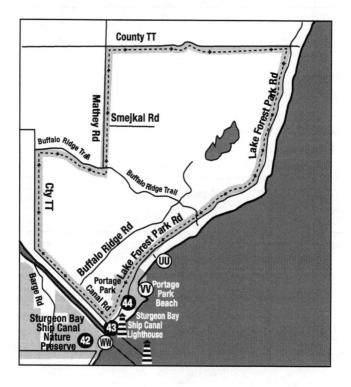

Buffalo Ridge Trail for 1.1 miles to Mathey Road. Turn left and head north on Mathey Road for 1.2 miles to County TT. Turn right and follow County TT for 1.8 miles to Lake Forest Park Road. Turn right and head south on Lake Forest Park Road/County TT for 3.5 miles back to the U.S. Coast Guard Station.

CONTACT INFORMATION

United States Coast Guard Station–Sturgeon Bay, 2501 Canal Rd., Sturgeon Bay, WI 54235-9103, (920) 743-3366, http://www.uscg.mil. No fee.

PADDLING ROUTES

P18. Portage Park to Shivering Sands
(2.0–12.0 miles round-trip—moderate)

Intermediate paddlers can launch kayaks from Portage Park and paddle north along the sandy beaches of the Shivering Sands complex. While

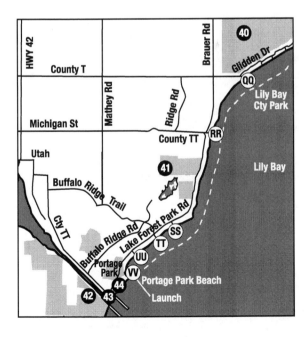

this area doesn't have any particularly noteworthy features, the views of the beaches and large homes can be mildly interesting. This area can have tricky currents, but stopping for a break along the beach is always an option. Stay below the high water mark in this area to avoid upsetting local property owners. Portage Park has parking and is an easy launching point. Take appropriate safety precautions along this route—you may want to consider wearing a dry suit even during the summer months.

ROUTE

From Portage Park, proceed north along the shore up to Lily Bay (about 3.0 miles). From here you can continue north up to the Glidden Drive beaches. There are no facilities, but paddlers can stop at any of the sand beaches along the route. Retrace your route to return to Portage Park.

DIRECTIONS TO LAUNCH SITE

From the Bayview Bridge in Sturgeon Bay, go north on Highway 42/57 for 0.4 mile to Utah Street. Turn right and follow Utah Street for about 0.4 mile to Cove Road. Turn right heading south on Cove Road for about 0.2 mile to County TT/Canal Road. Turn left and follow County TT/Canal Road east for 0.2 mile. Take a right to stay on County TT/Canal Road and proceed southeast for 2.4 miles along the ship canal toward the Coast Guard station at Lake Forest Park Road/County TT. Turn left at the Coast Guard station onto County TT/ Lake Forest Park Road and go about 0.3 mile to the entrance road for the park, which is marked with a large boulder with a plaque that says Portage Park, 2650 Lake Forest Park Road. (Note that it is easy to miss this marker.) No fee.

P19. Dolan's Creek and Dunes Lake

(2.2 miles round-trip—easy)

When water levels are sufficient, paddling Dolan's Creek and Dunes Lake should be at the very top of any Door County kayak or canoe trip list. Wildlife viewing in this area can be spectacular, and it is truly one of the last "wild" places in Door County. The roadless 6,000-acre wetlands area west of Glidden Drive known as the Shivering Sands State Natural Area

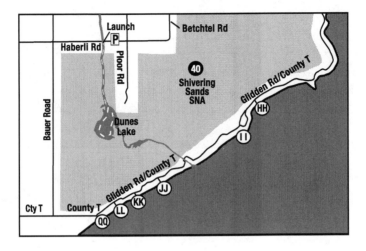

contains three small lakes: Dunes Lake, Schwartz Lake, and Arbter Lake. While Schwartz and Arbter are inaccessible from public roads, Dunes Lake, fed by Dolan's Creek to the north, is reachable. This area is all private land, much of it protected for its high ecological values by The Nature Conservancy, Door County Land Trust, and other private landowners. Foot access is restricted to protect the sensitive species that make their homes here, and leaving your boat is prohibited. The scenery is spectacular, with emergent marsh wetlands, northern sedge meadows and shrub carr communities along the winding route from the Haberli Road bridge to Dunes Lake. Along the creek and Dunes Lake, look for Sandhill Crane, Virginia Rail, Sora, Bald Eagle, and Osprey, along with Hine's emerald dragonfly, muskrat, striped skunk, pygmy shrew, beaver, and occasionally river otter.

ROUTE

When water levels are high enough, you can put in at Dolan's Creek from the bridge off Haberli Road and paddle down the creek to the north end of Dunes Lake, about 1.1 miles. Dunes Lake then drains toward Lake Michigan via Shivering Sands Creek to the south. When conditions are right, you can go further past Dunes Lake and head a bit down along Shivering Sands Creek. Note that Shivering Sands Creek is typically too shallow to paddle much past Dunes Lake.

CONTACT INFORMATION AND DIRECTIONS TO LAUNCH SITE

Door County Land Trust, P.O. Box 65, Sturgeon Bay, WI 54235, (920) 746-1359, http://www.doorcountylandtrust.org/. The Nature Conservancy, 242 Michigan St., Ste. B103, Sturgeon Bay, WI 54235, (920) 743-8695, http://www.nature.org. To the Haberli Road bridge put-in from downtown Sturgeon Bay: Head north on Highway 42/57 to County T. Turn right and head east on County T for 3.6 miles to Brauer Road. Turn left and follow Brauer Road for 2.0 miles to Haberli Road. Turn right and follow Haberli Road for about 0.5 mile to the bridge over Dolan's Creek. Park well off the shoulder of Haberli Road on either side of the bridge, and put in boats on the right side of the road. Proceed south along Dolan's Creek from the bridge. No fee.

8

Sturgeon Bay Area

Sturgeon Bay is known to many visitors as the gateway to Door County, a place to shop and sightsee before heading to points farther north. However, this vibrant little city is a great base for outdoor recreation. City parks offer surprisingly good wildlife-watching opportunities, the harbor teems with birdlife, and it's an easy hop to biking on the Ahnapee State Trail or hiking at Potawatomi State Park.

Originally home to the Menominee and Chippewa Indians, Sturgeon Bay was a waypoint and safe harbor for French fur trappers and traders during the 1670s. Increase and Mary Claflin, generally credited as the first white settlers in Door County, set up a residence near Little Sturgeon Bay around 1835, but after ten years of skirmishes with local Menominee and Chippewa, they decamped to Fish Creek. Other settlers, including Peter Rowley, who settled at the mouth of Sturgeon Bay, and Peter Sherwood, who settled nearby on what is now Sherwood Point, came shortly after. As the population gradually grew, with more migrants from the East Coast, along with Norwegian Moravians and German, French, and English settlers, the Menominee and Chippewa were driven out. Today, the only reminder of their presence around the Sturgeon Bay region is found in a few place-names, such as Nasewaupee, named for a Menominee chief in the 1860s.

The abundant natural resources of the area and safe harbor soon made Sturgeon Bay a hub for shipbuilding, quarrying, timbering, trapping, and trading. By the 1880s, the Sturgeon Bay Ship Canal had been completed, providing an alternative to Death's Door and firmly establishing Sturgeon

Bay as the commercial center for the region. Today, Sturgeon Bay is the largest city in Door County, with a year-round population of just under ten thousand people. Despite its small size, the city has a number of excellent local parks, a waterfront geared toward boaters, and easy access to a number of beaches and biking and hiking trails. Opportunities for wildlife-watching also abound—watch for American White Pelicans soaring in formation past your car as you travel across the Bayview Bridge, gulls and terns fishing along the waterfront, and migratory Canada Geese honking overhead in the fall.

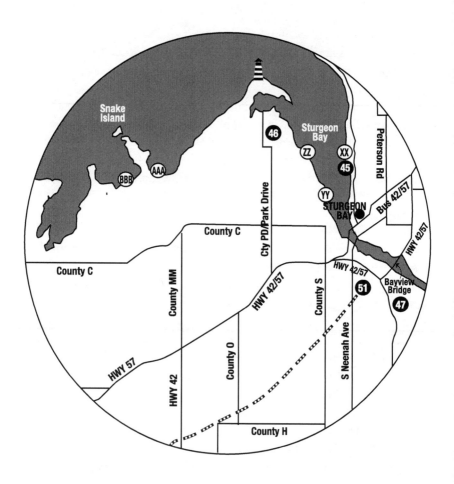

MAJOR POINTS OF INTEREST
45. Sunset Park

This 41-acre urban park includes a small freshwater lake, Bradley Lake, and excellent views of the bay on this side of the peninsula. The park is well developed, with many amenities, including a Frisbee golf course, a dock, playgrounds, two boat ramps, basketball courts, tennis courts, swimming beach, and a picnic pavilion, along with 0.5 mile of paved trails. It is also popular for fishing, boating, and swimming, and you can put in kayaks at one of two ramps to access Sturgeon Bay. It is also a good spot to watch the sunset or have a picnic during the warmer months. Given the park's popularity, early morning and early evening visits are recommended if you want to avoid crowds during the busy season.

Despite its urban setting, Sunset Park can be surprisingly good for wildlife-watching. In the warmer months, look for Black-crowned Night Heron, Green Heron, Common Yellowthroat, and Chimney Swift. The park also provides an excellent vantage point to watch for American

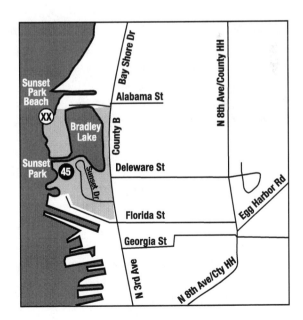

White Pelicans, Double-crested Cormorants, gulls, and terns, roosting on sandbars offshore to the south or navigating up the Sturgeon Bay Ship Canal. This area can also be an excellent spot during spring and fall migration, where warblers, vireos, and other songbirds stop over along Green Bay. During the fall, winter, and spring, Bradley Lake can be good for a diversity of dabbling ducks and large flocks of Canada Geese.

CONTACT INFORMATION AND DIRECTIONS

City of Sturgeon Bay Parks and Recreation, 421 Michigan St., Sturgeon Bay, WI 54235, (920) 746-2900, http://www.sturgeonbaywi.org/. From the intersection of South Third Avenue and Michigan Street in downtown Sturgeon Bay, head northeast on South Third Avenue for 0.75 mile to Sunset Drive. Take a left on Sunset Drive into the park. Sunset Park is located off Third Avenue in downtown Sturgeon Bay, next to the shipyard, at 747 North Third Avenue. No fee.

46. Potawatomi State Park

This popular 1,200-acre state park, with its steep ravines, rocky beaches, and towering limestone cliffs along Sturgeon Bay, provides year-round wildlife-viewing, hiking, camping, and boating opportunities. Its 75-foot observation tower high above the treetops provides an excellent vantage point for watching and listening for migrating warblers and raptors. The tower also provides panoramic views of Green Bay, Chambers Island, and the Upper Peninsula.

Potawatomi State Park is primarily northern mesic forest community, dominated by sugar maple and American beech. Along the lakeshore, the park has a moist cliff community comprised of northern wet-mesic forest with a well-developed native fern understory on the bluffs. During summer, along the 150-foot bluffs, look for Caspian Terns, gulls, American White Pelicans, and Double-crested Cormorants flying past. In the interior, northern hardwood, northern mesic, and northern wet-mesic forests, look for nesting Rose-breasted Grosbeak, Pileated Woodpecker, Black-throated Green Warbler, and Wood Thrush, as well as raccoons, gray squirrel, white-tailed deer, striped skunk, and meadow vole.

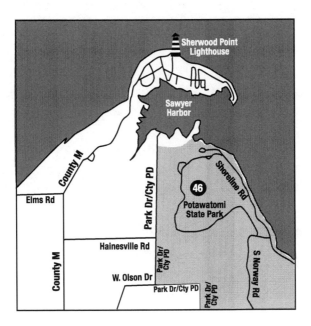

Trails, Access, and Facilities

Potawatomi State Park has a number of hiking trails, including the
Ancient Shores Trail (a 0.5-mile interpretive loop), the Hemlock Trail
(2.6 miles along the Green Bay shoreline and inland), and the Tower
Trail (3.6 miles to the observation tower across the Niagara Escarpment
and bluffs over Green Bay). If you're interested in getting a bit more off
the beaten path in this sometimes busy park, try the Tower Trail and the
Ice Age National Scenic Trail, a 2.8-mile trail along glaciated ridge, part
of the 1,000-mile national scenic trail, which continues outside the park
boundaries. There is also a network of mountain biking trails, as well as
groomed trails for cross-country skiing in the winter. Check at the visitors' center for specific trail information and conditions. Potawatomi
State Park also has camping, picnic areas, a nature center with interpretive programs, a boat ramp, and a rocky beach. Campsites may be
reserved through the Wisconsin State Parks system. This park can be
crowded during summer months and at the peak of fall colors.

Potawatomi State Park, 3740 County PD, Sturgeon Bay, WI 54235, (920) 746-2896. Wisconsin Department of Natural Resources, 101 S. Webster St., P.O. Box 7921, Madison, WI 53707, (608) 266-2621, http://www.dnr .wi.gov/. From the Michigan Street Bridge in downtown Sturgeon Bay, head southwest across the bridge to Maple Street. Turn right on Maple Street and go 0.6 mile to County S/County C/North Duluth Avenue. Turn right at County S/County C/North Duluth Avenue and proceed 1.5 miles to the entrance to the park. Fee area.

47. Franke Park

Franke Park, a 6.5-acre city park, has a 0.5-mile loop trail, with a few boardwalks, through a northern wet-mesic white cedar swamp, with small patches of northern hardwood swamp and northern sedge meadow wetlands. Primarily used by neighborhood residents for dog walking and jogging, it is an excellent choice for those who seek a wooded area but

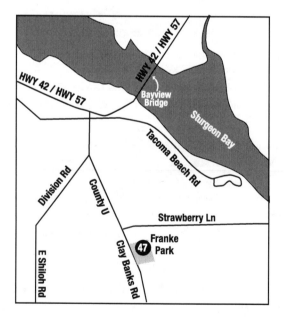

can't walk far or are walking with small children. It has many of the common woodland birds, including Blue Jay, Cedar Waxwing, White-breasted Nuthatch, and Black-capped Chickadee. There are no facilities.

CONTACT INFORMATION AND DIRECTIONS

City of Sturgeon Bay Parks and Recreation, 421 Michigan St., Sturgeon Bay, WI 54235, (920) 746-2900, http://www.sturgeonbaywi.org/. From the Bayview Bridge, head south on Highway 42/57 for 0.5 mile to Clay Banks Road/County U. Turn left and follow Clay Banks Road/County U southeast for 1.0 mile. The park is at 1700 Clay Banks Road, near the intersection of County U and Strawberry Lane. No fee.

BEACHES AND OVERLOOKS
XX. Sunset Park Beach

This small, urban beach with a swimming area along the Sturgeon Bay has a lifeguard in summer and numerous other facilities, including a boat ramp (see Major Point of Interest 45). It is a great choice for families with

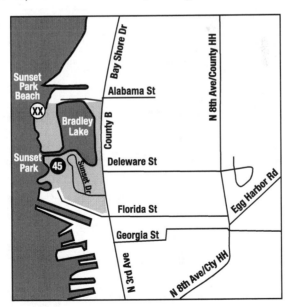

small children, because the area is well protected, and the waters of the bay are generally far warmer than Lake Michigan.

CONTACT INFORMATION AND DIRECTIONS

City of Sturgeon Bay Parks and Recreation, 421 Michigan St., Sturgeon Bay, WI 54235, (920) 746-2900, http://www.sturgeonbaywi.org/. From the intersection of South Third Avenue and Michigan Street in downtown Sturgeon Bay, head northeast on South Third Avenue for 0.7 mile to Florida Street. Take a left on Florida Street and follow it to the parking area (about 0.1 mile). The beach is located adjacent to the Florida Street parking lot. No fee.

YY. Otumba Park Beach

This small, protected, sandy beach has a marked swimming area with lifeguard staffing during the summer. The calm, protected, warm water beach is perfect for families with small children. Other facilities include

restrooms, a large picnic area, pavilions, tennis courts, basketball courts, and walking paths. The bay located directly off the park can also be an excellent place to see diving ducks in the fall and winter and provides a protected area to put in and paddle kayaks.

CONTACT INFORMATION AND DIRECTIONS

City of Sturgeon Bay Parks and Recreation, 421 Michigan St., Sturgeon Bay, WI 54235, (920) 746-2900, http://www.sturgeonbaywi.org/. From the Michigan Street Bridge in downtown Sturgeon Bay, head southwest across the bridge to Maple Street, merging onto Madison Avenue heading south. Turn right on Maple Street, and proceed 0.3 mile to North Joliet Avenue. Turn right on North Joliet Avenue and proceed for 0.1 mile to West Juniper. Otumba Park Beach is on the west side of Sturgeon Bay on West Juniper off North Joliet Avenue. No fee.

ZZ. Potawatomi State Park Beaches

The rocky beaches in Potawatomi State Park are not well suited to swimming, but they do provide scenic views of Green Bay and a place to launch kayaks for trips around Sturgeon Bay and Little Sturgeon Bay. For park facilities, see Major Point of Interest 46.

CONTACT INFORMATION AND DIRECTIONS

Potawatomi State Park, 3740 County PD, Sturgeon Bay, WI 54235, (920) 746-2896. Wisconsin Department of Natural Resources, 101 S. Webster St., P.O. Box 7921, Madison, WI 53707, (608) 266-2621, http://www.dnr .wi.gov/. From the Michigan Street Bridge in downtown Sturgeon Bay, head southwest across the bridge to Maple Street. Turn right on Maple Street and go 0.6 mile to County S/County C/North Duluth Avenue. Turn right at County S/County C/North Duluth Avenue and proceed 1.5 miles to the entrance to the park. Fee area.

AAA. Sand Bay Beach

This very narrow, sandy, 50-foot public beach is situated between two private beaches. Not a swimming beach, it is useful primarily for launching canoes and kayaks for trips around Sand Bay Point and Snake Island, a private 26-acre single-residence island just off the end of Sand Bay Point. There are no facilities.

DIRECTIONS

From the Bayview Bridge in Sturgeon Bay, head south on Highway 42/57 for 3.8 miles to Park Drive/County PD. Turn right and head north on Park Drive/County PD about 2.3 miles to Sand Bay Road. Turn left, heading west, and follow Sand Bay Road for about 3.7 miles to Sandy Bay Lane. Turn right and follow Sandy Bay Lane north for 0.3 mile. The beach is at the end of Sandy Bay Lane adjacent to private homes and resorts, so take caution to avoid trespassing. Parking is limited. If you can't find parking, try nearby Haines Park Beach instead. No fee.

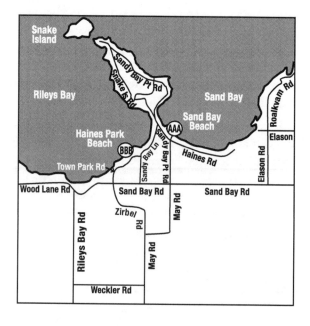

BBB. Haines Park Beach

Haines Park Beach has some sand, but it can be very mucky in places, with rotting Cladophora algae when lake levels are low. This is an excellent put-in point for canoeing or kayaking out around the end of Sand Bay Point and Snake Island, a private 26-acre island just off the end of Sand Bay Point. There are no facilities, but the town provides a seasonal portable toilet in some years.

CONTACT INFORMATION AND DIRECTIONS

The park is owned and operated by Nasewaupee Township. From the Bayview Bridge in Sturgeon Bay, head south on Highway 42/57 for 3.8 miles to Park Drive/County PD. Turn right and head north on County PD/Park Drive about 2.3 miles to Sand Bay Road. Turn left, heading west, and follow Sand Bay Road for about 3.7 miles to Sandy Bay Lane. Turn right and head north on Sandy Bay Lane for 0.3 mile to Town Park Road. Turn left and follow Town Park Road to the parking spaces on the right-hand side of the road. No fee.

LIGHTHOUSE

L11. Sherwood Point Lighthouse

This small lighthouse, light keeper's residence, and fog bell tower were built on Sherwood Point, a 30-foot bluff at the mouth of Sturgeon Bay, around 1883. Today, the red brick keeper's residence, white lighthouse tower, and white fog bell tower are owned by the U.S. Coast Guard and operated as a recreation facility for Coast Guard staff. The lighthouse is open to the public only during the Door County Maritime Museum's annual tour and is otherwise off limits.

CONTACT INFORMATION AND DIRECTIONS

United States Coast Guard Station–Sturgeon Bay, 2501 Canal Rd., Sturgeon Bay, WI 54235, (920) 743-3366, http://www.uscg.mil. Door County Maritime Museum, 120 N. Madison Ave., Sturgeon Bay, WI 54235,

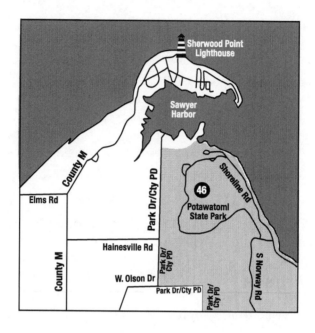

(920) 743-5958, http://www.dcmm.org/. From the Michigan Street bridge in downtown Sturgeon Bay, go southwest on Maple Street for 0.6 mile to North Duluth Avenue. Turn right and head north on North Duluth Avenue/County S for 0.4 mile to County C. Turn left and head west on County C for 3.0 milesto County M. Turn right and head north on County M for 4.1 miles to Sherwood Point Road. Turn left and follow Sherwood Point Road about 0.5 mile to the lighthouse. The lighthouse can be viewed at a distance from the road and from the water offshore, but the grounds are generally closed to the public. No fee.

BIKE ROUTES

B25. Sunset Park to Olde Stone Quarry County Park
(8.8 miles round-trip—easy)

This easy route follows the Sturgeon Bay shoreline from Sunset Park in Sturgeon Bay to Olde Stone Quarry County Park along Bay Shore Drive.

It primarily goes through residential areas of the city and ends with spectacular views of the bay, downtown Sturgeon Bay, and Potawatomi State Park across the bay. Restrooms are available at Sunset Park and Olde Stone Quarry County Park.

ROUTE

From Sunset Park in downtown Sturgeon Bay, off North Third Avenue, head north on Third Avenue/County B toward Alabama Avenue. Third Avenue becomes Bay Shore Drive. Continue on Bay Shore Drive/County B for 4.4 miles to Olde Stone Quarry County Park. Retrace your route to return to Sunset Park.

CONTACT INFORMATION

Door County Parks System, 3528 Park Dr., Sturgeon Bay, WI 54235, (920) 746-9959, http://map.co.door.wi.us/parks/. City of Sturgeon Bay Parks and Recreation, 421 Michigan St., Sturgeon Bay, WI 54235, (920) 746-2900, http://www.sturgeonbaywi.org/. No fee.

B26. Potawatomi State Park Mountain Biking Trails

(8.0 miles—moderate)

Potawatomi State Park has 8.0 miles of biking trails within its borders. These trails can be busy at times, particularly during summer and on weekends, but less busy than other state parks in Door County. They are best suited to mountain or hybrid bikes: generally moderate, winding through some hills, some flatter stretches. Cyclists in search of something a bit more challenging will enjoy the more difficult stretches around the now defunct downhill ski area and around the observation tower, in the northwest corner of the park.

Trails go through steep ravines and past towering limestone cliffs along Sturgeon Bay, through northern mesic forest community, dominated by sugar maple and American beech. Along the lakeshore are moist cliff

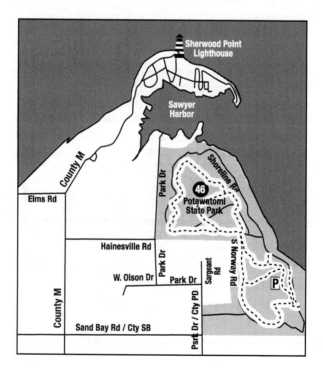

communities comprised of northern wet-mesic forest with a well-developed native fern understory on the bluffs. Restrooms are located throughout the park.

ROUTE

Potawatomi State Park maintains a specific "off-road cyclist" parking lot (Parking Area 1) off Shoreline Road, which is the best place for mountain bikers to pick up the trails. The trail system is a series of loops and can be accessed from Parking Area 1, the observation tower parking area, or any of the picnic areas. Pick up a trail map at the visitors' center for details.

CONTACT INFORMATION AND DIRECTIONS

Potawatomi State Park, 3740 County PD, Sturgeon Bay, WI 54235, (920) 746-2896. Wisconsin Department of Natural Resources, 101 S. Webster St., P.O. Box 7921, Madison, WI 53707, (608) 266-2621, http://www.dnr .wi.gov/. To reach Potawatomi State Park, from the Michigan Street Bridge in downtown Sturgeon Bay, head southwest across the bridge to Maple Street. Turn right on Maple Street and go 0.6 mile to County S/County C/North Duluth Avenue. Turn right at County S/County C/North Duluth Avenue and proceed 1.5 miles to the entrance to the park. Follow the park roads to designated parking areas. Fee area.

B27. Sturgeon Bay–Little Sturgeon Bay Loop

(17.3 miles—moderate)

This longer loop route, best suited for road cyclists, runs from downtown Sturgeon Bay, through miles of farm lands, up the shores of Little Sturgeon Bay, and back to downtown Sturgeon Bay. It is generally flat, but has a moderate rating for its length. You'll cruise past scenic views of the Green Bay and Little Sturgeon Bay and the surrounding farms and forests. Roads on this route generally have low traffic, except in the center of town, where you'll need to keep an eye out for cars, especially during busy summer weekends.

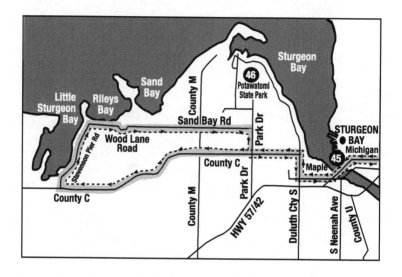

ROUTE

From the Michigan Street bridge in downtown Sturgeon Bay, head southwest across the bridge for 0.4 mile to Madison Avenue. Turn right and follow Madison Avenue 0.2 mile to West Maple Street. Turn right on West Maple Street and head west for 0.6 mile to Duluth Avenue/County S. Turn right and proceed on Duluth Avenue/County S for 0.4 mile to County C. Turn left and follow County C past the airport for 7.8 miles to Stevenson Pier Road. Turn right and follow Stevenson Pier Road north along Little Sturgeon Bay for 2.2 miles to Wood Lane Road. Take a right and follow Wood Lane Road for 0.6 mile. Wood Lane Road will turn into Sand Bay Road. Continue on Sand Bay Road for 4.6 miles until you reach the intersection with Park Drive. Turn right and head south on Park Drive for 1.0 mile (past the airport) to County C. Turn left and follow County C for 1.5 miles to Duluth Avenue/County S. Turn right and follow Duluth Avenue/County S for 0.4 mile to West Maple Street. Turn left and proceed on West Maple Street for 0.2 mile to Michigan Street. Cross the bridge and return to downtown Sturgeon Bay. No fee.

PADDLING ROUTES

P20. Otumba Park and Downtown Sturgeon Bay
(0.5–5.0 miles round-trip—easy)

Kayakers of all ability levels will find something of interest in the busy Sturgeon Bay, around the bustling waterfront of the City of Sturgeon Bay. Otumba Park on the south side of Sturgeon Bay is an ideal launching point for excursions. The area immediately off the swimming beach is well protected and is great for beginners. Experienced paddlers can use the beach as a starting point to head out to the other areas of Sturgeon Bay toward Green Bay. Note that while the areas off Otumba Park are fine for beginners, other areas require a bit more skill and a healthy dose of common sense. Sturgeon Bay can be very busy with power boat traffic, particularly on summer weekends. Kayakers should use common sense around larger and faster boats, stick to the shorelines, and avoid wakes from larger craft.

Despite the human activity in this area, the bay can also be a good place to watch for wildlife. Keep an eye out for American White Pelicans soaring, Ring-billed Gulls looking for handouts, and Caspian Terns and Double-crested Cormorants diving for fish.

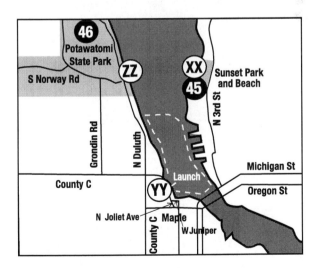

Contact Information and Directions to Launch Site

City of Sturgeon Bay Parks and Recreation, 421 Michigan St., Sturgeon Bay, WI 54235, (920) 746-2900, http://www.sturgeonbaywi.org/. From the Michigan Street Bridge in downtown Sturgeon Bay, head southwest across the bridge to Maple Street, merging onto Madison Avenue heading south. Turn right on Maple Street, and proceed 0.3 mile to North Joliet Avenue. Turn right on North Joliet Avenue and proceed for 0.1 mile to West Juniper. You can park along the local streets or in the park and carry your boat down to the beach area. You can launch directly from the beach. The park has restrooms and parking. No fee.

P21. Sunset Park and Downtown Sturgeon Bay

(1.0–4.0 miles round-trip—easy to moderate)

Sunset Park, on the north shore of Sturgeon Bay, is a good launching point for intermediate and experienced kayakers interested in a day trip

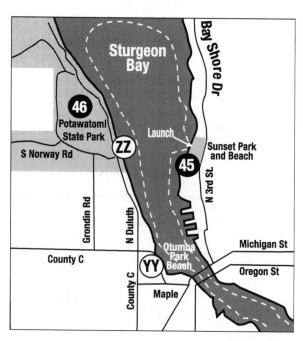

around the bay. From this launching point, you can explore the entire bay, including the docks and marinas that line both sides. Watch for gulls and Caspian Terns foraging in the shallows, paddle under the bridges, or enjoy the sunset from your boat. Keep an eye out for other boats of all kinds in the harbor, particularly on summer weekends when the area is busy. The park has parking and restrooms.

CONTACT INFORMATION AND DIRECTIONS TO LAUNCH SITE

City of Sturgeon Bay Parks and Recreation, 421 Michigan St., Sturgeon Bay, WI 54235, (920) 746-2900, http://www.sturgeonbaywi.org/. From the intersection of South Third Avenue and Michigan Street in downtown Sturgeon Bay, head northeast on South Third Avenue for 0.7 mile to Florida Street. Take a left on Florida Street and follow it to the end (about 0.2 mile) to the boat ramp. No fee.

P22. Rileys Bay and Snake Island

(4.0 miles round-trip—moderate)

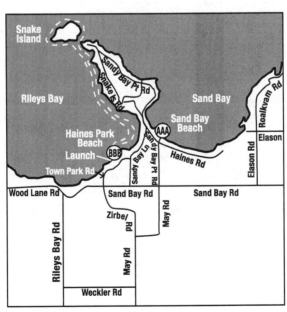

A trip around Rileys Bay, along Sandy Bay Point, and around Snake Island is a convenient and enjoyable trip for intermediate and experienced kayakers. The paddling is generally calm and protected, though weather can come up quickly here, so you want to take appropriate safety precautions. Consider wearing a wet or dry suit and carry foul weather gear. Points of interest are an offshore private island and the gulls and terns cruising past. Launch from Haines Park Beach, a small Nasewaupee Township beach. There are no facilities at Haines Park Beach, but the town puts in a seasonal portable toilet in some years. Note that Haines Park Beach can be very mucky in places, with rotting Cladophora algae when lake levels are low.

ROUTE

From the launching spot at Haines Park Beach, a small Nasewaupee Township beach, head around the shore of Rileys Bay to the northeast, which will take you along Sandy Bay Point, a distance of about 1.2 miles if you're following the shoreline. Snake Island, a 26-acre single-residence private island, sits right off the end of Sandy Bay Point. You can then kayak around Snake Island, another 0.5 mile, and return by retracing your route along the north side of Rileys Bay. The total trip is about 4.0 miles if you go out around Snake Island and follow the shoreline.

DIRECTIONS TO LAUNCH SITE

The beach and small township parking lot are located on Town Park Road on the west side of Sandy Bay Point. From the Bayview Bridge, head south on Highway 42/57 for 3.8 miles to Park Drive/County PD. Turn right and head north on County PD/Park Drive about 2.3 miles to Sand Bay Road. Turn left, heading west, and follow Sand Bay Road for about 3.7 miles to Sandy Bay Lane. Turn right and head north on Sandy Bay Lane for 0.3 mile to Town Park Road. Turn left and follow Town Park Road to the Nasewaupee Township parking spaces on the right-hand side of the road. No fee.

P23. Little Sturgeon Bay

(0.5–6.0 miles round-trip—moderate)

Robert M. Carmody County Park, a public boat-launching facility, provides an excellent launching point for intermediate and experienced paddlers to explore Little Sturgeon Bay, a paddle of about 6.0 miles round-trip, if you follow the shoreline around the bay. Appropriate safety gear is important—consider wearing a wet or dry suit. The sheltered Little Sturgeon Bay is generally quiet, although the park and its docks are popular with fishermen, so keep an eye out for power boats.

ROUTE

From the boat launch at Robert M. Carmody County Park you can paddle north to Claflin Rock, a popular diving location, just 0.2 mile north of the park; paddle south around Squaw Island Point, about 0.5 mile south; or

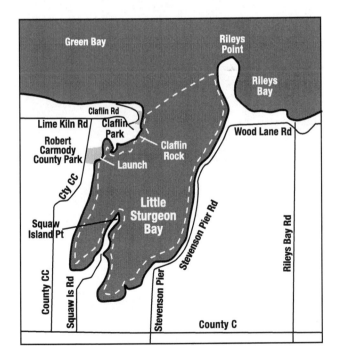

head directly across Little Sturgeon Bay to Rileys Point, a 1.0-mile crossing. Note that the water can be choppy crossing from the park to Rileys Point. You can also cruise along the shoreline of Little Sturgeon Bay, a trip of about 6.0 miles from the park, up around Squaw Island Point, up to Rileys Point, across the mouth of the bay, past Claflin Rock, and back to the park.

CONTACT INFORMATION AND DIRECTIONS TO LAUNCH SITE

Door County Parks System, 3528 Park Dr., Sturgeon Bay, WI 54235, (920) 746-9959, http://map.co.door.wi.us/parks/. From downtown Sturgeon Bay, head southwest on Michigan Street across the bridge to Maple Street, merging onto Madison Avenue heading south. Turn right on Maple Street and head west for 0.6 mile to Duluth Avenue. Turn right, heading north on Duluth Avenue for 0.4 miles to County C. Turn left on County C and proceed west for 8.8 miles to County CC. Turn right and follow County CC north about 2.0 miles to the park entrance. The park is located in the Town of Gardner at 3570 County CC. Small fee to use boat launch.

9

The Clay Banks

Clay Banks, Maplewood, and Forestville

The red clay cliffs that line Lake Michigan in this part of Door County—once a navigation aid for sailors—give the area its name. The Town of Forestville, established in the 1850s, was the first settlement in this part of the county. Early settlers began to clear Door County's vast forests, hauling trees by barge down the Ahnapee River to a sawmill in the center of town. Soon after, the town of Clay Banks split off from Forestville. There, along the lake, a shipping dock was built, and by the late 1880s the town was the site of several brick-manufacturing facilities. Inland, as the land was cleared, farmers from the East Coast, Germany, and Norway began to settle family farms.

While the brick factories and sawmills are gone, today the area looks much the same—with red clay banks along the lake and family farms inland. It is a welcome respite from the hustle and bustle found in much of Door County during the tourist season. The Legacy Nature Preserve at Clay Banks and the Ahnapee State Trail are major highlights, but the best activities in this region are also the simplest—paddling an empty stretch of Lake Michigan shoreline, taking a bike ride down to the beach at the end of an empty road, or walking a deserted expanse of Door County's quietest beaches. The best thing about the Clay Banks is that you'll have the place almost to yourself.

MAJOR POINTS OF INTEREST
48. Legacy Nature Preserve at Clay Banks

The Legacy Nature Preserve at Clay Banks was once the site of a historic sawmill and timber-shipping dock. Today it boasts one of the finest hikes in all of Door County. Straddling about three thousand feet of Lake Michigan shoreline, the preserve is an excellent place to watch a sunrise from atop the promontory near the parking area, or to find solitude at the small, scenic, sandy beach. The preserve includes pockets of northern wet-mesic and northern mesic forest communities, and wetlands areas. Look for breeding Black-throated Green Warbler, American Redstart, coyote, and white-tailed deer, as well as migrating raptors in the spring and fall and diving ducks offshore in the colder months. In the prairie areas, watch for Clay-colored Sparrow, Eastern Meadowlark, red fox, raccoon, striped skunk, and other smaller mammals.

TRAILS, ACCESS, AND FACILITIES

The Legacy Nature Preserve at Clay Banks offers one of the best hikes in all of Door County. The 1.0-mile loop trail, steep in some parts, begins at the parking area, at the top of a large red clay bank, traverses down through prairie and shrublands, and ends at the Lake Michigan shoreline, at a secluded, sand and rock Great Lakes beach and dune community. Bikes, horses, and motorized vehicles are prohibited. Hunting is authorized subject to Door County Land Trust (DCLT) guidelines and permission. There are no facilities.

CONTACT INFORMATION AND DIRECTIONS

Door County Land Trust, P.O. Box 65, Sturgeon Bay, WI 54235, (920) 746-1359, http://www.doorcountylandtrust.org/. From Highway 42 in Forestville, head east on County J (Main Street) for 3.0 miles. Follow County J as it jogs north for 0.5 mile and then heads east again for 2.8 miles until it ends at County U. Turn left on County U, heading north along Lake Michigan for 0.9 mile. County U forks at South Lake Michigan Drive. Bear right and follow South Lake Michigan Drive for 1.5 miles.

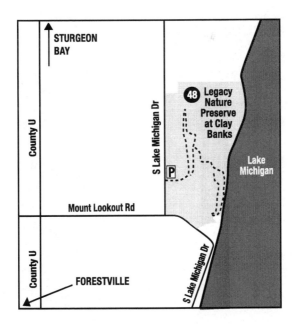

At the intersection of Mount Lookout Road, turn right to stay on to South Lake Michigan Drive and continue to follow it for about 0.1 mile to the preserve parking area and sign. (Watch for DCLT signs, as this is easy to miss.) Park along the shoulder of South Lake Michigan Drive or in the seasonally mowed parking lot, and hike east to access the preserve. No fee.

49. Robert La Salle County Park

Located just north of Door County's border with Kewaunee County, this 25-acre park, along County U on Lake Michigan, is named after the Great Lakes explorer who is thought to have landed here in the mid-1600s. A historical marker in the park provides details of the landing. This park is best suited for picnicking, sunbathing, and enjoying views of Lake Michigan. The parcels are owned and operated by the Door County Parks System. While primarily developed as a park, there is public lakefront access in a stretch of Lake Michigan that is primarily private property.

Robert La Salle County Park includes steep sand bluffs created by changes in Lake Michigan's water levels over geologic time, ravines, and

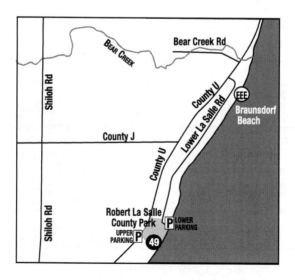

northern mesic forest. While the park lacks hiking trails, stairways connect the upper and lower sections of the park and provide access to the historical marker. The park also has some ephemeral creeks to the north and south, including Bear Creek, which bounds the park on the north.

CONTACT INFORMATION AND DIRECTIONS

Door County Parks System, 3528 Park Dr., Sturgeon Bay, WI 54235, (920) 746-9959, http://map.co.door.wi.us/parks/. From Highway 42 in Forestville, head east on Main Street/County J for 3.0 miles, and continue on County J as it jogs north for 0.5 miles and then heads east again for 2.8 miles until it ends at County U. Turn left on County U, heading north along Lake Michigan for about 0.5 mile to Lower La Salle Road. Turn right and follow Lower La Salle Road south for 1.0 mile until it ends at the park entrance and large "lower" parking lot. There is also an upper parking lot accessible by turning right on County U (instead of left at the end of County J) and following it for about 0.4 mile to the parking area on the east side of the road, located at 408 County U. No fee.

50. Forestville Dam County Park

Forestville Dam County Park, also known as Forestville Mill Pond Park, is a 79-acre park owned and operated by the Door County Parks System. Situated on the western banks of the Forestville Mill Pond, locally known as Forestville Flowage, a dammed stretch of the Ahnapee River, it offers ideal opportunities for relaxed and easy canoeing and kayaking along the protected waters of the flowage. This is also a popular spot for fishing. While there are no trails in the park itself, this is an excellent place to park for hiking or biking excursions on the Ahnapee State Trail, which runs along the edge of the park. The park is primarily developed with a boat launch, dock, playground, and picnic facilities, but also contains wooded northern wet-mesic forest areas with open grassy areas and playing fields. Look for Black-capped Chickadee, Chipping Sparrow, American Goldfinch, Red-breasted Nuthatch, White-breasted Nuthatch, Chimney Swift, and Ruby-throated Hummingbird.

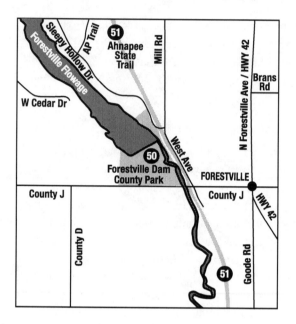

CONTACT INFORMATION AND DIRECTIONS

Door County Parks System, 3528 Park Dr., Sturgeon Bay, WI 54235, (920) 746-9959, http://map.co.door.wi.us/parks/. From the intersection of Highway 42 and Main Street/County J in Forestville, go west on Main Street/County J for 0.3 mile to West Avenue (Mill Road), where you'll see a brown sign for the park. Take a right and head north on Mill Road for 0.3 mile to the parking area. The park entrance, at 475 Mill Road, is just before Mill Road crosses the Ahnapee State Trail. This park and parking lot serve as a primary access point to the Ahnapee Trail. No fee.

51. Ahnapee State Trail

The Ahnapee State Trail is one of Wisconsin's premier examples of a successful rails-to-trails project. Developing this trail has been a collaborative effort of a large number of individuals and organizations over the years, and currently the Door County Parks System is the lead agency in maintaining the trail in Door County. This 27-mile corridor is a multiuse path along former railroad tracks that links up with hundreds of miles of bike routes in Door and Kewaunee Counties. The trail is well graded and surfaced for smooth riding conditions. It runs roughly between the Village of Luxemburg in Kewanee County and Peninsula State Park, with plans to add additional trail miles. In spring, summer, and fall, the trail is open for hiking, biking, and horseback riding, in winter for cross-county skiing and snowmobiling.

The trail spans just about all of southern Door County's interior community types, including northern wet-mesic, northern mesic, and northern dry-mesic forests, along with scattered pockets of wetlands and old fields. It is an excellent place to observe spring wildflowers and plants and animals that favor edges and disturbed successional communities,

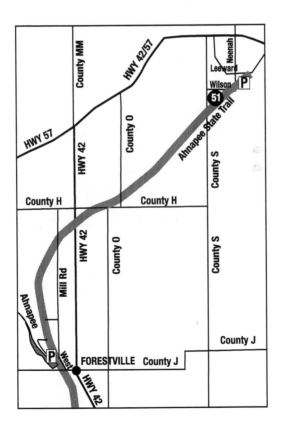

including aspen stands and old fields. Particularly in the quiet early morning and at dusk, watch for Wild Turkey, monarch butterfly, Mourning Warbler, Clay-colored Sparrow, white-tailed deer, spotted salamander, raccoon, Virginia opossum, and red fox.

TRAILS, ACCESS, AND FACILITIES

There are a number of places to access the trail. One of the easiest is the trailhead parking lot just south of downtown Sturgeon Bay off Neenah Avenue between Leeward Street and Wilson Road. Easy access and parking are also available at Forestville Dam County Park (see preceding entry, Major Point of Interest 50).

CONTACT INFO

http://www.ahnapeetrail.org/. Door County Parks System, 3528 Park Dr., Sturgeon Bay, WI 54235, (920) 746-9959, http://map.co.door.wi.us/parks/ or Kewaunee County Promotion and Recreation Department, 613 Dodge St., Kewaunee, WI 54216, (920) 388-7199, http://www.kewaunee.org/. No fee.

BEACHES AND OVERLOOKS
CCC. Clay Banks Beach #1

You will encounter very few other people along this extensive, secluded, sandy, windswept Lake Michigan beach southeast of Sturgeon Bay. It is perfect for quiet solitude. The area just inland from the beach is part of the southernmost Great Lakes ridge and swale complex in Door County.

North of this beach along South Lake Michigan Drive are a series of narrow beaches, as well as numerous private homes. It is important to park well off the road and not block driveways or trespass on private land. When in doubt, ask permission.

DIRECTIONS

From the Bayview Bridge in Sturgeon Bay, go south on Highway 42/57 for 0.6 mile to County U. Turn left and head south on County U for 4.2 miles to Hornspier Road. Turn left and follow Hornspier Road east for

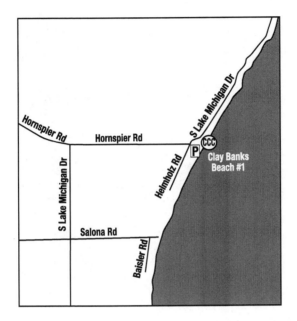

1.5 miles to South Lake Michigan Drive. Turn left; in 0.1 mile South Lake Michigan Drive will meet Lake Michigan and begin heading northeast along the lake. About 100 feet past a bend in the road is a sandy parking area. No fee.

DDD. Clay Banks Beach #2

You will find very few other people in this area, an ideal spot to enjoy a bit of solitude next to Lake Michigan. This sandy, exposed beach is just north of Braunsdorf Beach off County U, between Bear Creek Road and Lake Michigan Drive. It can be accessed by walking along the beach from La Salle County Park, which is located south of Braunsdorf Beach, or by parking off County U in a sandy lot and walking directly down to the lake. There are a number of private homes in this area, but the land on the lake side of County U is state property and accessible to the public. If in doubt, ask permission from local landowners.

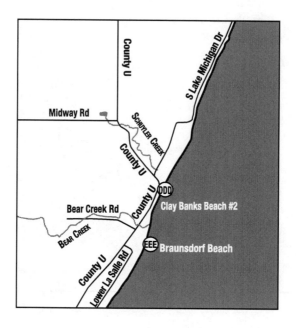

DIRECTIONS

From the Bayview Bridge in Sturgeon Bay, head south on Highway 42/57 for 0.6 mile to County U. Turn left and head south and east on County U for 8.0 miles. In the last 0.3 mile, just past the Clay Banks Cemetery, County U will start heading east and end at the beach. Park off the shoulder in a sandy parking area, where County U makes a sharp bend inland. No fee.

EEE. Braunsdorf Beach

Braunsdorf Beach is an exposed sand and rock beach, primarily used by residents of the neighborhood of the same name. You can park at Robert La Salle County Park and walk north, or ask permission of private landowners living along Lower La Salle Road. The county park has parking, restrooms, a playground, and picnic areas.

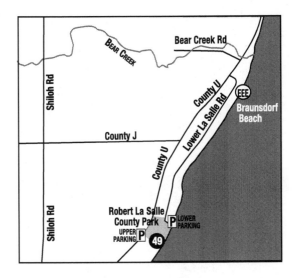

CONTACT INFORMATION AND DIRECTIONS

Door County Parks System, 3528 Park Dr., Sturgeon Bay, WI 54235, (920) 746-9959, http://map.co.door.wi.us/parks/. To reach Robert La Salle County Park, from Highway 42 in Forestville, head east on County J (Main Street) for 3.0 miles. Follow County J as it jogs north for 0.5 mile and then heads east again for 2.8 miles until it ends at County U. Turn left on County U, heading north along Lake Michigan for about 0.5 mile to Lower La Salle Road. Turn right and follow Lower La Salle Road for 1.0 mile south until it ends at the park entrance, 408 County U, and large parking lot. No fee.

BIKE ROUTES

B28. Ahnapee State Trail to Maplewood
(9 miles round-trip—easy)

This short section of the Ahnapee State Trail is suitable for cyclists of all ages, and is especially good for families with young children. It is well graded and runs through a variety of fields, residential areas, and forests.

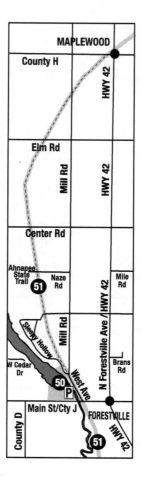

This route can be extended for those interested in a longer ride. A trip along the entirety of the trail can be completed as a day trip, or broken into several segments. The riding is easy, so adjust your mileage depending on your interest and endurance.

ROUTE

Park at Forestville Dam County Park and pick up the trail adjacent to the park. Head north on the Ahnapee State Trail for about 4.5 miles to the intersection of the trail with County H. Retrace your route to return to Forestville Dam County Park.

Contact Information and Directions

Door County Parks System, 3528 Park Dr., Sturgeon Bay, WI 54235, (920) 746-9959, http://www.ahnapeetrail.org/. From the intersection of Highway 42 and Main Street/County J in Forestville, take Main Street/County J west for 0.3 mile to West Avenue (Mill Road), where you'll see a brown sign for the park. Take a right and head north on Mill Road for 0.3 mile to the parking area. The park entrance, at 475 Mill Road, is just before Mill Road crosses the Ahnapee State Trail at Forestville. The park and parking lot serve as a primary access point to the Ahnapee Trail. The park has restrooms. No fee.

B29. Forestville Dam County Park to Robert La Salle County Park

(14.6 miles round-trip—moderate)

This straightforward and mostly flat route, past a mix of agricultural areas, is flat, easy, and suitable for cyclists of all ages and abilities, but is rated moderate for its length. The roads have generally light traffic.

Route

From Forestville Dam County Park, head southeast on Mill Road and cross the Ahnapee State Trail. Continue onto West Avenue for 0.1 mile and turn left onto Main Street/County J. Follow Main Street/County J for 3.4 miles. Turn left to stay on County J for 0.5 mile, then right on County J and proceed 2.8 miles to County U. Take a right on County U, and continue on County U for 0.5 miles to the upper entrance of Robert La Salle County Park. Here you can walk your bike down the steps and into the park or retrace your route back to Forestville. Both parks have restrooms.

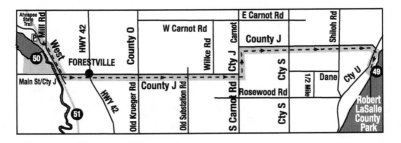

CONTACT INFORMATION AND DIRECTIONS

Door County Parks System, 3528 Park Dr., Sturgeon Bay, WI 54235, (920) 746-9959, http://map.co.door.wi.us/parks/. From the intersection of Highway 42 and Main Street/County J in Forestville, go west on Main Street/County J for 0.3 mile to West Avenue (Mill Road). Take a right and head north for 0.3 mile to the parking area. The park's entrance, 475 Mill Road, is just before Mill Road meets the Ahnapee State Trail. No fee.

B30. Robert La Salle County Park to Salona Road Beach

(9.9 miles round-trip—easy)

This bike route covers a sparsely populated stretch of Lake Michigan shoreline, past summer cottages, with views of Lake Michigan. It has light car traffic and is a good choice for a family bike ride with older children, though cyclists should be aware that there are some minor hills, particularly leaving Robert La Salle County Park. There are beaches at the beginning and end of the route. La Salle County Park has restrooms.

ROUTE

From the lower parking lot of Robert La Salle County Park, head west on Lower La Salle Road toward County U, about 1.0 mile. Turn right on County U and proceed for 0.4 mile to South Lake Michigan Drive. Turn right and continue on South Lake Michigan Drive for 1.5 miles. At the Legacy Nature Preserve at Clay Banks, at the intersection with Mount Lookout Road, turn right to stay on South Lake Michigan Drive and proceed for 1.5 miles to Salona Road. Turn right and follow Salona Road to the end, where there is a small public lake access point. Depending on lake levels, a small beach may be worth visiting. Retrace your route to return to La Salle County Park.

CONTACT INFORMATION AND DIRECTIONS

Door County Parks System, 3528 Park Dr., Sturgeon Bay, WI 54235, (920) 746-9959, http://map.co.door.wi.us/parks/. To reach Robert La Salle County Park, from Highway 42 in Forestville, head east on Main

Street/County J for 3.0 miles. Follow County J as it jogs north for 0.5 miles and then heads east again for 2.8 miles until it ends at County U. Turn left on County U, heading north along Lake Michigan for about 0.5 mile to Lower La Salle Road. Turn right and follow Lower La Salle Road for 1.0 mile south to the park entrance and large parking lot. There is also an upper parking lot accessible by taking a right on County U, and following County U for about 0.4 mile to the parking area on the east side of the road, 408 County U. No fee.

PADDLING ROUTES

P24. Clay Banks Beaches to Robert La Salle County Park
(2.0–8.0 miles round-trip—moderate)

This sandy, exposed stretch of Lake Michigan beach, north of Braunsdorf
Beach, provides launching opportunities for experienced paddlers interested in getting away from the crowds. Generally deserted, this stretch
of coastline is starkly beautiful, with sand beaches and towering red clay

banks. Rarely will you find other boaters. During windy weather the shoreline can be tricky paddling, but under calm conditions the gradual shallow waters and sand beaches provide easy paddling, with plenty of empty beaches in between to stop off for a break or a swim. Carry appropriate safety equipment and consider a wet or dry suit no matter the month of the year.

ROUTE

From the launching spot at Clay Banks Beach #1, head south for about 1.5 miles and you'll pass the Legacy Nature Preserve at Clay Banks. Continue another 1.0 mile and you'll pass Clay Banks Beach #2, followed by Braunsdorf Beach, and proceed an additional 1.0 mile to Robert La Salle County Park. Retrace your route to return to Clay Banks Beach #1. The total distance from Clay Banks Beach #1 to La Salle County Park and back is about 8.0 miles.

DIRECTIONS TO LAUNCH SITE

To reach the launching spot at Clay Banks Beach #1, from the Bayview Bridge in Sturgeon Bay head south on Highway 42/57 for 0.6 mile to County U. Turn left on County U and head south for 4.2 miles to Hornspier Road. Turn left and follow Hornspier Road east for 1.5 miles to South Lake Michigan Drive. Turn left on South Lake Michigan Drive. After 0.1 mile, South Lake Michigan Drive will meet the lake and begin heading northeast along the lake. About 100 feet past the bend is a sandy parking area. No fee.

P25. Forestville Flowage

(2.0 miles round-trip—easy)

Forestville Dam County Park is situated on the western banks of the Forestville Mill Pond, locally known as Forestville Flowage, a dammed stretch of the Ahnapee River. This park offers outstanding opportunities for relaxed and easy canoeing and kayaking along the protected waters of the flowage for paddlers of all ages and ability levels, as well as ample wildlife-viewing opportunities along the marshes that line the banks of the flowage upriver from the park. This spot is good for beginners and

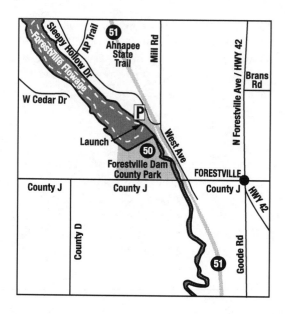

provides enough interest for those with more paddling experience. You can launch kayaks or canoes from the boat launch and dock area adjacent to the parking lot.

ROUTE

From the dock at Forestville Dam County Park, proceed northwest along the shoreline. The round-trip journey up the flowage and back is about 2.0 miles.

DIRECTIONS TO LAUNCH SITE

From the intersection of Highway 42 and Main Street/County J in Forestville, take Main Street/County J west for 0.3 mile to West Avenue (Mill Road), where you'll see a brown sign for the park. Take a right and head north on Mill Road for 0.3 mile to the parking area. The park's entrance is just before Mill Road meets the Ahnapee State Trail.

CONTACT INFORMATION

Door County Parks System, 3528 Park Dr., Sturgeon Bay, WI 54235, (920) 746-9959, http://map.co.door.wi.us/parks/. Small fee to use boat launch.

10

Southern Door

Gardner, Namur, and Brussels

Once home to bands of Menominee and Chippewa, today Southern Door has a distinctly Belgian flavor. The area was settled in the late 1850s by Belgian farmers, who named the settlements of Brussels and Namur after cities in their homeland. Nearby Gardner was named after Freeland Gardner, who ran a highly profitable shipbuilding and lumber business

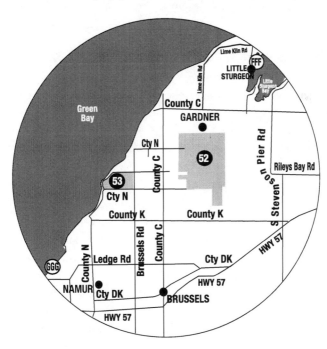

and employed many of the local Belgians. Today this area is primarily agricultural, populated mostly by Belgian-American dairy and wheat farmers. The landscape here probably looks much as it did 100 years ago.

Southern Door is generally off the radar of most summer visitors to Door County, and while the area lacks the extensive woodlands and marshes of other parts of the county, it retains a certain rural charm, without crowds. This area also has a different feel from the rest of Door County—perhaps because of the oak trees that grow in patchy savannahs throughout the area, which are absent north of the Bayview Bridge. The fall colors of these oak woodlots around farms can be spectacular, and this region is well suited to long bike rides down low-traffic roads, no matter the season. Additionally, the beaches along Green Bay are generally used only by a few locals, so you'll have them to yourself. If you're truly looking to get off the beaten path in Door County, Southern Door is a sure bet.

MAJOR POINTS OF INTEREST

52. Gardner Swamp State Wildlife Area

Gardner Swamp, also known as Gardner Marsh, is a classic northern hardwood swamp with extensive wetlands flowing into Kayes Creek. The Gardner Swamp State Wildlife Area includes a 1,200-acre tract managed by the Wisconsin Department of Natural Resources (WDNR), as well as a nearby 400-acre private tract known as Brussels Hill and Kayes Creek Preserve, protected by the Door County Land Trust (DCLT). The WDNR tract is open to the public and has a network of rustic trails, but they may not be well maintained. Along Kayes Creek are extensive emergent and submergent cattail marshes, bordered by mature northern mesic forests. Around Brussels Hill are some steep ravines bordering drier upland northern dry-mesic forests. Gardner Swamp contains some of the largest oak woodlands in Door County, along with American elm, American beech, hemlock, and sugar maple.

Gardner Swamp is a breeding location for Hine's emerald and other dragonflies, chorus frogs, and northern spring peepers, and is a great place to find Wood Duck, Ruffed Grouse, Sandhill Crane, Wild Turkey,

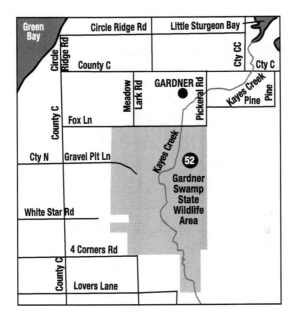

and white-tailed deer. In the spring and fall, look for a variety of migrating wood warblers, including Bay-breasted, Blackpoll, Nashville, Canada, and Golden-winged. The section owned by WDNR is primarily maintained for wildlife, hunting (waterfowl and white-tailed deer), and trapping. The fall colors are often spectacular, but hikers should be especially cautious during fall hunting seasons.

TRAILS, ACCESS, AND FACILITIES

The WDNR property has some trails, but they may not be well maintained. There are no facilities. Contact WDNR for information on hunting regulations, closures, and access. The DCLT sites are currently undeveloped and accessible by permission only. Contact DCLT for information on access.

CONTACT INFORMATION AND DIRECTIONS

Wisconsin Department of Natural Resources, 101 S. Webster St., P.O. Box 7921, Madison, WI 53707, (608) 266-2621, http://www.dnr.wi.gov/. Door County Land Trust, P.O. Box 65, Sturgeon Bay, WI 54235, (920)

746-1359, http://www.doorcountylandtrust.org/. From the intersection of County DK and County C in Brussels, go north on County C for 4.6 miles to County N/Gravel Pit Road. Head east on Gravel Pit Road for about 1.0 mile until it dead-ends. The marsh can also be reached via 4 Corners Road off County C, or Pickeral Road off Fox Lane. The WDNR area is roughly bounded by Fox Lane to the north, Pickeral Road to the east, and 4 Corners Road to the south. No fee.

53. Sugar Creek County Park

Sugar Creek County Park occupies 40 wooded acres along Green Bay, with a small boat launch when lake levels are adequate, and picnic areas. While there are no formal hiking trails, the exposed location of the park makes it a popular spot to watch winter storms along Green Bay, and the mature northern mesic forest can sometimes be productive in the spring and fall for migrating songbirds and raptors. Look for breeding Chipping Sparrow, Red-eyed Vireo, and American Robin. Sugar Creek, which flows into Green Bay at the park, is a high quality 10-mile-long stream that is popular with anglers when the smelt are running. This park may host huge concentrations of migrant Canada Geese, along with diving ducks in the winter, which forage on zebra and quagga mussels.

TRAILS, ACCESS, AND FACILITIES

Sugar Creek County Park has parking, restrooms, a boat launch, a picnic area with grills, and lake access. The undeveloped portion of the property is well wooded, with some trails created by public use over time.

CONTACT INFO AND DIRECTIONS

Door County Parks System, 3528 Park Dr., Sturgeon Bay, WI 54235, (920) 746-9959, http://map.co.door.wi.us/parks/. From the intersection of County N and County DK in Namur, go north on County N for 3.7 miles to Sugar Creek Drive and the entrance to the park. No fee.

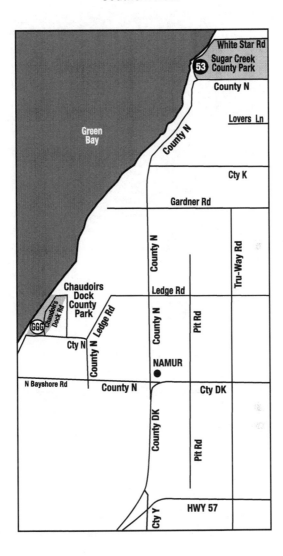

BEACHES AND OVERLOOKS
FFF. Robert M. Carmody County Park

This six-acre county park on the western shore of Little Sturgeon Bay, recently developed in cooperation with the Wisconsin Department of

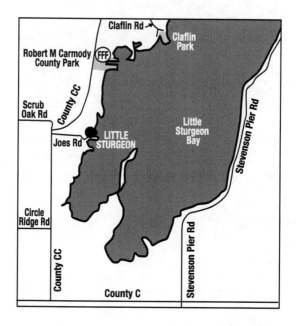

Natural Resources, was designed to serve as a large boat launch facility for anglers. Robert M. Carmody County Park has a large boat ramp and dock complex, fishing pier, restrooms, and a large parking lot. This is a good place for experienced kayakers to launch for trips around Little Sturgeon Bay or out to Rileys Point.

CONTACT INFORMATION AND DIRECTIONS

Door County Parks System, 3528 Park Dr., Sturgeon Bay, WI 54235, (920) 746-9959, http://map.co.door.wi.us/parks/. From the Michigan Street bridge in downtown Sturgeon Bay, head southwest to Maple Street, merging on to Madison Avenue. Turn right on Maple Street and head west for 0.6 mile to Duluth Avenue. Turn right and head north on Duluth Avenue for 0.4 mile to County C. Turn left and go west on County C for 8.8 miles to County CC. Turn right and follow County CC north for about 2.2 miles to the park entrance. The park is located in the Town of Gardner at 3570 County CC. No fee, except to use the boat launch.

GGG. Chaudoirs Dock County Park

This five-acre county park, near the town of Namur, has a small picnic area with grills, restrooms, a boat ramp, and breakwater along Green Bay.

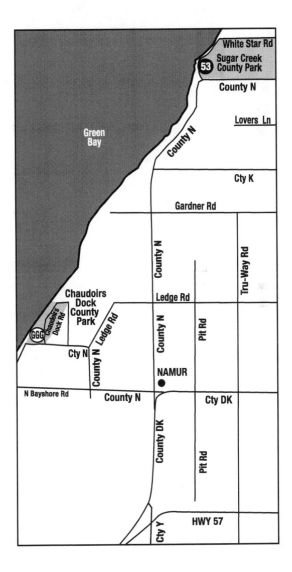

There is no beach, but this is an excellent lookout point, a good launching point for boating, and a great spot to look for mixed gull and tern flocks roosting on the breakwater and diving ducks in winter. This park is very popular for fishing and boating, particularly in the summer months. The operation of the boat ramps and docks depend on lake levels.

CONTACT INFORMATION AND DIRECTIONS

Door County Parks System, 3528 Park Dr., Sturgeon Bay, WI 54235, (920) 746-9959, http://map.co.door.wi.us/parks/. From the Bayview Bridge in Sturgeon Bay, head south on Highway 42/57 for 18.1 miles, to County Y. Turn right on County Y and proceed 0.2 mile north, past Woods Road. When County Y dead-ends, turn right on County DK and proceed for 0.9 mile. Turn left on County N and follow it for 0.1 mile before again turning left to continue on County N for 0.7 miles. Take a right to stay on County N (don't follow Bayshore Road) and proceed 1.0 miles, and then another slight right on County N and proceed 0.3 mile to Chaudoirs Dock Road, the entrance road to the park. The park is located at 1552 County N. No fee, except to use the boat launch.

BIKE ROUTES

B31. Brussels to Chaudoirs Dock County Park
(16.8 miles round-trip—moderate)

This easy bike route passes through the extensive agricultural areas around the farming hamlet of Brussels and ends with views of Green Bay at Chaudoirs Dock County Park. The route is generally flat and has little car traffic. The park has restrooms.

ROUTE

From downtown Brussels, at the intersection of County DK and County C, head north on County C for 2.4 miles to County K. Turn left and follow County K west for 2.5 miles to County N. Turn left and follow County N south for 1.5 miles to Ledge Road. Turn right and follow Ledge Road west and then south for 1.0 mile to County N. Turn right and proceed west on County N for 0.2 mile to Bent Road. Turn right and head

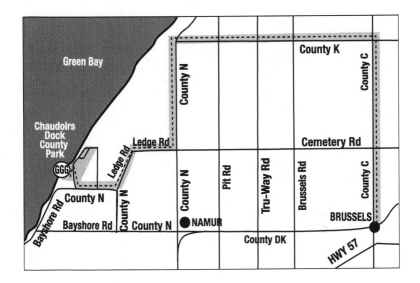

north on Bent Road for 0.7 mile to Chaudoirs Dock County Park. Retrace your route to return to Brussels.

CONTACT INFORMATION

Door County Parks System, 3528 Park Dr., Sturgeon Bay, WI 54235, (920) 746-9959, http://map.co.door.wi.us/parks/. No fee.

B32. Brussels to Sugar Creek County Park

(11.6 miles round-trip—easy to moderate)

This easy to moderate route is generally flat and runs along lightly traveled roads and farmland, ending along the shores of Green Bay. The county park has restrooms.

ROUTE

From the intersection of County DK and County C in downtown Brussels, head north on County C (toward Cemetery Road) for 3.4 miles to 4 Corners Road. Turn left and proceed for 1.0 mile straight onto County

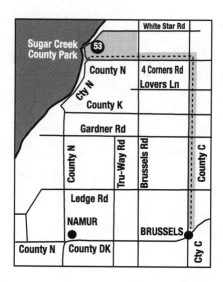

N, and stay on County N for 0.9 mile to the Sugar Creek County Park entrance. Retrace your route to return to Brussels.

CONTACT INFORMATION

Door County Parks System, 3528 Park Dr., Sturgeon Bay, WI 54235, (920) 746-9959, http://map.co.door.wi.us/parks/. No fee.

B33. Brussels to Robert M. Carmody County Park

(21.8 miles round-trip—moderate)

This moderate route through farmland and northern mesic and northern hardwood forests is best suited to road cyclists. The roads tend to be lightly traveled, and the route is ideal for those interested in gaining mileage with minimal traffic congestion. Robert M. Carmody County Park has restrooms.

ROUTE

From the intersection of County DK and County C in Brussels, head north on County C (toward Cemetery Road) for 5.8 miles. County C will

jog east here, so continue on County C another 1.3 miles to Lime Kiln Road. Turn left on Lime Kiln Road and proceed 1.4 miles. Bear right to stay on Lime Kiln Road, and go another 1.9 miles to County CC. Turn right and head south on County CC for 0.1 mile to the entrance of Robert Carmody County Park.

CONTACT INFORMATION

Door County Parks System, 3528 Park Dr., Sturgeon Bay, WI 54235, (920) 746-9959, http://map.co.door.wi.us/parks/. No fee.

PADDLING ROUTE

P26. Chaudoirs Dock County Park to Sugar Creek County Park
(7.0 miles round-trip—moderate)

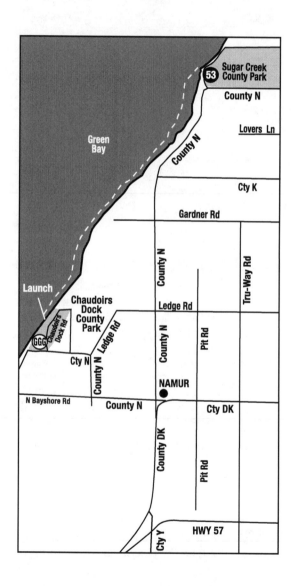

A trip between these two county parks, located along Green Bay just north of the Kewaunee County border, provides a quiet paddle in a low traffic part of Door County. It's a good choice for those seeking solitude. Paddling on this stretch of lake is perfect for experienced paddlers looking for an uncrowded excursion, but there are no real noteworthy features in this area, beyond a few homes and farms. While conditions can be rough during periods with strong onshore winds, this stretch of Green Bay is generally easy to navigate. Appropriate safety gear is a must. You should also consider wearing a wet or dry suit in any month of the year. Chaudoirs Dock County Park provides plenty of parking, and you can launch boats from the dock or from the beach.

ROUTE

From here you can head north up the coastline to Sugar Creek County Park, 3.5 miles north, or head south down the shore to Kewaunee County. Round-trip from Chaudoirs Dock to Sugar Creek County Park is about 7.0 miles round-trip.

DIRECTIONS TO LAUNCH SITE

To reach Chaudoirs Dock County Park, from the Bayview Bridge in Sturgeon Bay, head south on Highway 42/57 for 18.1 miles, to County Y. Turn right on County Y and proceed 0.2 mile north, past Woods Road. When County Y dead-ends, turn right on County DK and proceed for 0.9 mile. Turn left on County N and follow it for 0.1 mile before again turning left to continue on County N for 0.7 miles. Take a right to stay on County N (don't follow Bayshore Road) and proceed 1.0 miles, and then another slight right on County N and proceed 0.3 mile to Chaudoirs Dock Road, the entrance road to the park. The park is located at 1552 County N.

CONTACT INFORMATION

Door County Parks System, 3528 Park Dr., Sturgeon Bay, WI 54235, (920) 746-9959, http://map.co.door.wi.us/parks/. Small fee to use boat launch.

REFERENCES

Bay-Lake Regional Planning Commission. 1980. "Green Bay West Shore Study: Summary Report." Green Bay, WI: Bay-Lake Regional Planning Commission. Available at http://unicorn.csc.noaa.gov/docs/czic/QH545.C65%5FG74%5F1980/ 2800.pdf.

Burton, Paul, and Frances Burton. 2009. *Door County's Islands*. Ephraim, WI: Stonehill Publishing.

Curtis, John T. 1959. *The Vegetation of Wisconsin*. Madison: University of Wisconsin Press.

Door County Land Use Forum, Inc. 1999. "Door Peninsula, Wisconsin Critical Habitat and Natural Areas Land Protection Plan—Project Prospectus." Sturgeon Bay, WI: Door County Land Use Forum.

Grimm, M. 1994. "The Door Peninsula Conservation Initiative: A Resource Guide for Local Conservation Partners with Site Reports." Madison, WI: The Nature Conservancy.

Harris, H. J. 1993. "The State of the Bay—A Watershed Perspective." Green Bay: Institute for Land and Water Studies, University of Wisconsin–Green Bay.

Herdendorf, Charles E., Suzanne M. Hartley, and Mark D. Barnes, eds. 1981. *Fish and Wildlife Resources of the Great Lakes Coastal Wetlands within the United States*. 6 vols. Washington, DC: U.S. Fish and Wildlife Service. FWS/OBS-81/02.

Jackson, Hartley H. T. 1961. *Mammals of Wisconsin*. Madison: University of Wisconsin Press.

Judziewicz, Emmet, and David Kopitzke. 1999. "Wisconsin's Lake Michigan Islands Plant Survey II (1998 and 1999)." PUB ER-801-01. Madison: Wisconsin Department of Natural Resources. Available at http://dnr.wi.gov/wetlands/cw/pdfs/mich igan_islands.pdf and http://dnr.wi.gov/wetlands/cw/pdfs/Phase3_report/site_de scriptions.pdf.

Kasprzak, Candice M., and Mark A. Walter. 2001. "An Inventory and Assessment of the Resources of the Niagara Escarpment in Wisconsin." Green Bay, WI: Bay-Lake Regional Planning Commission. Technical report 7. Great Lakes National Program Office of the U.S. Environmental Protection Agency. Available at http://nefoundation.ca/pdfs/Wisconsin_Escarpment_Inventory.pdf.

Lukes, Roy. 2004. *Toft Point: A Legacy of People and Pines*. Egg Harbor, WI: Nature-Wise.

Martin, Charles I. 1881. *History of Door County, Wisconsin: Together with Biographies of Nearly Seven Hundred Families and Mention of 4,000 Persons*. Sturgeon Bay, WI: Expositor Job Print. Available at http://content.wisconsinhistory.org/cdm4/document.php?CISOROOT= /wch&CISOPTR=29730&REC=2&CISOSHOW=29578.

Merryfield, Nicole. 2000. "A Data Compilation and Assessment of Coastal Wetlands of Wisconsin's Great Lakes." PUBL-ER-002-00. Madison: Wisconsin Department of Natural Resources. Available at http://dnr.wi.gov/wetlands/cw/pdfs/Phase1_report.pdf.

Pohlman, John D., et al., eds. 2006. *Wisconsin Land Legacy Report: An Inventory of Places to Meet Wisconsin's Future Conservation and Recreation Needs*. Publication number LF-040-2006. Madison: Wisconsin Department of Natural Resources. Available at http://dnr.wi.gov/Master_Planning/land_legacy/report.html.

Salamun, Peter J., and Forest W. Stearns. 1978. *The Vegetation of the Lake Michigan Shoreline in Wisconsin*. Madison: University of Wisconsin Sea Grant College Program.

Shideler, Gerald L. 1992. *Critical Coastal Wetland Problem Areas along the Michigan-Wisconsin Shoreline of Lake Michigan, and Their Prioritization for Further Study*. Denver, CO: U.S. Geological Survey.

Tans, William, and Raphael Dawson. 1980. *Natural Area Inventory: Wisconsin Great Lakes Coast*. Madison: Office of Coastal Management, Wisconsin Department of Natural Resources.

Tessen, Daryl D. 2009. *Wisconsin's Favorite Bird Haunts*. 5th ed. Waukesha: Wisconsin Society for Ornithology.

Thwaites, Fredrik T. 1943. "Pleistocene of Part of Northeastern Wisconsin." *Bulletin of the Geological Society of America* 54, no. 1: 87–144.

Thwaites, Fredrik T., and Kenneth Bertrand. 1957. "Pleistocene Geology of the Door Peninsula, Wisconsin." *Bulletin of the Geological Society of America* 68, no. 7: 831–79.

U.S. Fish and Wildlife Service. 1993. *Green Bay Special Wetlands Inventory Study (SWIS) Data Base and Manual*. Chicago: U.S. Environmental Protection Agency.

Valvassori, Danielle. 1990. "Door County Basin Water Quality Management Plan." Madison: Wisconsin Department of Natural Resources. PUBL-WR-205-90-REV.

Wardius, K., and B. Wardius. 2000. *Wisconsin Lighthouses: A Photographic and Historical Guide*. Madison, WI: Prairie Oak Press.

Wisconsin Coastal Management Program. 1996. *Wisconsin Coastal Zone Management Profile—Protection of Estuaries and Coastal Wetlands*. Madison: Wisconsin Department of Administration.

Wisconsin Department of Natural Resources. 1993. *Guide to Wisconsin's Endangered and Threatened Plants*. Madison: Bureau of Endangered Resources, Wisconsin Department of Natural Resources.

———. 2003a. "Door County Comprehensive Forest Plan." Available at: http://www.forestguild.org/ecological_forestry/Door_County_Comprehensive_Forestry_Plan.pdf.

———. 2003b. "A Guide to Significant Wildlife Habitat and Natural Areas of Door County, Wisconsin: A Review of the County's Natural Areas and the Plants and Animals That They Support." Available at http://map.co.door.wi.us/swcd/Guide%20to%20Significant%20Wildlife%20Habitat%20&%20Natural%20Areas%20of%20Door%20County.pdf.

INDEX